DESERTS ARE NOT EMPTY

COLUMBIA BOOKS
    ON ARCHITECTURE
        AND THE CITY

SAMIA HENNI

DESERTS
ARE NOT
EMPTY

Samia Henni is assistant professor of history of architecture and urban development at Cornell University's College of Architecture, Art, and Planning. She is the author of the multi-award-winning *Architecture of Counterrevolution: The French Army in Northern Algeria* (gta Verlag, 2017), the editor of *War Zones*, gta papers 2 (gta Verlag, 2018), and the curator of the exhibitions "Archives: Secret-Défense?" (ifa Gallery Berlin, and SAVVY Contemporary, Berlin, 2021), "Housing Pharmacology" (Manifesta 13, Marseille, 2020), and "Discreet Violence: Architecture and the French War in Algeria" (ETH Zurich; New Institute, Rotterdam; Archive Kabinett, Berlin; Graduate School of Architecture, University of Johannesburg; La Colonie, Paris; Galerie VI PER, Prague; Cornell Architecture, Art, and Planning, Ithaca, NY; and University of Virginia Arts, Charlottesville, 2017–2022). She was formerly Albert Hirschman Chair at the Institute of Advanced Study in Marseille, a visiting Geddes Fellow at Edinburgh School of Architecture and Landscape Architecture, and a visiting professor at the Institute of Art History at the University of Zurich.

SAMIA HENNI

AGAINST THE
REGIME OF
"EMPTINESS"

The term "desert" stands in for a complex locus of imageries, imaginaries, climates, landscapes, spaces, and histories. The territories of both hot and cold deserts embody various forms of anthropogenic exploitation, such as colonial dispossession, resource extraction, and civil and military occupation. And yet, among the most common platitudes about the desert are ideas that "deserts are empty," that "the desert is absent of life," or that "there is nothing at all in the desert." This misleading *conceptualization* of the desert has served to legitimize its transformation, manipulation, toxification, and destruction. This stereotype was, for instance, the justification offered by the French army to defend its choice to use the Algerian Sahara—then a French colonized territory—as the firing field for France's first atomic bombs between 1960 and 1966. According to General Charles Ailleret, the head of France's nuclear program, the Sahara was "a land of thirst and fear, from which all life was reputedly absent," the designated desert characterized by "the total absence of animal and vegetal lives."[1]

1   Charles Ailleret, *L'aventure atomique française: Comment naquit la force de frappe. Souvenirs et réflexions* (Paris: Editions Bernard Grasset, 1968), 229. Translated by the author. ["Pays de la soife et de la peur, d'où toute vie était réputée absente dans les espaces immenses qui séparent Reggane de Tessalit."]

Contrary to this imaginary, the Sahara is not devoid of life. Desert territories—which comprise approximately one-third of the Earth's land surface—host human, nonhuman, biological, microbiological lives. They support sedentary, nomadic, animal, vegetal, mineral forms of existence. Even though the presence of life in desert territories might seem evident, to this day, one is repeatedly hearing and reading the same old colonial platitudes. This is because industrialized subjectivities and exploitative authorities are constantly searching for and in need of so-called "empty" places to be "filled" through occupation, extraction, mining, production, and accumulation. These mechanisms are often intertwined with implicit or explicit forms of *coloniality* and *toxicity*, which result in racializing, altering, damaging, or destroying the living, natural, and built environments present in the desert.

Deserts Are Not Empty is concerned with these processes of anthropogenic construction and destruction that have occurred in various deserts over the last century. This book does not offer comprehensive histories of affective and romantic approaches to the desert, nor does it deal with artistic, literary, philosophical, and theological theories of the desert.[2] Instead, it seeks to scrutinize and comprehend the deeds and practices of modern nation-states, corporations, and institutions—both civil and military—and the harm they cause by "filling" desert territories, spaces, and atmospheres. It is interested in undoing the ramifications of colonial projects in the desert and unfolding the politics of representation, extraction, forced displacement, infrastructure, and "desertification" narratives.[3]

The essays and conversations that constitute *Deserts Are Not Empty* question the dynamics of *coloniality* and *toxicity*—both environmental and sociopolitical. Introduced by sociologist Aníbal Quijano in the 1990s, the concept-term *coloniality* can be defined as a process of domination and dispossession, which began with the devastation of the Americas in 1492 and continues to this day. Such extractive and destructive practices have been

2   See, for example, Elizabeth A. Povinelli, *Geontologies: A Requiem to Late Liberalism* (Durham, NC: Duke University Press, 2016); Lyle Massey and James Nisbet, eds., *The Invention of the American Desert: Art, Land, and the Politics of Environment* (Berkeley: University of California Press, 2021); David Jasper, *The Sacred Desert: Religion, Literature, Art, and Culture* (Malden, MA: Blackwell Publishing, 2004); Aidan Tynan, *The Desert in Modern Literature and Philosophy: Wasteland Aesthetics* (Edinburgh: Edinburgh University Press, 2020); Reyner Banham, *Scenes in America Deserta* (Cambridge, MA: MIT Press, 1989).
3   On desertification, see, for example, Diana K. Davis, "Desert 'Wastes' of the Maghreb: Desertification Narratives in French Colonial Environmental History of North Africa," *Cultural Geographies* 11, no. 4 (October 2004): 359–387.

particularly reinforced over the course of the Cold War and the Nuclear Age, as well as with the continuous rise of right-wing nationalists around the world. According to Quijano, one of the fundamental principles of *coloniality* "is the social classification of the world's population around the idea of race, a mental construction that expresses the basic experience of colonial domination and pervades the more important dimensions of global power."[4] Nomadic, semi-nomadic, and nonnomadic populations living in deserts, fallaciously deemed "empty," have been, and still are, racialized—continuously subjugated to the violent racial and racist dynamics that underpin colonial *conceptualizations* of the desert. Their lands, too, were, and in many cases still are, occupied, exploited, and heavily damaged.[5]

On the other hand, the production of *toxicity* is embedded in processes of colonialization and mechanisms of *coloniality*.[6] The structures that allow lives, soils, matters, and atmospheres to be polluted and toxified are based on colonial land conditions, which serve colonial projects, military rivalries, industrial goals, and economic incentives. These conditions include occupation, expropriation, dispossession, and in some cases massacres. In desert territories, they operate through the search for and extraction and transportation of natural resources, such as oil, gas, and lithium, as well as via the construction of company towns, infrastructures, and energy, climate, aerospace, chemical weapons, and atomic weapons research centers. Under the banner of "emptiness," and the inanity that "there is nothing at all in the desert," those living in occupied deserts have been forcibly displaced, denomadized, and in some cases exterminated—either immediately or gradually. As environmental critic Rob Nixon argues in his book *Slow Violence and the Environmentalism of the Poor*, maintaining media attention on the temporalities of toxicity is challenging: "not only because it is spectacle deficient, but also because the fallout's impact may range from the cellular to the transnational and (depending on the specific character of the chemical or radiological hazard) may stretch beyond the horizon of imaginable time."[7] In addition to struggling to imagine,

---

4   Anibal Quijano, "Coloniality of Power, Eurocentrism, and Latin America," *Nepantla: Views from South* 1, no. 3 (September 2000): 533.
5   See, for example, Nick Estes, *Our History Is the Future: Standing Rock versus the Dakota Access Pipeline, and the Long Tradition of Indigenous Resistance* (London: Verso, 2019).
6   On this relationship, see, for example, Max Liboiron, *Pollution Is Colonialism* (Durham, NC: Duke University Press, 2021).
7   Rob Nixon, *Slow Violence and the Environmentalism of the Poor* (Cambridge, MA: Harvard University Press, 2011), 47.

measure, and capture the temporalities of harm imposed on the desert and its population, the lack of attention is also triggered by the absence, scarcity, and classification of resources.

However, as a way to imagine "the horizon of imaginable time" of both the *coloniality* and *toxicity* that haunt desert populations, territories, and beyond, it is worth returning to the specific case of France's nuclear program in the colonized Algerian desert. Between February 1960—about five years after the outbreak of the Algerian Revolution, or the Algerian War of Independence (1954–1962), and four years after the first exploitation of Algerian oil—and February 1966, France designed and built two military bases in the Algerian Sahara: the Centre Saharien d'expérimentations militaires (CSEM, or Saharan Center for Military Experiments), built for 10,000 workers in Reggane in the Tanezrouft Plain, approximately 1,150 kilometers south of Algiers; and the Centre d'expérimentations militaires des Oasis (CEMO, or the Center of Military Tests of Oasis), designed for 2,000 people in Ecker, about 600 kilometers southeast of Reggane.[8] Despite Algeria's referendum on self-determination, which was approved by 75 percent of voters on January 8, 1961, and its independence after 132 years of French colonial rule in March 1962, France detonated seventeen nuclear bombs and tested other nuclear technologies and weapons.[9] These atmospheric bombs and underground atomic explosions caused irreversible contamination, spreading radioactive fallout across Algeria, Central and West Africa, and the Mediterranean (including southern Europe).[10]

To secretly prepare for and execute its first atomic bomb, the French army demarcated an area of about 100,000 square kilometers around Reggane. It erected a *base-vie* (life base) called Reggane-Plateau to house civil and military personnel, with underground laboratories and workshops; an advanced

8   Bruno Barrillot, *Les irradiés de la république: les victimes des essais nucléaires français prennent la parole* (Brussels: Editions GRIP, 2003), 19–23.
9   In 1966, France moved its nuclear weapons testing from Algeria to another territory under French rule: the Mururoa and Fangataufa atolls in colonized Tahiti Nui (French Polynesia) in the southern Pacific Ocean. Despite objections and protests, the French colonial authorities conducted nearly 200 atmospheric and underground nuclear experiments there between 1966 and 1996, further toxifying colonized environments.
10   For an overview of these atomic bombs, see, for example, Samia Henni, "Toxic Imprints of Bleu, Blanc, Rouge: France's Nuclear Bombs in the Algerian Sahara," in "Toxic Atmospheres," special issue, *The Funambulist* 14 (November–December 2017): 28–33.
11   Barrillot, *Les irradiés de la république*, 19–20. France Ministry of Defense, *Rapport sur les essais nucléaires français (1960–1996)*, vol. 1, *La genèse de l'organisation et les expérimentations au Sahara (CSEM et CEMO)*, classified report (1998), 57–71, http://www.obsarm.org/essais-nucleaires.pdf.

base named Hamoudia; and ground zero zones where the bombs would be detonated.[11] After approximately two-and-a-half years of design and construction in the desert, most of the constructions planned for the CSEM in the colonized Algerian Sahara were completed, comprising 82,000 square meters of buildings, 7,000 square meters of underground works, 100 kilometers of roads, 1,200 cubic meters of water per day, 4,400 kilovolts of power in three power plants, more than 200 kilometers of underground cables and pipes, and 7,000 cubic meters of reinforced concrete in the ground zero zones.[12] On February 13, 1960, the first atomic bomb—codenamed Gerboise bleue (Blue Jerboa) after a tiny jumping desert rodent—was successfully detonated. The bomb had a blast capacity of about 60 to 70 kilotons, roughly four times the strength of Little Boy, which was dropped by the United States on Hiroshima on August 6, 1945, about a month before the end of World War II.[13] Additional bombs were exploded on the soil of the Sahara until February 1966, which caused a few uncontained atomic "accidents."[14]

In 1966, the French army moved its nuclear program to the atolls of Mururoa and Fangataufa, another colonized territory in the southern Pacific Ocean. They dug large holes in the Sahara and buried radioactive remains, engines, equipment, objects, and materials, covering them with contaminated soil and sand. Over the years, the winds and people living in the Sahara uncovered this toxic matter, contaminated debris, and radioactive pieces of architecture.[15] Testifying to the scars of the French atomic bombs in the Sahara, a witness published in Bruno Barrillot's *Les irradiés de la république: les victimes des essais nucléaires français prennent la parole* (The Irradiated of the Republic: The Victims of the French Nuclear Tests Speak Out), in a chapter titled "Enfouissement des matériels contaminés" (Burying of Contaminated Materials), asserted that "there was no particular medical follow-up of the population around Reggane."[16] The *toxicity* and *coloniality* of France's nuclear program—which severely damaged and contaminated the human, animal, vegetal, and mineral lives of the desert—did not disappear with the departure of the French colonial authorities and with Algerian independence. On the contrary, they are engraved on the

12   *Rapport sur les essais nucléaires français,* 1:46–47.
13   Ailleret, *L'aventure atomique française,* 382.
14   On one of these "accidents," see, for example, Louis Bulidon, *Les irradiés de Béryl: L'essai nucléaire français non contrôlé* (Paris: Editions Thaddée, 2011).
15   Barrillot, *Les irradiés de la république,* 43–44.
16   Barrillot, *Les irradiés de la république,* 43–44. ["Il n'y a pas eu de suivi médical particulier de la population autour de Reggane."]

particles of the desert for thousands of years, if not forever.
The temporalities of France's (and other modern nation-states')
coloniality and *toxicity* in the Sahara (and in other deserts) must
be imagined, re-imagined, voiced, presented, and re-presented
despite institutional obstacles, including, in the case of France,
the classification of the great majority of military archival records
of the nuclear program, which are deemed "top-secret military
documents."

Thanks to the extensive work of two independent associations of nuclear victims, France's secrecy was questioned and
challenged. The partial lifting of this secrecy occurred with a
legal case initiated in 2004 by the associations Moruroa e tatou
and AVEN (Association des vétérans des essais nucléaires, or
Association of the Veterans of Nuclear Tests) in the context of
a complaint against X[17] filed with the Health Unit of the Paris
Public Prosecutor's Office.[18] Following a favorable response from
the French Commission consultative du secret de la défense
nationale (Advisory Board on National Defense Secrets) on
March 21, 2013, the French Minister of Defense opened access
to 154 documents on the nuclear bombs in the Sahara.[19] The
documents include various charts and tables of air radioactivity
records at CSEM and CEMO desert sites. For example, thirty-eight
documents titled "radioactivity of the air" and ninety-five
documents titled "radioactivity measurements" show only
graphs and weekly or monthly reports of air radioactivity at
both sites; the great majority of these documents do not contain
any comments. The most useful documents, when they are
legible, are those that report on air radioactivity after each of the
seventeen atmospheric and underground detonations. However,
as Barrillot stated, "Certainly, the radiological and biological
and other monitoring services have developed more detailed
reports, but they are not part of the documents declassified

---

17   In French, filing "a complaint against X" means that the complaint is lodged against
      unknown persons.
18   Bruno Barrillot, *Essais nucléaires français: à quand une véritable transparence?*
      (Obsarm: February 2014), 1, http://obsarm.org/spip.php?article226.
19   Copies of these documents can be freely consulted at the Observatoire des
      armements (Centre de documentation et de recherche sur la paix et les conflits) in
      Lyon, France. See http://obsarm.org.
20   Barrillot, *Essais nucléaires français*, 2. ["Il est certain que les services de contrôle
      radiologiques et biologiques et autres ont élaboré des rapports plus circonstanciés
      mais ils ne font pas partie des documents déclassifiés en mars 2013. On ne dispose
      donc que d'informations partielles, voire tronquées et difficilement exploitables."]
      Barrillot is referring, particularly, to the 129 official reports on the French tests in the
      Sahara quoted in the confidential defense report *La genèse de l'organisation et les
      expérimentations au Sahara (CSEM et CEMO)* of 1998, which were not declassified in
      March 2013.

in March 2013. This means that only partial or even truncated information is available, which is difficult to use."[20] These sources are not that useful for writing the history of France's nuclear bombs in colonized Sahara and thereby for making the French government accountable for its harm imposed on the desert and its population.

The institutional obstruction of history-writing and the denial of social and environmental justice are embedded in France's *coloniality* and *toxicity*, as well as in its attempts at delaying and unsettling the "horizon of imaginable time": the imaginable time and temporality of the medical care of the victims, the decontamination of the sites, the detoxification of the radioactive materials and infrastructure left on site, and the cleaning of the undergrounds and overgrounds of the desert. What happened to the populations living in the desert during and after the fact? Where did those colossal cubic meters of concrete and other construction materials come from? What happened to the toxic matters after their employment? Who is responsible and accountable for social reparation and environmental decontamination? What are the legal devices that existed, or exist today, to impose or reject these colonial conditions? How do colonial built, dismantled, destroyed, displaced, toxified, buried, unearthed, or wasted environments operate within these conditions? How to constitute alternative archives, sources, and evidence to narrate these histories?

These lines of inquiry inform some of the essays and conversations included in this volume. They also guided the 2020 Preston Thomas Memorial Lectures at the Department of Architecture, Cornell University, as well as two conference panels: "Designing in the Desert" at the International Conference of the Society of Architectural Historians in 2020 and "Colonial Spatiality in African Sahara Regions" at an International

21   The Preston Thomas Memorial Lecture Series, "Into the Desert: Questions of
      Coloniality and Toxicity," were held online for the Department of Architecture, Cornell
      University, between October and November 2020. Speakers included: Ariella Aïsha
      Azoulay, Dalal Musaed Alsayer, Paulo Tavares, Asaiel Al Saeed, Aseel AlYaqoub,
      Saphiya Abu Al-Maati, Yousef Awaad Hussein, Nadim Samman, Menna Agha,
      Alessandra Ponte, Solveig Suess, and Zoé Samudzi. See https://aap.cornell.edu/
      news-events/desert-questions-coloniality-and-toxicity#open-sec-7. The "Designing
      in the Deserts" panel included Secil Binboga, Timothy Hyde, Fernando Luis Martinez
      Nespral, Dalal Musaed Alsayer, and Alla Vronskaya, and convened at the Society of
      Architectural Historians, 73rd Annual International Conference, Seattle, Washington,
      April 29–May 3, 2020. The "Colonial Spatiality in African Sahara Regions" panel
      included Maria Gonzalez Pendas, Enrique Bengochea Tirado, José Rodriguez-
      Esteban and D. Barrado-Timón, Violeta Ruano Posada, Gemma Jennings, and Paul
      Bouet, and met at the International Congress: Colonial and Postcolonial Landscapes:
      Architecture, Cities and Infrastructure, Lisbon, January 16–18, 2018.

Congress in Lisbon in 2018.[21] The majority of these presentations and papers have critiqued the imposed "regime of emptiness" and demonstrated that research on desert territories requires a variety of sources, including oral history, literature, films, fictions, personal accounts, art projects, and field visits. *Deserts Are Not Empty* thus also invites readers to challenge their reading habits and reconsider the modalities of and the relationships between and across desert zones as well as between deserts and urban, rural, and other areas, including oceans. It aspires to voice this critique and divulge these methodologies, which are, in many cases, the only plausible way to record desert stories and histories. Some of these accounts evidence how the imaginaries and imageries of "empty" deserts get propagated and carried over time through materials, bodies, institutions, archives, poems, plans, maps, so on, and how they fulfill state and corporate interests in "filling" desert landscapes and their desires to do so.

The aim of scrutinizing state- and corporate-led transformations of deserts is three-fold. It intends first to expose the relationships between architecture and the politics of colonization, wars, forced displacement, ethnic cleansing, representation, and logistics; second, to elicit that the supply of sand, fossil fuels, lithium, and other resources and goods comes from the desert's underground and overground strata; third, to call for reparation and ask authorities and stakeholders to pay off their debts, their accumulated debts. The scale, space, and time of these relationships are multiple, sometimes broken, sometimes illegible, sometimes unimaginable, sometimes incomplete. In "Indent (To Serve the Debt)," a chapter in their book *All Incomplete*, critical theorists Stefano Harney and Fred Moten argue that:

> The impossible and impossible-to-satisfy master is dazzled by it [indebtedness], would open it, wants total access to it, but what they do in the absence of that access, which will have been endured as enclosure, is conceptualize it, place a value on it, impose terms upon it that are meant to approach and explain and regulate the invaluable, the incalculable, while also submitting it to the wasteland of credit, the outer depths of usury, the desert, the slough, the plantation, the prison of the eternally payable.[22]

22   Stefano Harney and Fred Moten, *All Incomplete* (Colchester, NY: Minor Compositions, 2021), 83.

In other words, the colonizer, the officer, the exploiter, the administrator, so on, is obsessed with obtaining "total access to" the desert. Given that such totality is not possible, the desert is occupied, militarized, conceptualized, capitalized, transformed, or destroyed. While the "regime of emptiness" imposed on desert populations and territories obeys precisely these dynamics, this volume, *Deserts Are Not Empty*, interrogates them and stages the "dazzle of indebtedness."

This book invites readers to subvert the analysis of the *conceptualization* of the desert. The essays and conversations spatialize economic, environmental, political, social, health, psychological, and military debts. As in the poem *Sahara: Visions atomoniques* (Sahara: Atomic Visions), in which the Tuareg poet and painter Hawad, originally from the Saharan Aïr Mountains in northern Niger, bears witness to the devastating effects of France's nuclear bombs in the desert, referencing debt, death, radiated bodies, toxified environments, and (still-) contaminated sand, soil, water, and human and nonhuman lives, the essays and conversations herein remember, testify to, and confront various temporalities of *coloniality* and *toxicity* that desert terri-tories and populations have been, and are still, facing. Hawad writes:

> *Agag gag garet!*
> This is no longer an innocent game
> hide and seek
> between nature and denature.
> Neither is it
> of three jerboas leaping
> in spikes of mirages.
> Blue mirages
> green mirages
> purple mirages
> swallowing six jerboas
> turned into a rainbow
> of sulfur and mercury,
> which consume the resin
> of their own essence.
> No, the game exceeds
> the cynical pretense,
> the military poetry
> of enumeration and attribution
> from reference numbers to jerboas
> and to hallucinatory pantings
> of mirages and desert wind.[23]

The volume echoes—among other reverberations—that architecture is not only what is designed and built but also what is indebted, destroyed, dismantled, contaminated, displaced, buried, unearthed, and wasted. *Deserts Are Not Empty* insists: "This is no longer an innocent game."

23   Hawad, *Sahara: visions atomiques* (Paris: Paris-Méditerranée, 2003), 16–17.
       Translated by the author.
       [Ce n'est plus un jeu innocent
       de cache-cache
       entre nature et denature.
       Pas plus qu'il ne s'agit
       de trois gerboises bondissant
       en épis de mirages.
       Mirages bleus
       mirages verts
       mirages violet
       avalant six gerboises
       transformés en arc-en-ciel
       de soufre et de mercure,
       qui consument la résine
       de leur propre essence.
       Non, le jeu dépasse
       le faux-semblant cynique,
       la poésie militaire
       d'énumération et d'attribution
       de matricules aux gerboises
       et aux halètements hallucinés
       des mirages et du vent du désert.]

Acknowledgments

I would like thank Isabelle Kirkham-Lewitt and Joanna Joseph for their tireless reading, careful editing, delightful patience, and esteemed engagement in this collective endeavor.

I would also like to thank all the authors and interlocutors for their determined work and delightful commitment, as well as Andrea Lee Simitch, Meejin Yoon, and the Preston Thomas Memorial Lecture Series Fund at the Department of Architecture, Cornell University, for their generous support.

My gratitude also goes to Patrice Bouveret, the co-founder of the Observatoire des armements in Lyon, France, for agreeing to publish Bruno Barrillot's photographs and for his hospitality in Lyon, and to Pascal Schwaighofer for his tireless support and intellectual inspiration.

Note on translation

Several authors have been invited to select poems to precede their contributions, which appear both in their original language and in English. The translations and reproductions reflect the various ways the poems are found and shared across communities and formats. Some have been scanned from their original source, some handwritten, and some typed. Unless mentioned otherwise, all translations in the volume are by the authors.

Note on visual evidence

Photographs of the environmental impacts of France's nuclear weapons program in the Algerian Sahara are included on pages 368–383. These images were taken by Bruno Barrillot, the co-founder of the Observatoire des armements in Lyon, France, during a visit to France's nuclear sites in Reggane and Ecker in the Algerian Sahara, with the filmmaker Larbi Benchiha and his team in November 2007. Benchiha directed the documentary *Vent de sable, Le Sahara des essais nucléaires* (Sandstorm, The Sahara of Nuclear Tests), which was released in 2008, and *L'Algérie, De Gaulle et la bombe* (Algeria, De Gaulle, and the Bomb), which was released in 2010. Other photographs of this environmental colonial disaster can be found in *At(h)ome*, a film directed by Elisabeth Leuvrey and released in 2013, which documents Bruno Hadjih's photographs.

Brahim El Guabli is assistant professor of Arabic studies and comparative literature at Williams College, and the author of *Moroccan Other-Archives: History and Citizenship after State Violence* (Fordham University Press, forthcoming). He is currently completing a second book, provisionally titled "Saharan Imaginations: Between Saharanism and Ecocare." El Guabli is also the co-editor of *LAMALIF: A Critical Anthology of Societal Debates in Morocco during the "Years of Lead" (1966–1988)*, which is forthcoming from Liverpool University Press. An interdisciplinary scholar, El Guabli's scholarly articles have appeared in *Interventions, The Cambridge Journal of Literary Inquiry, Arab Studies Journal*, and the *Yearbook of Comparative Literature*, among others.

Jill Jarvis is assistant professor in the Department of French and an active member of the councils on African Studies and Middle East Studies at Yale University. Her first book, *Decolonizing Memory: Algeria & the Politics of Testimony*, was published by Duke University Press in 2021; her next book, *Signs in the Desert: Aesthetic Cartographies of the Sahara* (University of Chicago Press, forthcoming), builds a case for how contemporary writers and filmmakers from across the African Sahara transform the reductive ways in which this desert has long been mapped. Other writing appears in *New Literary History, Representations, PMLA, The Journal of North African Studies, Yale French Studies, Expressions maghrébines, Public Books*, and elsewhere.

Francisco E. Robles is assistant professor of English at the University of Notre Dame, where he is a faculty affiliate in the Institute for Latino Studies and a concurrent faculty member in the Gender Studies Program. His writing can be found in *MELUS: Multi-Ethnic Literature of the United States, Post45: Peer Reviewed, Latino Studies*, and *Twentieth-Century Literature*; other essays appear in *Killing the Buddha, Post45: Contemporaries, sxsalon, the Journal of Popular Music Studies*, and the collection *Decolonizing Latinx Masculinities* (University of Arizona Press, 2020).

DESERT FUTURES COLLECTIVE

A CONVERSATION WITH BRAHIM EL GUABLI, JILL JARVIS, AND FRANCISCO E. ROBLES

Samia Henni (SH):

>   You three founded the Desert Futures Collective: "a
>   growing network of scholars, activists, and artists whose
>   shared goal is to chart new paradigms for interdisciplin-
>   ary humanities scholarship through a comparative focus
>   on the poetics and politics of desert spaces."[1] Could you
>   tell us about the genesis of this collective?

Jill Jarvis (JJ):

>   The collective began in a surreptitious, informal,
>   and organic way. Your question about genesis
>   makes me stretch to think back to what might have
>   been the first spark, perhaps nearly a decade ago
>   now. I recall a series of late-night conversations
>   that I had with Brahim and Francisco—separately,
>   before they knew each other—while we were
>   graduate students. I faintly remember a conversa-
>   tion with Brahim in the East Pyne basement café
>   (Brahim had just started in the Comparative Litera-
>   ture program at Princeton, where I was a few years
>   in) about all the different ways our interests in
>   Maghrebi places and poetics were connected. He
>   may or may not remember this but, at some point,
>   Brahim started talking about the Sahara as a living
>   space of connection across the African continent,
>   and how this has been shadowed out of the disci-
>   plinary frames of African studies, Francophone
>   studies, and Maghrebi studies. The idea just stayed
>   with me. In 2013, I applied for a fellowship to go to
>   Algiers for the first time with the American Institute
>   of Maghrib Studies (AIMS), and also submitted an
>   abstract to this intriguing conference called "Carre-
>   fours Sahariens/Saharan Crossroads," organized by
>   the AIMS-affiliated research institute in Oran called
>   the Centre d'Etudes Maghrébines en Algérie. The

1   "Desert Futures," Yale MacMillan Center, published March 4, 2020, https://desert
       futures.yale.edu.

conference was supposed to happen in Ghardaïa, in the Algerian south in 2013—I remember feeling so excited to visit the desert city—but it was cancelled because of, I think, some political complications. It was held instead the following year in Oran, in May 2014. I participated. The experience of this interdisciplinary, multilingual conversation, which recast the African Sahara as a center rather than a periphery, and the impromptu bus trip I took with a friend to Aïn Sefra stirred something in me that I started to write and talk more about years later. Francisco and I had been friends since, quite literally, our first day at Princeton—he was getting his PhD in English—but it wasn't until the end of the program, when we were trying to figure out how to narrate future versions of our professional selves to face the job market, that we really started to talk about deserts together. I remember the energy of our first conversations about the resonances between the Sahara and the Sonoran Desert spaces and histories. This was incredibly vivid and grounding and exciting—especially during the anxious and uncertain process of applying to academic jobs. We came up with a title right then and there: SAHARA | SONORA. The collective itself formed only after each of us had found institutional work—Brahim at Williams, Francisco at Notre Dame, me at Yale—but since you asked about genesis! It started without our knowing what it could grow into.

Francisco E. Robles (FER):

Our answers have two things in common: the informality of the initial conversation, and the excitement we felt when discovering our shared sensibilities and the connections in and across the diverse desert geographies we were studying. I remember feeling this after teaching a section for a class led by Professor Wendy Belcher at Princeton University: Jill and I went to a bar called Winberies after. We were both on the academic job market and were talking about our application materials. In particular, we were telling each other about our hopes for projects beyond the dissertation—the dreaded and often expected "second project" we'd embark upon after significantly revising our dissertations into first books. Hearing Jill describe her second project, I kept noting all the connections between her comments on the Sahara Desert and the ways the Sonoran Desert is both depicted and understood in the US and Mexico. We had both been in a graduate seminar on the postcolonial novel taught by Professor Simon Gikandi, and, in that course, my final paper considered a broader conceptual geography of the so-called "US Southwest," comparing Anglo-American, Chicanx, and Indigenous literatures and their engagements with the desert spaces of the Sonoran and Chihuahuan Deserts.[2] Gikandi's class was exceptionally exciting to us. It offered the space to think through what "postcolonial" and "the novel" meant within a global, comparative methodology. The seminar continues to inform my work. In discussing Gikandi's class as well as the new work we hoped to take up, Jill and I kept building this incredible set of connections, realizing that there was so much to say through a comparative framework that considered how the Sahara and Sonoran Deserts became (or, rather, have become) spaces of wilderness, terror, and emptiness within the imaginaries of the Global North, in particular Europe and the United States. Why was it that both of these landscapes were nearly always conceptualized as cultureless, barren zones of death—especially when each has housed humans for millennia, and have thriving ecologies?

We even tried, but failed, to organize a panel on this topic at the American Comparative Literature Association conference. But with that failure came two of the collective's early collaborators: Natalie Koch (a geographer at Syracuse University), and Daniela Johannes (a literary and cultural critic at West Chester University).

---

2   Some of the novels we read included (and this is not a complete list): Rabindranath Tagore, *The Home and the World*, trans. Surendranath Tagore (London: Macmillan and Co, 1919); Mulk Raj Anand, *Untouchable* (London: Wishart Books, 1935); George Lamming, *In the Castle of My Skin* (London: Michael Joseph, 1953); Chinua Achebe, *Arrow of God* (London: Heinemann, 1964); Ngũgĩ wa Thiong'o, *A Grain of Wheat* (London: Heinemann, 1967); and V.S. Naipaul, *The Enigma of Arrival* (London: Viking Press, 1987).

Natalie presented in the first of the 2021 workshops we held, which yielded a powerful and fruitful conversation.[3] Daniela organized a panel at West Chester University as part of the Ethnic Studies Seminar Series titled "Borders, Barriers, Separation, and Immigration," and the discussion featured Daniela, Eda Pepi (an anthropologist, ethnographer, and gender studies scholar at Yale, and Jill's colleague), Samer Abboud (a scholar of politics and area studies at Villanova), and myself. The panel, titled "Sonora/Sahara/Syria: Immigration and Borders," took place on April 4, 2019, and was an interdisciplinary blend of scholarship ranging across literary studies, border studies, anthropology, migration studies, and political science.

Brahim El Guabli (BEG):

By the time I met Jill in graduate school, the desert had started to shape my thinking in ways that pushed me to reconsider my own positionality. I was born and raised in a small pre-Saharan village in the governorate of Ouarzazate, Morocco. My mother is Black and my father is Sahrawi, but I was raised among Imazighen (Berber people). Thus, while my family's identity was shaped by memories of desert origins and multiple histories of passage between sub-Saharan Africa and the Maghreb, my Berberness/Amazighity complicated these forms of inheritance. However, the Sahara did not become a real scholarly issue for me until I read *Nazīf al-Hajar* (The Bleeding of the Stone) and the two volumes of *al-Majūs* (The Fetishists) by Libyan novelist Ibrahim al-Koni and *Mudun al-milḥ* (Cities of Salt) and *al-Nihāyāt* (Endings) by exiled Saudi novelist Abdelrahman Munif.[4] These

---

3   This workshop, titled "Wastelanding Arabia: America's 'Garden of Eden' in Al-Kharj, Saudi Arabia," discussed a pre-circulated paper by Natalie Koch, which examined connections between the University of Arizona, Aramco, and the Kingdom of Saudi Arabia. The respondent was Eda Pepi of Yale University. The workshop took place virtually on March 26, 2021.

4   Ibrahim al-Koni, *Al-Majūs*, 2 vols. (Limassol, Cyprus: Dār al-Tanwīr li-al-Ṭibāʿa wa-al-Nashr, 1992), translated by William M. Hutchins as *The Fetishist* (Austin: University of Texas Press, 2018); Ibrahim al-Koni, *Nazīf al-ḥajar* (Miṣrātah: al-Dār al-Jamāhīrīya li-al-Nashr wa-al-Tawzīʿ wa-al-

two writers helped me process the significance
of my indigeneity and how I was connected to the
land and the people. Munif also wrote *Sharq al-
mutawassiṭ* (East of the Mediterranean) and *al-Ān,
hunā, aw sharq al-mutawassiṭ marratan ukhrā*
(Here and now, east of the Mediterranean again)—
two novels that depict the dehumanization of
political prisoners in a desert jail in an unnamed
Arab country located on the eastern side of Mediterranean.[5] *Sharq al-mutawassiṭ* evokes Morocco's
most notorious prison during the "Years of Lead,"
a period of prolonged state violence that began
with the country's independence in 1956 and
lasted until the passing of King Hassan II in 1999.
The prison camp of Tazmamart, which was built
in a military garrison in the desert of southeast
Morocco, was a horrible jail where the Moroccan monarchy detained fifty-eight soldiers and
officers—known as the putschists—who participated in the two consecutive coups d'état against
the king in 1971 and 1972.[6] Although these prisoners were sentenced by a military court to prison
terms ranging from three years to life in prison,
they were kidnapped from their jail cells and taken
to the desert, which was ice cold in the winter
and scorching hot in the summer. After eighteen
years in Tazmamart, only twenty-eight prisoners survived and emerged to tell the traumatizing
story of their forced disappearance. The Moroccan

I'lān, 1996), translated by May Jayyusi and Christopher Tingley as *The
Bleeding of the Stone* (Northampton: Interlink Books, 2002); Abdelrah-
man Munif, *Mudun al-milḥ* (Beirut: al-Mu'assasah al-'Arabīyah li-al-
Dirāsāt wa-al-Nashr, 1985), translated by Peter Theroux as *Cities of Salt*
(London: Jonathan Cape, 1988); Abdelrahman Munif, *Al-Nihāyāt* (Beirut:
al-Mū'assasah al-'Arabīya li-al-Dirāsāt wa-al-Nashr, 1999), translated by
Roger Allen as *Endings* (London: Quartet Books, 1988).
5   Abdelrahman Munif, *Sharq al-Mutawassiṭ* (Beirut: al-
Mu'assasah al-'Arabīyah li-al-Dirāsat wa-al-Nashr, 1975); and
al-Ān, hunā, aw Sharq al-mutawassiṭ marrah ukhrā (Beirut:
al-Mu'assasah al-'Arabīyah li-al-Dirāsāt wa-al-Nashr, 1991).
6   See Brahim El Guabli, "Theorizing Intergenerational
Trauma in Tazmamart Testimonial Literature and Docu-
testimonies," *Middle East – Topics & Arguments* 11
(2018): 120–133; and Brahim El Guabli, "The Absent
Perpetrators: Morocco's Failed Accountability,
Tazmamart Literature and the Survivors' Testimony for
their Jailers (1973–1991)," *Violence: An International
Journal* 1, no. 1 (2020): 80–101.

state drew on the colonial imaginary, which used deserts and islands as spaces of indefinite detention and banishment—weaponizing the southeast desert to disappear the undesirable and insurgent. In fact, the weaponization of the desert is embedded in a long history of violence committed by early explorers, colonial states, and post-independence dictatorships. Somehow, deserts allowed impunity, which is something that continues even today in border areas. So, when I met Jill in 2014, my mind was bursting with questions about imprisonment, about geographies of exclusion and the desert, about mobility, and about the impetus for creating spaces in which people are literally left to decay. The same year, I had a chance to take a course titled "Problems in North African History" with Professor M'hamed Oualdi, which really encouraged creative and interdisciplinary thinking about history and space. This was the first history course that I took in graduate school, and it allowed me to use this literature to think about archives and archiving. Desert Futures Collective officially formed in 2018, and I am always amazed at how such a fortuitous encounter shaped our collaborations. I have since offered two Saharan Imaginations courses at Williams College, where I have been appointed as an assistant professor of Arabic studies and comparative literature, and organized a Comparative Deserts Imaginations Conference in May 2021, and each time my learning about the desert continues to be informed by different encounters across different geographies and pedagogies.

SH: How would you define or describe a "desert"? Are there notions associated with the desert that concern you or inspire you?

BEG: For me, the desert summons many things. Most importantly, however, the desert means home. It means a place of origin, an indigeneity that is grounded in relationship to place rather than space. I see the desert as a place because, unlike geometrical space, places have affective and emotional importance. Approaching the desert as home or as a place changes the stakes from a purely scholarly interest into an investment in the desert as a center of human existence and civilization. Also, the desert summons my childhood, and—thinking about the bare minimum resources that we had to survive— it summons the multiple forms of generosity that adhere to an ethics of survival. The desert is an epistemic space that extends my own existence as an individual into an infinite archive of Arabic and Islamic literary heritage. This geographic extension from the Maghreb to Arabia is nourished by a rich poetic and cultural tradition that sustains a local Saharan imagination; a Saharan *ummah* of sorts.

The word *ṣaḥrā'* (desert) itself is not the only word used in Arabic or Berber/Amazigh to describe this landscape. *Bādiyya*, *barriyya*, *baydā'*, *sabsab*, *'arā'*, *flāt*, *mafāza*, *fayfā'* do too—and, perhaps, with more nuance, depending on the topography or the "sandiness" or "stoniness" of the place. It is very important to underline that the English and French meanings that stem from the word "desert" have no equivalents in the root (ṣ-ḥ-r). This root allows us to generate several verbs and verbal nouns that are closely related to the desert, including cooking (*ṣaḥara*), leaving land unattended, and desertifying. While French and English definitions of the word "desert" insist on emptiness and inhabitability, the Arabic origin of the term does not point to emptiness at all; it rather emphasizes an interaction between different elements. So, the desert is not really *deserted* (*khālin/khāliyya*).[7] It is a locus for the millennial production and transmission of knowledge, traditions, and know-how. This misconception—whose history is embedded in Western encounters with deserts—reduces the richness of the etymology of *taṣaḥḥar* (to become desertified)

---

7   Note here that *khālin* (deserted/empty) and *khalā'* (wilderness) are from the root kh-l-w, which is different from ṣ-ḥ-r.

and extrapolates that there is nothing in the desert. In Amazigh language, the desert is described as *iyar, amrdul, anezraf, anezruf, tanzruft, tama, asnzruf, tiniri,* and *tinariwin*. It is important to note here that *tinariwin* means deserts in plural, thus adding a layer of complexity by pluralizing a space that is misconceived as being singular. Instead of being a void, deserts, by virtue of their plurality, are full, both materially and immaterially. By conceptualizing the desert as both a physical and a metaphysical space as well as a space that is constantly filled with other forms of existence, including spirits and ghosts, we are able to reframe the discussion and subvert some of the longstanding misconceptions about deserts in general.

My current work endeavors to construct the concept of "Saharanism" (*al-istiṣḥār*). Saharanism, which I define as a universalizing imaginary and discursive practice about deserts, perceives desert spaces as empty, dead, and inherently dangerous. It transforms deserts into death traps for immigrants, into sites in need of policing, and legitimizes all forms of destruction, from the material and immaterial extraction of resources and knowledge to the testing of lethal military equipment and the dumping of waste. Rooted in Greek, Arab, and Western racializing encounters with desert spaces, Saharanism has had the perverse effect of creating global desert imaginaries, which erase the morphological richness, ecological liveliness, and millennia-old human-nature relations that have sustained the fine balance between life and death within deserts. Saharanism has morphed over time into a powerful extractive ideology that manifests in a range of ways, from the most mundane activities, like taking pictures with camels and sand dunes, to complicated extractive enterprises, such as oil drilling. It draws on Edward Said's *Orientalism*, which examines how the Orient was invented through scholarship and politics, and Valentin Mudimbe's *The Invention of Africa*, which addresses the conditions that make some discourses possible, to offer

a conceptual framework that will help us understand what it is that connects the ways in which
people perceive deserts as a place onto which to
project their romanticism, nostalgia, fears, and
wild dreams.[8] My research has revealed that Saharanism harks back to the earliest racialization of
Africans by the Ancient Greeks, who called them
Ethiopians, which means "the land of burned
faces."[9] Unlike Orientalists, who have been almost
exclusively Euro-American, Saharanists (the orig-
inators and propagators of Saharanism) hailed
from all parts of the world, including North Africa
and China, before it became a predominantly
Euro-American enterprise. Yet regardless of where
they hail from (Fez, London, or Beijing), Saharanists have been ambassadors, travelers, explorers,
priests, enslavers, geologists, and army officers,
and their writings have circulated and informed
their intellectual trajectories.

Saharanism also sheds light on the ardent desire to
segment and compartmentalize the desert to stave
off fictitious security threats. Compartmentaliza-
tion is connected to notions of death and waste.
Drawing on histories of place and space as well as
travelogues and photography, Saharanism reveals
the institutionalized ideologies that produce the
desert as an inherently unsafe and irredeemably
dead space. As a result, we can talk about various
forms of Saharanism. There is cultural Saharanism, which manifests in a fascination with desert
cultures, dress codes, and people. There is environmental Saharanism, which takes the form of
environmental onslaught on desert spaces through
multifold forms of extraction, experimentation, and
militarization. This is evidenced by airplane and

8   Edward Said, *Orientalism* (New York: Vintage Books, 1994); and V. Y. Mudimbe,
     The Invention of Africa: Gnosis, Philosophy, and the Order of Knowledge
     (Indianapolis: Indiana University Press, 1988).
9   For a longer explanation of this racial slur and its origins in Ancient
     Greek literature, see Frank M. Snowden, *Blacks in Antiquity: Ethiopians
     in the Greco-Roman Experience* (Cambridge, MA: Harvard University
     Press, 1970), 174–175.

tire graveyards.[10] Saharanism has also informed security projects in deserts, such as the European Border Control Agency's delocalization of the European Union's border to the Sahara.[11] What makes Saharanism dangerous is its banality. Things as simple as the seemingly most benign pictures that visitors take in the desert are inherently framed by a long tradition of more overtly violent Saharanist imaginaries.

I am very interested in the notion of archiving and dis-archiving. If prevalent notions of the archive emphasize stability, at least in theory, then desert archives are dis-archives. That means they uncover and disrupt that which is supposed to be preserved for eternity in the commonsensical conceptualization of archive. Nothing is stable in the desert. The wind moves sand dunes, bones, landmarks. Roads get buried, train tracks get lost, and paths do not survive the next gust of wind. I am very excited about the archiving and dis-archiving created by this instability. Dis-archiving is this continuous movement to uncover and recover that which would have been stabilized if it was kept in a heav-

10   The Sulaibiya graveyard in Kuwait is one of the largest landfills on Earth, holding over forty-two million used tires; see Kaushik Patowary, "Biggest Tire Graveyard in Sulaibiya, Kuwait," January 19, 2015, https://www.amusingplanet.com/2015/01/worlds-biggest-tire-graveyard-in.html. The Sonoran Desert hosts the largest graveyard for retired airplanes; see Stephen Dowling, "The Secrets of the Desert Aircraft 'Boneyards,'" *BBC*, September 17, 2014, https://www.bbc.com/future/article/20140918-secrets-of-the-aircraft-boneyards.

11   Through intergovernmental agreements that tie monetary aid to migration control, such as the Rabat Process (2006), Khartoum Process (2014), and Valletta Summit (2015), the EU has virtually moved its borders to the Sahara and the Sahel, outsourcing border enforcement to African nations in exchange for millions of euros. While the real borders have not moved, the zone of border control and the deadly threats it entails have been offloaded from European to African land. For more on this topic, see Oriol Puig, *The Sahel: Europe's Other Border*, Notas Internacionales 230 (Barcelona: Centre for International Affairs, 2020), https://www.cidob.org/en/publications/publication_series/notes_internacionals/n1_230/el_sahel_la_otra_frontera_de_europa; Andrea Stäritz and Julia Stier, eds., *The Sahara: EUrope's New Deadly External Border* (Berlin: borderline-europe – Menschenrechte ohne Grenzen, 2018), https://www.bildungswerk-boell.de/sites/default/files/the_sahara.pdf; and Amgad Fareid Eltayeb, "Why Is the EU-Khartoum Process So Wrong on So Many Levels," *Sudan Tribune*, November 6, 2017, https://www.sudantribune.com/spip.php?article62098.

ily guarded official archive. The desert lays bare everything and even the things that may be hidden will, for sure, be dis-archived when the right wind or storm hits. The desert archive is mobile and transnational, carried through by, among other things, dust storms that sometimes reach as far as the east coast of the United States. I continue to think about the desert Gothic as a generative genre for thinking about archiving and dis-archiving.[12]

All these interrogations come together in my pedagogical practice. I have taught Saharan Imaginations: Reflections on Mobility, Ethics, and Environmentalism twice now. Each time I teach this class, I feel that my students have been able to overcome the pitfalls of Saharanism and emerge more vigilant about their assumptions regarding deserts. Students always express their surprise at how much they did not know or how much their ideas about the place were informed by the very misconceptions we aim to deconstruct. All in all, I see desert studies as a space for a different kind of active pedagogical praxis that proactively pushes our thinking beyond the ordinary notions of space and place.

JJ: The whole idea of "desert" worries me for the reasons that Brahim has outlined. Because I found my way into this work by researching the occluded history of French nuclear imperialism in the Sahara, I'm pretty preoccupied with the colonizing forces and uses that inhere in defining the "desert" as empty, uninhabited, and therefore useful space. Whether or not we choose to know about it, we are all still living with the enduring effects of nuclear bombs detonated in desert places. I come from deserts, or rather from a history of white settlers occupying desert places in the US Southwest. I was born in Utah. One of my parents was from a very small town in

12   Brahim El Guabli, "Saharan Gothic: Desert Necrofiction" in *Maghrebi and Middle Eastern Desert Literature for Middle Eastern Gothics*, ed. Karen Grumberg (Wales: Wales University Press, forthcoming).

arid southern Idaho; the other from a different small town in the central Idaho mountains. My early sensibilities were shaped by a deep sense of Mormon cultural history in which cultivating "unwanted" and "uninhabitable" desert land—which was of course already very much inhabited and sacred—was an act of survival central to the cultural identity of the community into which I was born. When I was in college, I also read Terry Tempest Williams's memoir *Refuge* and learned in an unsettling way about the residual impact of nuclear imperialism quite close to my cultural home and birthplace.[13] I also spent a good part of my young life living near the toxic Hanford Nuclear Site in a corner of southeastern Washington State. These experiences have shaped my path.

In 2014, when I was a graduate student living in Algiers, I took an overnight bus with a friend to Aïn Sefra and learned a number of rather obvious but important things. This was—shockingly, considering that I was working on a PhD project that focused on the effects of French colonial violence in contemporary Algeria—the first time I had ever heard about the seventeen nuclear bombs detonated by the French in Algeria between 1960 and 1966. These bombs left a toxic legacy whose effects are still unknown and whose traces have been persistently erased from history and public knowledge. It became clear to me that (of course) the Sahara is anything but empty and also that the consequences of seeing it *as* empty are lethal, in a quite unmetaphorical and enduring way. That haunted me too, and has prompted my current work, both in this collective and in a new book project that I am drafting called *Signs in the Desert: Aesthetic Cartographies of the Sahara*.

"Desert" is an idea with a long and violent colonial history. It is an English word, with cousins in French and Spanish, distinct from the myriad other Arabic and Berber words used to name the topography, as Brahim has explained. This is a point that I try to bear always in

13   Terry Tempest Williams, *Refuge: An Unnatural History of Family and Place* (New York: Vintage, 1991).

mind when undertaking the kind of comparative work that is a central ambition of our collective. For now, I think of "desert" first as a verb rather than a noun. Here my thinking has been nourished by Ariella Aïsha Azoulay's talk in Fall 2020 about *deserting* the Negev ("Palestine is there, where it has always been").[14] She very memorably listed the verb forms and senses of the word "desert" — to leave, to abandon, to leave without permission (in a military sense of desertion), to undo, to sever connection, to forsake, to give up. It comes from Latin: *de* (undo) + *serere* (join together, put in a row), so that to *desert* is to unmake and disconnect what is connected, ordered, sensible, joined together.

Thus I understand "desert" as a colonizing term, difficult if not impossible to separate from the ongoing processes and histories of settler colonizing (Utah; Algeria; Palestine) that are disruptive, violent, destructive. I have also been thinking about the epistemological effects of the ongoing activity of abandoning, evacuating, and *making deserted*—framing certain places as desert has the effect of vanishing them from our mental maps, our disciplinary geographies. "Desert" has been and continues to be useful (or, really, absolutely central) to colonizing projects, which seem to *need* spaces that can be mapped out as wasteland in order to function and extract as they do. This exceptionally powerful and motivating idea of empty space has shaped nation-states, defined borders, justified wars and genocides, and continues to generate and sustain ideas about what does and does not count as life worth living and protecting. This is tragic. It should not be this way, but it is. At the moment, I am thinking through Elizabeth Povinelli's claim in *Geontologies* that the "Desert" is an organizing figure for our time, a place for working out the unstable distinction between Life and Nonlife: "The Desert," she writes, "holds on to the distinction between Life and Nonlife and dramatizes the

14   Ariella Aïsha Azoulay, "Palestine Is There, Where It Has Always Been" (talk, Preston Thomas Memorial Lecture Series, "Into the Desert: Questions of Coloniality and Toxicity," Cornell University Department of Architecture, Ithaca, NY, October 5, 2020). The lecture has been adapted for this volume, see pages 109–141.

possibility that Life is always at threat from the creeping, desiccating strands of Nonlife. The Desert is the space where life was, is not now, but could be if knowledges, techniques, and resources were properly managed."[15]

I think we in the collective agree that it is time to think deeply—together—about all of this and to work together in a sustained and serious way to correct it. Each in different and distinctive ways, we aim to contribute to shifting what presently qualifies as lives worthy of attention and care; these lives are both human and nonhuman, and some are surely ghosts and spirits. So I suppose what we are trying to do together is not only to worry over the violent, extractive, colonizing effects of these ways of thinking and talking about deserts but also to learn together to think and construct knowledge otherwise—in particular, to learn from the perspectives and epistemologies and aesthetics that come from desert places and lives. So I suppose we are taking on a kind of *resignifying* practice, in the hope that we can contribute to fundamentally changing perceptions about what "desert" means, how deserts mean, and cultivate sustained attention to how those who live in deserts contest their own erasure and *create* meaning. We have so much to learn.

FER: I love what both Jill and Brahim have said. I'll describe a very straightforward concern of mine, which builds on their responses: emptiness. I'm concerned with the discourses of emptiness—what Brahim refers to as the void and what Jill connects to the verb "to desert" and the adjective "deserted"—that define so much of how deserts are imagined and approached. Deserts can certainly be dangerous places, but empty, they are not. The increasing danger of deserts, however, is largely due to the biopolitical and practical effects of sovereign borders, which seek to reshape long-standing migration and economic patterns that precede the very idea of nation-states. Look at how the US-

15   Elizabeth A. Povinelli, *Geontologies: A Requiem to Late Liberalism* (Durham, NC: Duke University Press, 2016), 16.

Mexico border has become defined in so many ways by migrant death: these deaths are manufactured by the combination of competing state and economic interests with the coerced traversal of dangerous desert terrains.

Emptiness is not only a means of refusing to acknowledge who lives in deserts, as well as the incredibly important and environmentally necessary flora and fauna of deserts—it's also a means of asserting and proving dominant cultural ideas. To teach this point, I often turn to the writings of Zane Grey (such as his 1924 novel *The Call of the Canyon*) and Edward Abbey (the *Edward Abbey Reader* is a great place to start, though *Desert Solitaire* is a must-read in terms of getting a sense of his understanding of the Sonoran Desert), as well as to Hollywood's mid-century Western films (most any film will do, honestly, though I've found that *True Grit* and *The Searchers* are exceptional studies of how deserts in the US Southwest serve as proving grounds for white masculinity).[16] In short, the desert becomes a place where men can go to prove that they're men, where white people go to prove that they're white, where survival means proof of one's worth.[17] One of the first Anglo writers to push against this sensibility, even though her thought was still sustained by a sense of exceptionalism, was Mary Hunter Austin. There's a passage from *The Land of Little Rain* (1903) that has stuck with me since I first read it, in which Austin claims, that in the desert, "the land favors the sense of personal relation to the supernatural."[18] She continues, a bit later:

16   Zane Grey, *The Call of the Canyon* (New York: Grosset & Dunlap, 1924); Edward Abbey, *Slumgullion Stew: An Edward Abbey Reader* (New York: Dutton, 1984); Edward Abbey, *Desert Solitaire* (New York: Ballantine, 1994); True Grit, dir. Henry Hathaway (Los Angeles: Paramount, 1969); *The Searchers*, dir. John Ford (Burbank: Warner Bros., 1956).
17   For an excellent examination of how cultural texts—from paintings to novels to essays to films—shape this imaginary, see Lee Clark Mitchell, *Westerns: Making the Man in Fiction and Film* (Chicago: University of Chicago Press, 1996).

Western writers have not sensed it yet; they smack the savor of lawlessness too much upon their tongues, but you have these to witness it is not mean-spiritedness. It is pure Greek in that it represents the courage to sheer off what is not worthwhile. Beyond that it endures without sniveling, renounces without self-pity, fears no death, rates itself not too great in the scheme of things; so do beasts, so did St. Jerome in the desert, so also in the elder day did gods. Life, its performance, cessation, is no new thing to gape and wonder at.[19]

Austin points out the absurdity of "the savor of lawlessness" that so often defines the US and Mexican deserts, a definitive impression of rawness and danger and violence. In this passage she also undermines claims to the special or exceptional status of the white witness in the desert, even if she relies on this sense of privilege in much of the rest of her book. For Austin, the wilds of the desert suggest endurance and humility, whether empty or shot through with desert life.

In short, and in contradistinction from what I've described above (and in ambivalently considering Austin an exception to the dominant Anglo perspective of deserts as bleak and empty), what inspires me is the magnificent fullness of deserts—the many people across the world who have made homes in deserts for millennia, whose artistic cultures speak powerfully to the lives they have built. I'm also deeply moved, odd as it is to say, by the specialized flora and fauna that have made xeriscapes (that is, dry landscapes) their preferred zones of habitation. One thing that desert plants, the desert animals, and desert people have in common, however, is a deep understanding of what is possible and impos-

18   Mary Hunter Austin, *The Land of Little Rain* (New York: Houghton, Mifflin and Company, 1903), 120.
19   Austin, *Land of Little Rain*, 121.

sible, what is deadly and what is not. For the people of the desert, there is often a deep admiration of the desert, an attachment to its fierce beauty and a recognition of how limited human existence and knowledge can be. In her essay "Where the Wilderness Begins," the Tohono O'odham poet and linguist Ofelia Zepeda writes:

> Because we know where the desert ends, we also know *what* is in that desert. Sometimes we know these things firsthand, sometimes not. As O'odham, we know the desert is the place of wilderness. It is the place of dreams for those who must dream those kinds of dreams, and it is the place of songs for those who must sing those kinds of songs. But it is also the place where nightmares hide, nightmares so fierce that one can believe one has seen a guardian angel.
> For the O'odham, the desert is certainly a place of power. Because we know this essence of the desert, although sometimes we do not fully understand it, we are able to live in it.[20]

Zepeda's insistence on the futility of controlling the desert as a requirement for living in it speaks to the astonishing fullness of the desert and points to a mode of understanding and inhabitation that isn't about comprehensiveness and control. This is so capacious and generative, the recognition that we cannot dominate or grasp the desert through either comprehension or power. This is a fundamental rejection of the desert as an emptiness or a blank slate that can be filled in with whatever we'd like. Deserts are *not* what we want them to be, and they are what they must be as part of an ecological network of relation and interdependence—this, precisely, is why they function as geological, biological, and cultural keystones.

20   Ofelia Zepeda, "Where the Wilderness Begins," *ISLE: Interdisciplinary Studies in Literature and Environment* 4, no. 1 (Spring 1997): 85–86.

SH: Along with the term "desert," you included the terms "futures" and "collective" in the title of the network you are creating. Could you please highlight the significance of these inclusions? I can't help but think of time and the right to imagine and believe in what I have called elsewhere "the possibility of an otherwise."[21]

FER: The collective aspect of this project is very invigorating. Knowing what we don't know is crucial to sustaining scholarly engagement. If we don't know something, we can rely on each other to determine a means of getting to know it or develop a method or protocol, or we can work together to figure out who has already been asking and considering the questions that we're asking. In many ways, the second workshop we held—with you [Samia], Jill, and Roxanne Panchasi—was, for me, an example of how collectively oriented conversation yields a comparative and shared language, which continues beyond the space of that initial conversation.[22] To build a flexible and uncountable set of methods for discussing deserts—methods that gesture globally even as they're attuned to localities and specificities—requires an open and willfully collective scholarly sensibility. That's a future and an otherwise that I'd love to participate in, for sure!

As I mentioned in earlier, in the March 2021 workshop we held, Natalie Koch presented on desert agriculture and the decades-long relationship between the University of Arizona, Aramco, and the Saud family.[23] Her research shows what's at stake in the collective imagination of a desert future we want to pursue: a desert whose future is also

21   Samia Henni, "The Coloniality of an Executive Order," Journeys and Translation, Canadian Centre for Architecture, June 21, 2020, https://www.cca. qc.ca/en/articles/issues/5/journeys-and-translation/73571/the-coloniality-of-an-executive-order. See also Catherine E. Walsh, "Decoloniality in/as Praxis," in Walsh and Walter D. Mignolo, On Decoloniality: Concepts, Analytics, Praxis (Durham, NC: Duke University Press, 2018), 15–104.
22   This workshop was titled "Archives & Afterlives: On Researching French Nuclear Imperialism in the Sahara," and was held virtually on April 30, 2021.

its past, whose local knowledges should not be steamrolled in the search for efficiency and land-use maximization, whose indigenous agricultures are not shunted aside in favor of goods and crops whose values are seen as more important to the global market, whose spaces are not converted into prisons and other carceral settings, whose flora and fauna are not negated but valued. We can find different modes of value, especially those that are not acquisitive or forceful or predicated upon separation and destruction, in the collective past—both in the scale of the human story on Earth and in the particularities of the local—and, I hope, in the collective future.

JJ: We are, in some fundamental way, trying to resignify "desert," which is a point that Francisco demonstrates beautifully in his reflection about the ecological intricacy and fullness of desert places. Of course deserts are not empty: they are incredibly full. One must learn to listen and perceive in new ways. And, as I hear it, this kind of resignifying is also at play in the name "Desert Futures Collective." It often strikes me that people pick up something surprising, perhaps counterintuitive, in the very notion of "desert futures." It can have a certain ominous valence—it taps into a fear of desertification, a sense that the warming planet is becoming hostile to life, as if to suggest or confirm that the future looks bleak.

But I think we are working together to articulate and defend a vision that the *inverse* is actually true—to be able to envision futurity through caring for and listening to knowledge that is grounded in desert histories, archives, places, ecologies, lives. Our futures depend on cultivating this kind of counter-knowledge. Deserts have been framed as places outside history, or without history—so not only

23 To read Koch on this topic, see Natalie Koch, "Desert Geopolitics: Arizona, Arabia, and an Arid-Lands Response to the Territorial Trap," *Comparative Studies of South Asia, Africa and the Middle East* 41, no. 1 (2021): 88–105; as well as Koch, *Arid Empire: The Entangled Fates of Arizona and Arabia* (New York: Verso, forthcoming).

are we insisting that deserts are full, we are also asserting that deserts are central to the flows that have made history possible, that deserts are quite literally essential to all our futures. May Joseph recently explained this in such a powerful way in her exhilarating talk "Harmattan Wind as Decolonial Morphology," which she delivered at a conference that Brahim organized at Williams College in May 2021—our planet's health depends on the sand and winds carried from the Sahara, she insisted; the Amazon rainforest biome relies on this wind and sand in order to properly breathe.[24] What would have to change about our relation to deserts if we were all really to let that knowledge sink in?

Calling this a "collective" was aspirational. We were a collective of three who then became five and seven and so on... We wanted to create a focal point and space to gather many other voices, to find out who else was out there asking these questions, and to invite them in so that we could have conversations together and create new ways of talking together. As we've been alluding to, we began by designing a series of conferences meant to be held in 2020 at each of our respective institutions. Then 2020 happened, and everything changed as we weathered the pandemic. In that chaotic and lonely summer, or perhaps fall, the three of us got in touch, after our conferences had all been indefinitely postponed and the future looked so blurry, and decided to gather online in the hopes of creating community that could help us through the isolation. We held a series of small and lively workshops over the winter, as Francisco has mentioned, which culminated in the Comparative Desert Imaginations digital conference organized by Brahim—and assembled the growing multitude of scholars, activists, and artists working across ages, languages, and geographies. In the fall, Francisco will host a conference at Notre Dame, and in April 2022, I will host another conference at Yale; so we are picking up the threads and extending them to all our various institutions. The collective is growing beyond us in a way that I find so deeply energizing and inspiring, gathering a momentum as it goes.

BEG: Your phrase, Samia, the "possibility of an otherwise" indicates the open futurity of the desert: the desert as a place that has a history, but which is also open into a possible, different future. When I think about the name "Desert Futures Collective," I am inclined to parse it into its constitutive parts: "desert" as a generic word that describes arid and dry regions across the globe; "futures," which definitely orients the desert and the project as a projective endeavor that is not limited to the present condition; and "collective," which, in my eyes, is a clear assertion of our attempt to create an ecumenical community. The name is thus a kind of approach to the examination of deserts, one that spans across time, disciplines, languages, and geographical locations. However, futurity does not mean ignorance of the past or lack of engagement with the present.

Inscribing the desert in a future project goes against its current theorizations as a symbol of civilization's negation in Western philosophy. Michael Marder, a professor of philosophy at the University of the Basque Country in Spain, cites German Philosopher Martin Heidegger's saying that "'Devastation' ["Verwüstung"] means for us, after all, that everything—the world, the human, and the earth—will be transformed into a desert [Wüste]."[25] Drawing on the distinction Heidegger makes between destruction and devastation in terms of the possibility (with the former) and the impossibility of a future (with the latter), Marder interprets the desert as "vast, unoccupied, desolate, vacant, vacated of beings."[26] This Western-centric theorization of the desert—as the opposite of civilization—is not just problematic but also the rationale for the continued extraction,

24   May Joseph, "Harmattan Wind as Decolonial Morphology" (talk, Comparative Desert Imaginations: Place, Mobility, and Environment Symposium & Student Workshop, Williams College Center for Foreign Languages, Literatures & Cultures, Williamstown, MA, May 21, 2021).

25   Martin Heidegger, *Country Path Conversations*, trans. Bret W. Davis (Bloomington: Indiana University Press, 2010), 136, quoted in Michael Marder, *Heidegger: Phenomenology, Ecology, Politics* (Minneapolis: University of Minnesota Press, 2018), 94.

weaponization, and annihilation of the desert. Using desert imagery to describe what the world will look like without civilization diminishes the desert to civilization's "Other" and, in doing so, paves the way for the devastation of the desert itself. If the future of humanity is desert, then everything that comes from the desert threatens the current civilization. Whether the fight against the desert takes the form of nuclear and chemical testing or the use of drones to track and prevent immigrants from crossing the Sahara, the war on and in the desert is really about fending off the catastrophic future that Euro-American philosophers, like Heidegger, associate with the space. So, imagining a futurity in which the desert is not threatening is crucial for the kind of work that I am personally invested in. What does it look like to think of a desertic future for humanity? How can the word "desert" be resignified to mean civilization in its own terms and context?

It always helps to think about the future from the perspective of local authors. Unlike the prevalent tendency to draw solely on Euro-American theory in European languages, the desert future, as I understand it personally, is inherently multilingual and informed by Indigenous theories, which I propose to "read with" (instead of being "read through") the prevalent theorizations of the desert. There is a critical difference between a future scholarship that starts with local texts and reads them in conversation with, say, Deleuze and Guattari and an approach that reads local theory through Deleuze and Guattari.[27] While the first kind of reading recenters the

26   Marder, *Heidegger*, 94.
27   I am referring to the celebrated distinction between "smooth" and "striated" in *A Thousand Plateaus: Capitalism and Schizophrenia*, trans. Brian Massumi (Minneapolis: Minnesota University Press, 1987); see especially "Treatise on Nomadology—The War Machine," 351–423, and "The Smooth and the Striated," 474–500. The hegemony of the framework offered by Deleuze and Guattari in this book has for a long time overshadowed other conceptualizations of deserts that exist beyond their binaries, hence my call to "read with" them and "not through" them.

desert as both a producer and object of knowledge, the second approach subjugates the desert to theorizations that have been produced elsewhere, like the Heideggerian musings above. For example, instead of merely presenting a counterpoint to the dichotomy that opposes the desert to Western civilization, Ibrahim al-Koni, a local, Tuareg theorist and novelist, provides a different, intrinsic view of the desert as being not only full but also fully alive:

> The oil wells have become, for the people of the Sahara, a bottomless abyss since the day they brought their paralysis upon the people of this virgin homeland. The paralysis of the soul before that of the body. The blessing [of oil] turned quickly into a curse because of lassitude, which did not only kill their innate love of work but also shook their moral values. The bleeding of the earth, which is called oil, has managed to bring a curse on the people of the land because this liquid was really never petrol. In fact, it was the blood of our mother earth. Drilling it is a violation of the belly of this mother and a defiling of its sacred soul.[28]

Al-Koni's words refute the ideas underlying the desert's desolation by humanizing it and by describing it as a mothering force contingent on respect. This mothering opens up space what I call "Ecocare" (ecological care), which is rooted in Indigenous traditions of desert dwellers. Most importantly, however, is al-Koni's argument that "if the world is a body, the desert is its soul."[29] Unlike Heidegger, who argues that humanity without a future becomes a desert, al-Koni sees no future for humanity without the desert, for the desert is co-constitutive of the very possibility of humanity. So the desert future al-Koni imagines is inclusive

28   Ibrahim al-Koni. *Waṭanī ṣaḥrāʾ kubrā* [My homeland is a great desert] (Beirut: al-Mu'assasa al-'Arabiyya li-al-Dirāsāt wa-al-Nashr, 2009), 8.
29   Al-Koni, *Waṭanī*, 49.

whereas Heidegger's is exclusive. I tend to agree with al-Koni and believe that Desert Futures is about the possibility of seeing beyond what has already been seen—the possibility of shattering the framework of the "has-already-been-thought" to rethink the desert and its ramifications through voices that have been eclipsed in prevalent Western-centric approaches to the study of formerly disregarded or coveted spaces in general. Hopefully, *reading with* desert sources and local thought will become a generalized practice in the future.

Menna Agha is assistant professor of design and spatial justice at Carleton University. She is an architect and researcher and holds a PhD in Architecture from the University of Antwerp and a MA in Gender and Design from Köln International School of Design. Menna was a 2019/2020 Spatial Justice Fellow and visiting assistant professor at the University of Oregon, as well as the coordinator of the 2021 spatial justice agenda at the Flanders Architecture Institute. She is a third-generation displaced Fadichka Nubian who frames and grounds her research in race, gender, space, and territory. Her writing includes "Nubia Still Exists: The Utility of the Nostalgic Space" (*Humanities*, 2019); "The Non-Work of the Unimportant: The Shadow Economy of Nubian Women in Displacement Villages" (*Kohl: a Journal for Body and Gender Research*, 2019); and "Liminal Publics, Marginal Resistance: Learning from Nubian Spaces" (*IDEA Journal*, 2017).

MENNA AGHA

IT IS NOT
A DESERT WHERE
GRANDMOTHER
SITS[1]

---

1   The title in Nubian is: ΔΝΝᾹ   ω-ιΝ ᾱ   ΓεΝ ΔΓΔρ ΟγΜΜΙΓ(Δ) Φᴀ ΝΔ𝑏𝑏ᴀᴄᴄΙ ΜΟγΝ.

ⲉⲗⲉⲗ̄   ē̄   ⲉⲗⲉⲗ̄   ē̄   .. ⳣⲁⲥⲉⲃⲁⲗ̄   ⲁ ⲱⲉⲇ̄ⲁ̄   ⲛ̄ⲁ̄   ⲕⲁⲗ̄   ⲁ

ⲥⲟⲩⲕⲁ ⲇ̄   ⲟⲩⲱⲁ ⲓ̄   ⲅⲁ ⲧⲓⲣⲁⲛⲁ ⲇ̄   ⲟⲩⲱⲁ ⳟⲉⲅⲓ̄   ⲣ ⲉⲗ ⲇⲁ   ⲥⲕⲁ

ⲩⲁⲗⲁⲱⲓ̈ⲓ̈ⲉⲗⲓ ⲇⲟⲩⲕ̄   ō̄   ⲇⲁ ⲟⲕ̄   ⲓⲥ̄   ⲛ̄ⲇⲟ ⲁ̄   ⲅⲛ̄ⲁ̄   ⲛⲓ

ⲕⲟⲩⲥⲁ ⳟⲁⲗⲕⲁ ⲇⲟⲩⲕ̄   ō̄   ⲇⲁ ⲟⲕ̄   ⲓⲥ̄   ⲛ̄ⲇⲟ ⲁ̄   ⲅⲛ̄ⲁ̄   ⲛⲓ

ⲕⲉ̄   ⲣⲁ-ⲧ̄ⲁ̄   ⲣⲉ-ⲙⲁⲅⲓⲛⲛⲁ ⳟⲉⲅⲓ̄   ⲣ ⲉⲗ ⲇⲁ   ⲥⲕⲁ

ⲉⲓⲛ ⲙⲁⲥⲣ ⲉⲧⲓ̄   ⲅⲁⲗⲓ ⲉⲓⲃ̄ō̄   ̓ⲛ ⲙⲉⲧ̄   ⲁ ⲓ̈ⲓⲛⲙⲟⲩⲛⲛⲁ̄   ⲛⲓ

ⲕⲟⲩⲡⲣⲓ ⲩⲟⲩⲡⲣⲁ ⲗⲓ ⲓⲡ̄ō̄   ⲛ ⲙⲉⲧⲧⲁ ⲓ̈ⲓⲙⲙⲟⲩⲛⲁⲛⲓ..

ⲕⲉ̄   ⲣⲁ-ⲧ̄ⲁ̄   ⲣⲉ-ⲙⲁⲅⲓⲛⲛⲁ ⳟⲉⲅⲓ̄   ⲣ ⲉⲗ ⲇⲁ   ⲥⲕⲁ

ⲙⲟⲩⲗⲟⲩⲭⲓ̈ⲓ̈ⲉ̇ ⳟⲁ̄   ⲱⲉ̄   ⲣⲕⲁ ⲉⲱⲓⲣō̄   ⲥⲕ ⲁⲛⲅō̄   ⲛⲓ

ⲉⲓⲇ̄   ⲁⲛⲓ ⲅⲉⲛⲁ ⲱō̄   ⲃⲁⲛⲕ̓ⲛ ⲁ̄   ⲧⲉ̄   ⲗⲁ ⲁ̄   ⲅⲓ

ⲕⲉ̄   ⲣⲁ-ⲧ̄ⲁ̄   ⲣⲉ-ⲙⲁⲅⲓⲛⲛⲁ ⳟⲉⲅⲓ̄   ⲣ ⲉⲗ ⲇⲁ   ⲥⲕⲁ

Elele, elele... we trust God in you.
Go descend and tell Fagir Algas
Shalaweye is waiting by the running waterwheel
In the time of its untying turns
Tell him to ascend, Fagir Algas
[Egypt] is not his father's house...
Shoubra Bridge is not his inheritance
Tell him to ascend, Fagir Algas
In our land, there is a Molokhia Basin
It gives more good than the bank he sits by
Tell him to ascend, Fagir Algas[2]

2   This is an excerpt of a Nubian song composed by Shalaweye, a renowned female Nubian poet. The song is part of the oral history of Fadichka Nubians. The song has been sung by many, most notably Abu Simbel native Fekry Kashef, who presents this song and an analysis in a recording uploaded by Nubiantv on March 30, 2012, https://www.youtube.com/watch?v=dr7S_G4b8RY. The Nubian transcription is courtesy of Dr. Hassan Nour, as part of his seminal project "Dore Kolod," "DORE KOLOD - النوبية والفنون اللغة," YouTube," https://www.youtube.com/channel/UCxSA8V vGSrAFoPT7ytdkLug/videos. Dore Kolod is an independent translation and archiving project situated outside any state, academic, or institutional umbrella, but rather in a Nubian episteme in which archival practices rely on living records. Dore Kolod puts Nubian songs back on our tongues to sustain our language.

About the Nubian font: Sawarda is a Nubian typeface designed by Hatim-Arbaab Eujayl, a Nubian designer who took on the task of producing a Nubian font that represents the Indigenous characteristics of Nubian scripts: the lack of capitalization, the slant, the letter proportions with two classes of ascenders, a letterform ductus that differs from Greek and Coptic counterparts. The Sawarda font allows Nubian text to follow Nubian phonetics and eliminates the reliance on Greek fonts for electronically produced transcripts. See https://unionfornubianstudies.org/projects/sawarda.

I write this to honor Nubian womanhood, the political project that is sustaining Nubian lives today and has throughout a century of displacement. Here I tell the stories of two Nubian icons, whose Indigenous methods of analysis, praxis, and resistance have ushered waves of return and reinforced Nubian landback claims. The first is the Nubian poet Shalaweye, whose verses prelude this text and have continued to linger on Nubian tongues for decades. The second is Hagga Tahra, who decided to return to her emptied ancestral land and lived there on her own for over forty years. Both women lived across the river from the Abu Simbel Temple, which was rescued by UNESCO from the High Dam reservoir. Nubian peoplehood, unlike monuments, were not regarded as worthy subjects of these international institutionalized rescue campaigns. Instead, as people, we had women like Shalaweye and Tahra, who helped Nubians salvage our cultural and material lives.

Nubia, my ancestral land, is the area on the Nile banks spanning between the first and the fifth Nile cataracts, in the area straddling the border between Egypt and Sudan. Today, as we mourn the loss of our land and Indigenous territories due to a series of damming projects over the Nile River, we also work towards a Nubian agenda of return and reparations. Young Nubians like myself identify as displaced despite never having

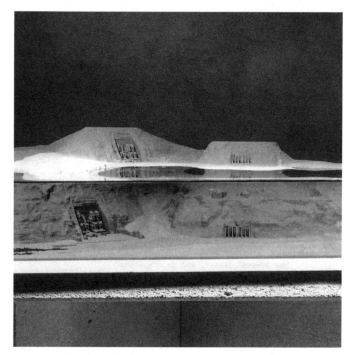

A model of the Abu Simbel Temples showing the previous site (below) and the new site above water level, produced for the UNESCO exhibition on the International Campaign to Save the Monuments of Nubia, 1960. Courtesy of Creative Commons.

encountered our ancestral land.[3] But our grandmothers render its image vivid in our minds through storytelling. I rely on and connect to this storytelling here, binding this text to a Nubian episteme that I stand within in my attempts to make sense of both this world and worlds yet to come.

There is what seems to resemble a consensus among Indigenous scholars across regions about the importance of inserting oneself into Indigenous research methodologies. The desire to ground one's sense of "self" is further articulated and expanded on in both Paul Whitinui's and Onowa McIvor's analyses of Indigenous autoethnography.[4] In this way, knowledge-seeking through Indigenous realms rejects individualization politics that otherwise allow the researcher to sever ties with

3   Menna Agha, "Nubia Still Exists: On the Utility of the Nostalgic Space," *Humanities* 8, no. 1 (2019): 24.
4   Paul Whitinui, "Indigenous Autoethnography: Exploring, Engaging, and Experiencing 'Self' as a Native Method of Inquiry," *Journal of Contemporary Ethnography* 43, no. 4 (2014): 456–487; Onowa McIvor, "I Am My Subject: Blending Indigenous Research Methodology and Autoethnography through Integrity-Based, Spirit-Based Research," *Canadian Journal of Native Education* 33, no. 1 (2010): 137–151.

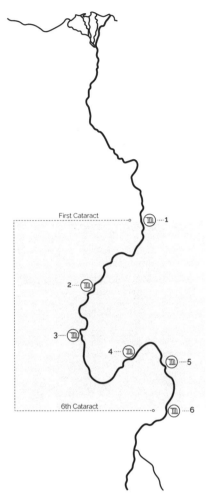

A map showing the historical limits of Nubian land beyond modern-day borders and nation-states. Courtesy of the author.

their kin. This means I am part of these stories and they are part of me. On this path, I implicate my knowledge, intuition, dreams, and desires to make sense of my own Nubian womanhood.

Nubian Struggle, Nubian Resistance

The Nubian struggle with dams and large hydropower projects started with the construction of the Low Dam in 1902, which raised the Nile's water level and flooded swaths of our land. The dam was heightened in 1912, and again in 1933, each time reducing agricultural land and disenfranchising Nubian economic

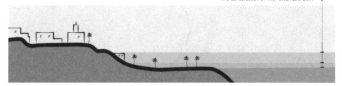

1964
The Construction of The High Dam and The Displacement of Nubians

1933
The second heightening of Aswan Low Dam

1902
The Construction of The Aswan Low Dam

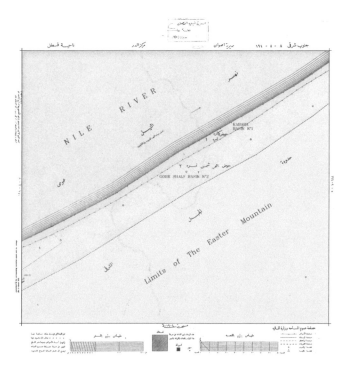

Section illustrating water levels rising over Nubian land during the twentieth century. Water levels started rising in 1902 following construction of the Low Dam, which submerged vast areas of arable land. Courtesy of the author.

In this 1904 map, we can see the raised water level over arable basins. The Kabara basin belonged to the family of my maternal grandmother Fawzeya Kabara, and was, according to my grandmother, partly submerged after the construction of the Low Dam. Base map sourced from the archive of the Egyptian Survey Authority. Courtesy of the author.

and social life.[5] These hydropower ventures were rooted in a colonial project that perceived Nubia as an empty desert.[6] Although the Low Dam and its modifications were devastating to our ways of life, perhaps our most intense loss came from the construction of the High Dam in Aswan in the 1960s. The dam created Lake Nasser, which engulfed the entirety of Nubian land within Egypt, triggering a large development-induced displacement that resulted in a resettlement project, for no fewer than one hundred thousand Nubians, in the Kom Ombo Valley, where I was born and raised.[7] This resettlement project was dubbed "New Nubia" by the Egyptian state, but we call it *Tahgeer*, meaning the site of displacement.[8] Tahgeer is where I was told by my grandmother that my ancestral land is elsewhere, underwater, and where I must return.

It is important for me to recite Nubian resistance against different damming projects, to remind myself that my people were not passive or silent but rather silenced and rendered vulnerable. Nubians protested the dam and its heightening in the early twentieth century, as evident through their letters of protest to the British High Commissioner.[9] They also rejected the High Dam through numerous Nubian songs that were composed at the time of its construction. Nubians were successful in halting the work on the Sudanese-Kajbar Dam in 2007, after four Nubians were killed and twenty were injured by state police agents at a protest there.[10] Nubian women in particular have performed several forms of resistance, including the rejection of the resettlement project in displacement villages, which led to the alteration and the rebuilding of almost every state-issued housing unit. My grandmothers were able to claim such powers over the built environment by mobilizing their emotional resources towards community-making.[11]

5   Ezzeldin Sakoury, *Highlights of Nubian Society* (Al Salam Al Gadida Press, 1988).
6   Eustace Alfred Reynolds-Ball, in his account of his trip to the south of the First
      Cataract, describes Lower Nubia as if it exists in a different continent from the
      northern Nile Valley, as "practically empty" and dangerous, with potential brigands
      and "dervishes." He quotes Arthur Conan Doyle, who also describes Nubia as this
      kind of deserted land, where there are "traces of vanished races." Eustace Alfred
      Reynolds-Ball, *The City of the Caliphs: A Popular Study of Cairo and Its Environs and
      the Nile and Its Antiquities* (Boston: Estes and Lauriat, 1897), 304–305 and 308–331.
7   There is no trusted demographic information that mentions the true count of
      Nubians who underwent displacement due to the High Dam.
8   Menna Agha and Els De Vos, "Liminal Publics, Marginal Resistance: Learning from
      Nubian Spaces," *IDEA Journal* 16, no. 1 (2017): 88–101.
9   Such as Mahmoud Hamed Taha to the British High Commissioner in Egypt, May
      24, 1932, FO 141/699/3, National Archives, London; in which Taha writes on behalf of
      Nubians and titles this letter "Who is responsible for these victims."
10   "Kajbar Dam, Sudan," International Rivers, https://archive.internationalrivers.org/
      campaigns/kajbar-dam-sudan.

The series of Nubian displacements are linked directly to
the Colonial perception of Nubian land as a desert, a designation
rooted in racism and used as a mechanism to subjugate and
modify lands classified as "desert." The term "Nubian Desert" is
found in Western literature about Nubia, especially in the early
nineteenth century, with travelers like the Swiss Johann Ludwig
Burckhardt, who, when writing about his journeys in his book
Travels in Nubia, mentions "making perhaps some lateral excur-
sions into the Nubian Desert. This journey will, I hope, make me
acquainted with the character of the Negroe."[12] In a white colonial
imaginary, Nubian people were considered the threshold where
any resemblance to white or "Mediterranean stock" is no longer
perceptible.[13]

There has always been a gap between my understanding
of my homeland and its depiction in literature, first because
Nubians are rarely allowed to write the terms of their own story,
and second because academic literature about Nubia existed
mainly to serve colonial and national interests. The first time I
learned that our land is classified as a desert was in college from
an English geography book in which the term sat uncontested
as a scientific definition. In this context, all the materialities
of Nubian geographies were collapsed into simplified colonial
definitions. We come from sand and sun, but it was never
a desert. For Nubians, our land is not perceived as a desert,
primarily because the concept is ontologically inapplicable
within Nubian fields of meaning and language. There is no active
word equivalent to the word desert in our contemporary Nubian
languages. Further, there are no traces of an equivalent word in
old Nubian according to philologist Vincent van Gerven Oei.[14]
The word for "sand" in contemporary Nubian stems from the old
Nubian word for Earth.

Nubian women were racialized and gendered in both
colonial and postcolonial Egypt.[15] As migration became institutionalized after the construction of the Low Dam, the male

11   Menna Agha, "Emotional Capital and Other Ontologies of the Architect,"
      Architectural Histories 8, no. 1 (2020): article 23, https://journal.eahn.org/articles/
      10.5334/ah.381.
12   Burckhardt was sponsored by the Association for Promoting the Discovery of the
      Interior Parts of Africa. Johann Ludwig Burckhardt, *Travels in Nubia* (London:
      John Murray, 1819), xlix.
13   David Randall-MacIver and Charles Leonard Woolley, *Areika*, Publications of the
      Egyptian Department of the University Museum (Philadelphia: University of
      Pennsylvania Press, 1909), 1.
14   Vincent W.J. van Gerven Oei, "What is the word for desert in Old Nubian?" Email,
      2021.
15   In his accounts of his visits to Nubia in the 1840s, John Gadsby recounts Orientalist
      fantasies of Nubian women greeting him while wearing almost nothing but
      castor oil. See Leslie Greener, *High Dam Over Nubia* (London: Cassell, 1962), 42–44.

emigration rate at any moment was at least 60 percent, while the
women were left behind in the villages.[16] Nubian women did not
follow their menfolk to urban centers, which were sites of intense
racial hostility; instead, they stayed home and allowed their
bodies to become metaphors for the lost land—what I see
as yet another example of "strategic essentialism," a strategy by
which members of a given group suspend their fluid understandings to achieve a political goal.[17] In this case, Nubian women
suspended the dynamism of their gendered being to become
the essence of their land. During the 1960s displacement, the
Egyptian state further dispossessed women when state agents
only talked to men,[18] resulting in women's loss of material
wealth, as compensation land was registered only in men's
names, despite the existing Indigenous tradition of shared
ownership systems. In reading these histories of women and
land, I see how the land became a Nubian woman's struggle, and
I understand my grandmother's call for return.

Shalaweye's Song of Refusal

Shalaweye, the iconic Nubian poet, was—and remains—filled
with sadness in the song I cite at the opening of this text. In this
seminal Nubian song, she implores her husband Fagir Algas to
return to Nubian Land from Cairo. The song takes the form of
a dictated letter—a popular format in Nubian spoken word arts
that mimics the common practice in which a person dictates
their letters to one of the few formally educated people in any
given village. I learned a lot about Shalaweye through talking
to my elders.[19] I learned that she was from Fareeg, a short boat
ride from the Abu Simbel Temple.[20] I have also tried to locate her
in time using pieces of information in the longer version of her
song. I have come to the conclusion that Shalaweye must have
lived in the first and second decades of the twentieth century,
as her husband traveled to work in *Masr* (or Cairo), a common
practice after the building of the Aswan Low Dam had substan-
tially reduced Nubian arable land.[21]

16   Sondra Hale, "The Impact of Immigration on Women: The Sudanese Nubian Case,"
        Women's Studies 17, no. 1–2 (1989): 53–56.
17   Gayatri Chakravorty Spivak, "Subaltern Studies: Deconstructing Historiography," in
        The Spivak Reader: Selected Works of Gayatri Chakravorty Spivak, ed. Donna Landry
        and Gerald MacLean (New York: Routledge, 1996), 203–236.
18   This information came from many elderly Nubian women in my family and
        interviews with elderly Nubian women in Ffadicha villages.
19   Namely, I talked with my uncles, Fekry Kashef, the Nubian singer and song writer
        from Abu Simbel, and Nubian poet and language specialist Mr Mohamad Omar,
        from the village of Ibrim.
20   Fareeg is also known as the village of Abu Simbel.

As the men left for Masr, Nubian women had to stay and maintain what remained of Nubia. Shalaweye had put her husband's diaspora into an analytical work. She spoke from a Nubian epistemic position, a position young Nubians—like myself—are trying to reclaim. She starts from a point of resistance to Western geographies: as she asks her husband to ascend (from Cairo to Nubian land), she maintains Nubian cartography, which was turned upside down by Western knowledge. She had the clarity to know that her enemy was a seductive image of the city, the steel bridge in Shobra, banks, and the glamour of urbanization.[22] As a member of a Nubian community, she linked the induced diaspora of her husband and many of his fellow Nubian men with the blight of agriculture in her ancestral land, alluding that their absence caused further deterioration of the land. We see her position rooted in land politics and Indigenous agricultural practices as the opening image of the song is one of Shalaweye standing next to the waterwheel, a historical key feature of Nubian agricultural technology.

A Nubian waterwheel (*Eskaleeh*), the site of Shalaweye's calls to Fagir Algas. Courtesy of the Metropolitan Museum of Art's collection via Creative Commons.

21   Shalaweye specifies Cairo in the poem: the word "Egypt" or "Masr" in Egyptian peasant cultures often refers to the Egyptian capital, whose urbanization was ironically enabled by the controlled, dammed Nile.

22   Shobra Bridge is the popular name of one of the novel steel bridges built in Cairo around the late nineteenth century. I suspect that this mention refers to the bridge that precedes the current Imbaba bridge; the older one was constructed is 1890. *Cairobserver* offers a study of this bridge that once was a landmark; Mohamed Elshahed, "Old Imbaba Bridge, 1890," *Cairobserver*, November 8, 2011, https://cairo bserver.com/post/12492028959/old-imbaba-bridge-1890.

My foremother remains adamant in arguing for her homeland as she implores her husband to come back, audaciously
pitting Nubian Indigenous cosmogony against Egypt's modernity.[23] She reminds her husband that her small basin of edible
greens is all that they need for food security, more trustworthy
than the bank in Cairo—she refers to him sitting by the bank,
as most men at the time worked as doormen. In a reading
positioned in a Nubian episteme, I can hear Shalaweye telling
him that the basin works for us, but we have to work for the
bank. To counter the seduction of the city, she weaves an
alluring image saying, "The pottery from Sudan in our Diwani,
where She'reye swims in milk and melted butter."[24] Diwani is a
well-decorated room in Nubian houses, and she also references
her ornamented pottery for this image as a reminder that Nubian
material culture is still capable of sustaining a good life.

The story of Shalaweye still rings in Nubian ears and flows
from Nubian tongues today, even during what seems like the
least fitting times for songs about sad calls for return. I can't
remember a wedding dance party without the echo of her words.
Shalaweye's song remains an active Nubian story: the groom
from that wedding will probably travel to an Arab Gulf country,
the contemporary form of exile with its seductive, growing
urbanism. He will probably join the tens of thousands of Nubian
men who are part of the new serf class brought to yet another
site of economic inequality. The bride, on the other hand, will
remain in a displacement village as her body becomes a materialized proxy for a lost land.

Tahra Refuses to Leave

This second story is about Tahra Ali Naser, affectionately called
Hagga Tahra, who lived—and died—a few kilometers away
from Shalaweye's submerged home village. Tahra was a Nubian
woman from my village of Qustul. She was displaced with her
family in the 1960s to Tahgeer. In January 1970, the Egyptian
state allowed for the first trip back to Nubian land that was then
mostly submerged underwater from the dam's reservoir.[25] Abdel

23   "Foremother" here refers affectionately to Shalaweye. "Modernity" here refers to
      the project of modernization by the British colonizers as well as the Egyptian
      postcolonial state. See Timothy Mitchell, *Colonising Egypt* (Berkeley: University of
      California Press, 1991); and Timothy Mitchell, *Rule of Experts: Egypt, Techno-Politics,
      Modernity* (Berkeley: University of California Press, 2002).
24   She'reye is sun-dried noodles often connected to special occasions in Nubian
      consciousness.
25   Mohy-Eldeen Hassan Saleh, *Qustul, a Nubian Presence* (Cairo: Egypt Publishing
      House, 2012).

Nasser's successor, then-president Muhammad Anwar el-Sadat, was much more sympathetic to Nubians and more interested in reviving the area by the water reservoir that encompasses the remains of Nubian Land. He invested in the area around the Abu Simbel Temple, turning the adjacent archaeologist settlement into a livable town, now referred to as touristic Abu Simbel town.[26]

This touristic town provided simple services to reach the area closest to Qustul's submerged site, where Tahra lived and where Nubians from Qustul—as well as its neighboring town Adendan—wish to return. A group of Nubian activists began approaching Sadat and his government to support their dream of return, successfully earning its support in 1976. It is common knowledge among Nubians that Sadat's sympathy and support came from his Sudanese ancestry on his mother's side. In May 1978, a group of thirty-five Nubians from the villages of Qustul and Adendan arrived at the site of their old neighboring villages as part of the state-backed project of return.[27] The returned Nubians began farming on the 1,030 acres on the lake's shores. Nubians began ascending and descending from the Egyptian Nubian north and the Sudanese Nubian south, respectively.

The first wedding on Nubian ancestral land after displacement was in 1980; it was the wedding of Awatef Hussein, a schoolmate of my aunt. President Sadat personally attended and was a signing witness to the marriage. But despite the advocacy of Sadat, after his death in 1981, Nubians lost the support of the government and were forced to return to their displacement villages. Except for Hagga Tahra. She refused to return to the resettlement in Tahgeer and remained in her ancestral land for forty years until her passing in 2021.

Tahra's house became a site of Nubian pilgrimage—it became a portal linking Nubians to a dream of return. She became a fascinating topic for journalists and filmmakers, which she despised once she recognized the futility of media exposure for her agenda.[28] She inspired several failed and successful return attempts and was a catalyst for larger agricultural projects in 2010, in which Nubians formed co-ops and bought patches of their land from the Egyptian Ministry of Agriculture and Land Reclamation. While the co-operation project has faced many

26   This epithet differentiates it from the village of Abu Simbel, which is located among other displaced villages in the Kom Ombo Valley.
27   Saleh, *Qustul, a Nubian Presence.*
28   Filmmakers frequented her house, especially in the later years of her life, after film equipment became easier to transport on the long, rough trip to reach her. She is featured in films such as "Nefertari insists on staying" produced by Al Jazeera. Al Jazeera Documentary, ‏البقاء الجزيرة الوثائقية. نفرتاري تصر على‏, March 31, 2017, https://www.youtube.com/watch?v=OvW6oV0FSqg.

Near Hagga Tahra's house, the 2010 return through agricultural cooperatives. In this photo, Hagg Awad Saleh Ibrahim moves the first harvest in Nubian ancestral land. Courtesy of Mohamed Ezz, Nile Foundation for African and Strategic Studies.

Hagga Tahra's house as depicted in the documentary film *Women from the Land of Gold*, directed by filmmaker Fayza Harby, 2015. Courtesy of Fayza Harby.

struggles, it was the most successful return since that of 1978, and, in it, the resistance of Tahara lives on.

It Was Never a Desert

Defining a "desert" is a burden I shed off of my shoulders despite having to experience its ramifications as an imposition. Our land was deemed a desert by colonial powers, thus deemed worthy of desertion, emptiness, and de-peopling. I shed that burden because I divest from colonial knowledge and epistemically reposition myself into a place where I hear my grandmother's voice. This is in part because of an agenda of self-care though which I attempt to rid myself of colonial burdens that have been imposed on myself, my people, and my land. But more importantly, I divest from defining the desert because I cannot locate it as a concept in my grandmother's voice.

Nubian spatialities rely on politics of personhood and peopling. The sand dunes and the mountains around us are not vacant, they are occupied with Jinn. The Nile is always bustling with "the people of the river," storied yet unseen populations who live within the river's waters. Therefore, when situated within the Nubian episteme, I can only posit that Nubia was not a desert and was instead a space of Nubian life for which my foremothers fought. The notion of "Nubian Desert," brings a geographic project of epistemicide, designed to discount Nubian humanity and peoplehood and facilitate colonial modes of extraction.

In situating ourselves in our epistemologies and our land, Indigeneity becomes a potent political project. Despite the term "Indigenous" being an English word, which is a language lacking the ontological resources to encompass what we feel about ourselves, it is the closest in meaning to our position and is a term claimed by Indigenous people resisting colonial hegemony the world over. When considering Nubia through the lens of Indigeneity, I am reminded constantly that our struggle is a land-based project, and that the centrality of our land is embodied and defended by Nubian women.

My foremothers built and safeguarded Nubian places that continue to emotionally scaffold our world-making projects against a colonial imaginary that extracted and dispossessed our land. These women also left a wealth of analytical tools through which I can make sense of my places, but only if I listen to my grandmothers' voices that keep ringing in my head. Both Shalaweye and Tahra performed political work to prevent the reproduction of another Nubian Desert through mechanisms of dispossession. Shalaweye understood the insidious projects of dispossession. She stood on her waterwheel calling on Nubians hundreds of miles away to return. Her voice then traveled a hundred years to us as a reminder of our land and a continued call to return. Tahra tied her physical being to our ancestral land, becoming land herself. Tahra's return is praxis, rendering landback and projects of return into a matter of Afrowomanism, reclaiming powers that were dispossessed from Nubian women in their displacement. It is not a stretch to state that Shalaweye made similar claims. It is not a stretch to see Tahra as an extension of Shalaweye's political work a century earlier. It is certainly not a stretch to find my voice in the echo of their voices, in a Nubian struggle against colonial and neocolonial desert-making projects.

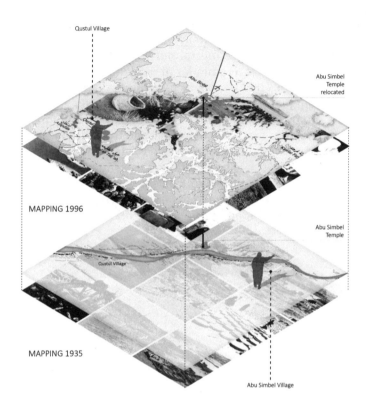

Qustul Village

Abu Simbel
Temple
relocated

MAPPING 1996

Abu Simbel
Temple

Qustul Village

MAPPING 1935

Abu Simbel Village

Mapping Nubian women's resistance across time and place. Courtesy of the author.

Bassam Ahmed, *Return*, digital illustration, November 2021. Courtesy of Bassam Ahmed.

Danika Cooper is assistant professor of landscape architecture and environmental planning at the University of California, Berkeley, where the core of her research centers on the geopolitics of scarcity, alternative water ontologies, and designs for resiliency in the world's arid regions. Her work incorporates historiographical research methods, data visualizations, and theories of urban infrastructure to evaluate and design for environmental and social justice. Cooper is specifically focused on emphasizing alternatives to the prevailing nineteenth-century conception that aridlands should be overturned through technocratic solutions and neoliberal politics. Her work has been published and exhibited around the world, and she has practiced architecture and landscape architecture in both the United States and India. Cooper holds degrees in landscape architecture, architecture, and design studies.

DANIKA COOPER

DRAWING DESERTS, MAKING WORLDS

Landscape

The early morning sounds are so clear.
Familiar in my memory.
The sound of boiling coffee.
The sound of shuffling feet, a step, a shuffle.
She didn't lift her feet when she walked.
She shuffled to her own rhythm.
Old wooden floors worn thin by her shuffling
and eight children.
She was short in stature.
Low to the ground.
She had joints that began
losing moisture and flexibility
when she first started to walk.
She didn't lift her feet.
She was in constant contact with the earth.
With each shuffle she pushed the earth along,
with each step she dragged time along.
She pushed bits of her past
and bits of her future
in uncertain amounts and
in uncertain directions.

Oig 'am si, 'oig 'am si	Come now, come now
Si g o 'e-keihi	Step lively
Si g o 'e-keihi	Step lively
Att o 'i-hudiñ g cewagï	We will pull down the clouds

| Att o 'i-wai g ju:kĭ | We will call the rain |
| Oig 'am si, 'oig 'am si | Come now, come now |

U:gk o himc g jeweḍ	We will make the dust rise
U:gk o himc g jeweḍ	We will make the dust rise
Att o 'i-hudiñ g cewagĭ	We will pull down the clouds

In awe I watch young men bound two,
sometimes three, steps at a time,
and young women as they virtually float
effortlessly across minor obstacles.
I, on the other hand, am a profiler.
I have no interest in ethnic distinctions.
Instead I survey with a biased eye
for uneven terrain before my journey.
I take special note of stairs, steps, tall curbs, grading.
I take note of minor ones,
breaks and seams of seemingly
smooth sidewalks,
roughness of asphalt and gravel walkways.
I consciously lift my foot with every step.
Unlike most, I am aware of the unevenness of landscape.
I know the earth has no smooth surfaces.
Primordial memories
store the memory of glacial movements
and carving of landscape.
I am aware of canyons reshaping themselves every moment.
Somehow I know water and air are not smooth
and molecules require speed bumps.
I am aware of strategically placed signs

for pedestrians of earth:
Hold onto handrails
Watch your step
Caution
Moving walkway will end
Please be prepared to step off
Keep shoelaces and straps away
from moving parts
Open-toed shoes not allowed
Please keep walkway clear.*

The deserts of the United States—the Great Basin, Mojave, Sonoran, and Chihuahuan—have been sites of genocide, territorial dispossession, and ecological devastation. Beginning in the fifteenth century, reaching a critical height during the nineteenth, and continuing to the present, millions of Europeans and Americans have moved through and settled in the deserts in pursuit of promised prosperity and opportunity. On these lands, the US has enacted its agenda for capital accumulation through landed systems of private property, extractive economies, and social exclusion, all of which have contributed to protracted and enduring violence against Indigenous peoples and the environment itself. Despite these histories, nineteenth-century maps, surveys, photographs, paintings, and other images made of desert landscapes masquerade as neutral artifacts, depicting "natural" conditions of the desert while simultaneously obscuring the violent sociopolitical context of US settler colonialism. These desert images thus help shape a historical account of the modern US nation-state as one built from achievement rather than from trauma, as Western Shoshone historian Ned Blackhawk has saliently articulated.[1] In his book, *Violence over the Land: Indians and Empire in the Early American*

1   Ned Blackhawk, *Violence over the Land: Indians and Empires in the Early American West* (Cambridge, MA: Harvard University Press, 2008), 1.

West, Blackhawk argues that violence was a precondition of US political formation: "From the initial moments of American exploration and conquest, through statehood, and into the stages of territorial formation, violence organized the region's nascent economies, settlements, and politics. Violence and American nationhood, in short, progressed hand in hand."[2] Arguing that violence is a corollary to colonialism, Blackhawk employs law historian Barbara Young Welke's theory that the "tools of civilization" in the nineteenth century were themselves "instruments of acute suffering."[3] In building from Blackhawk and Welke, it would follow that reckoning with the trauma of US imperialism then also requires critical engagement with the socio-environmental violence that desert landscape images have created and helped sustain.

Images are of course agentic instruments responsible for making and molding social worlds, materially, ideologically, and imaginatively.[4] As sociologists Gordon Fyfe and John Law contend, "Depiction, picturing and seeing are ubiquitous features of the process by which most human beings come to know the world as it really *is* for them."[5] In other words, the content of an image, as well as who has authored it, exists within particular cultural, political, and epistemological frameworks—all of which are impacted by, and have impact on, why the image is made and how it is interpreted. Notably, because landscapes are dynamic, characterized by their near-constant change, they can never be comprehensively represented by a static image.[6] As such, the crafting of landscape images requires deliberate acts of selection by their makers—privileging certain features,

2   Blackhawk, *Violence over the Land*, 9.
3   Barbara Young Welke, *Recasting American Liberty: Gender, Race, Law, and the Railroad Revolution, 1865–1920* (Cambridge: Cambridge University Press, 2001), 126, quoted in Blackhawk, *Violence over the Land*, 8.
4   Sebastian Vincent Grevsmühl, "Images, Imagination and the Global Environment: Towards an Interdisciplinary Research Agenda on Global Environmental Images," *Geo: Geography and Environment* 3, no. 2 (2016), https://doi.org/10.1002/geo2.20; Jeremy W. Crampton, "Cartography: Performative, Participatory, Political," *Progress in Human Geography* 33, no. 6 (December 2009): 840–848; A. Schlottmann and J. Miggelbrink, "Visual Geographies – An Editorial," *Social Geography* 4, no. 1 (2009): 1–11; John Pickles, *A History of Spaces: Cartographic Reason, Mapping, and the Geo-Coded World* (New York: Routledge, 2004); James Corner, "The Agency of Mapping: Speculation, Critique, and Invention," in *Mappings*, ed. Denis Cosgrove (London: Reaktion Books, 1999), 213–252.
5   Gordon Fyfe and John Law, "Introduction: On the Invisibility of the Visual," in "Picturing Power: Visual Description and Social Relations," ed. Gordon Fyfe and John Law, special issue, *The Sociological Review* 35, no. S1 (May 1987): 2. Emphasis in the original.
6   For more on the "incompleteness" of landscapes and how the production of images must inherently address this dynamism, see Ed Wall, "Incompleteness: Landscapes, Cartographies, Citizenships," research article, *Landscape Research* (2021), https://doi.org/10.1080/01426397.2021.1914011.

viewsheds, subjects, and temporal moments, while simultaneously rendering others invisible. Through this selection
process, the image itself becomes, as art critic John Berger has
claimed, an expression of the particular cultural and political
context in which it is created.[7] Desert images, as demonstrated
by those included in this essay, construct arguments that justify
socio-environmental violence, endorse extraction, and neutralize
disenfranchisement. In this way, the physical landscape and
visual representations of it are co-constitutive—they are
reciprocal and enmeshed, working together to cement specific
socio-spatial relations and power dynamics.[8] As landscapes are
eternally made and remade through temporal, environmental,
and anthropogenic processes, landscape images are themselves
agentic forces in this making, responsible for producing new
forms and visions. Thus, landscapes and their images are also
engaged in a recursive relationship—actively making and
remaking each other. When images are leveraged as instruments
for an imperial project, the visual archive reinforces, legitimizes,
and reproduces violence through its visual language of codes,
signifiers, and hierarchies; this language is culturally produced
and learned. Acknowledging that imperialism, as an economic,
political, and social phenomenon, depends on control over the
landscape and is a "complex ideology which had widespread
cultural, intellectual, and technical expressions," the visual
archive of landscape images is central to understanding how the
desert was imagined as a site to express and manifest imperial
power.[9] Three landscape drawing types—mapping, surveys,
and bird's eye perspectives—have been crucial to long-standing
perceptions and material transformations of the US's desert
lands as spaces for environmental and social exploitation by the
state.[10]

7   John Berger, *Ways of Seeing* (London: Penguin Books, 1972); Denis Wood,
        Rethinking the Power of Maps, illustrated edition (New York: Guilford Press, 2010);
        Denis Wood and John Fels, *The Power of Maps* (New York: Guilford Press, 1992).
8   Synne Movik, Tor A. Benjaminsen, and Tim Richardson, "Making Maps, Making
        Claims: The Politics and Practices of Visualisation in Environmental Governance,"
        Landscape Research 46, no. 2 (February 2021): 143–151.
9   Linda Tuhiwai Smith, *Decolonizing Methodologies: Research and Indigenous
        Peoples*, 2nd ed. (London: Zed Books, 2012), 23.
10   For more on the topic of landscape images as imperial tools, see Ed Wall, "Post-
        Landscape Or The Potential of Other Relations with the Land," in *Landscape and
        Agency*, ed. Ed Wall and Tim Waterman (London: Routledge, 2018), 144–163; Doreen
        Massey, "Landscape as a Provocation: Reflections on Moving Mountains," *Journal
        of Material Culture* 11, no. 1–2 (2006): 33–48; Corner, "The Agency of Mapping:
        Speculation, Critique, and Invention"; David Matless, "The Uses of Cartographic
        Literacy: Mapping, Survey and Citizenship in Twentieth-Century Britain," in
        Mappings, ed. Denis Cosgrove (London: Reaktion Books, 1999), 193–212; J.B.
        Harley, "Maps, Knowledge, and Power," in *The Iconography of Landscape: Essays
        on the Symbolic Representation, Design and Use of Past Environments*, ed. Denis

In the United States, the desert is perceived not as a valuable ecology but rather as a commodified object; as geographers Neil Smith and David Harvey, among others, have argued, the notion of nature itself is largely a product of commodification as it is deeply embedded in forms of imperial economic and political rationality.[11] Landscape images order the natural environment into hierarchies of use and value, with these categories figuring large in the imperial imagination and furthering the logics of capitalist extraction. Whether for use in environmental analysis, city land use and zoning, or social organization, the innumerable classifications that systematize the environment are encoded in images of the landscape. These categories are often leveraged to justify, legitimize, and sometimes even legalize environmental degradation and social exploitation in service of economic, political, and/or social agendas.[12] What's more, these categories are malleable, reinterpreted by sociopolitical actors to benefit changing objectives, intentions, and agendas for the landscape. Throughout US history, the desert has been imagined in binary terms—at times considered "empty," "barren," and "worthless," while at other moments brimming with economic potential. This binary is tied directly to a set of colonial beliefs and material manifestations that have registered the desert's value in terms of how effective it is when put to use toward imperial ambitions. Landscape visualizations of deserts that underscore this binary— "empty" on the one hand, and fruitful on the other—not only provide conceptual legitimacy of these categories but also rationalize the material transformations that respond to them: in other words, not only what is seen but also what *could* be seen. When maps, surveys, and bird's eye perspectives are examined in their sociopolitical context, not only do these desert images reveal histories of violence, dispossession, exploitation, and extraction, they also reveal how drawing the desert has the capacity to rationalize the making of desert worlds. Drawing the desert differently, specifically from a critical, anti-colonial, justice-oriented lens, has the potential to radically reconceptualize and restructure the desert as a world of radical social and ecological justice.

Cosgrove and Stephen Daniels (Cambridge: Cambridge University Press, 1988); Denis Cosgrove, "Prospect, Perspective and the Evolution of the Landscape Idea," *Transactions of the Institute of British Geographers* 10, no. 1 (1985): 45–62.

11   David Harvey, *Spaces of Capital: Towards a Critical Geography* (New York: Routledge, 2012); Neil Smith, *Uneven Development: Nature, Capital, and the Production of Space*, 3rd edition (Athens: University of Georgia Press, 2008).

12   Arturo Escobar, *Designs for the Pluriverse: Radical Interdependence, Autonomy, and the Making of Worlds* (Durham, NC: Duke University Press, 2017), 93–95; Valerie L. Kuletz, *The Tainted Desert: Environmental and Social Ruin in the American West* (New York: Routledge, 1998).

Cartographies of Emptiness

Emptiness is neither a geographical category nor an ecological feature; it is a culturally constructed, political instrument. When visualized through cartographic drawing, "emptiness" directs the perception of deserts, their ecologies, and the people who occupy them, and validates the social and ecological exploitation of desert environments. Mapping emptiness manipulates the perception of deserts; drawing the desert as a landscape of voids, gaps, and blank spots suggests that there is nothing there to pay attention to, simultaneously rendering invisible the past and present systems of exploitation occurring in desert landscapes. Discourses of deserts as empty, alongside the maps that spatialize this emptiness, have undergirded the United States' historic and contemporary imperial practices of territorial occupation and acquisition that encourage land dispossession, resource extraction, unequitable land use, and zoning practices. As scholar Scott Lauria Morgensen astutely notes, "'Empty land' reminds us that the ontology of settler colonialism has been premised on its own boundlessness: always projecting another horizon over which it might establish and incorporate a newest frontier."[13] In this way, drawings of "emptiness" construct new imaginative and material worlds.

These cartographies do not simply visualize—they are expressions of power that invent geographic, socio-material, and political knowledge of deserts. By embedding political and social agendas (whether intentionally or not), maps are encoded with numerous subjectivities, distortions, and hierarchies.[14] Historian John Pickles argues that maps have long asserted scientific and rational authority such that they can "signify the most important forms of reason."[15] But as the intellectual historian Mark Poster has discussed through his analysis of philosophers Friedrich Nietzsche and Michel Foucault, pursuits of reason are inseparable from pursuits of power; he argues that knowledge is a "form of power, a way of presenting one's own values in the guise of scientific disinterestedness."[16] Maps that visualize "emptiness"

13 Scott Lauria Morgensen, "Theorising Gender, Sexuality and Settler Colonialism: An Introduction," in "Karangatia: Calling Out Gender and Sexuality in Settler Societies," ed. Scott Lauria Morgensen and Michelle Erai, special issue, Settler Colonial Studies 2, no. 2 (2012): 2, quoted in Dian Million, "'We Are the Land, and the Land Is Us': Indigenous Land, Lives, and Embodied Ecologies in the Twenty-First Century," in Racial Ecologies, ed. Leilani Nishime and Kim D. Hester Williams (Seattle: University of Washington Press, 2018), 25.
14 Mark Monmonier, How to Lie with Maps (University of Chicago Press, 2014).
15 Pickles, A History of Spaces, 77.
16 Mark Poster, "Foucault and History," Social Research 49, no. 1 (1982): 119.

are thus deeply influential in constructing knowledge.[17] And yet, maps are often believed to be neutral, empirical, and rational.[18] It is this assumed objectivity that allows the map to appear impartial and viewers to frequently engage with its content uncritically, trusting that the represented features are true, factual, and accurate.[19] This scientific authority engendered by the map has been used by the United States to establish, expand, and maintain territorial authority.

In the nineteenth century, as the US charged west in search of new geographies to conquer, the map became ever more important in not only legitimizing the accumulation and administration of territories but also projecting and documenting future territorial claims.[20] The expanding geographic ambition of US imperialism hinged on propagating the west and its deserts as empty, and maps were central in disseminating this idea as instruments of governance. The perceived scientific objectivity and precise measurements of maps became a strategy of the state to assert claims to land and affirm new colonial boundaries, thus visualizing and establishing colonial expansion and exploitation as truth. The United States' modern political structure can be described, as argued by political scientist Jordan Branch, as the "result of the cognitive and social impact of cartography," wherein maps are entrenched in the political, social, and economic agendas of the nation-state.[21] Mapping the desert landscape as empty presented opportunity to actively imagine, interpret, and construct it into a place more economically and politically useful to the state and its priority to expand and exploit.

Surveys of Conquest

Land is both the material and metaphorical foundation of political and economic power in the United States, and imperial ambitions to both expand control over physical space and ideologically link territory to power have always been central to its nationhood.[22] In reflecting on the relationship between imperialism and territory,

17   Harley, "Maps, Knowledge, and Power"; Movik, Benjaminsen, and Richardson, "Making Maps, Making Claims."
18   Wood and Fels, *The Power of Maps.*
19   For an account of how the development of cartography in the sixteenth century paralleled the development of modern, Western science, see David Turnbull, "Cartography and Science in Early Modern Europe: Mapping the Construction of Knowledge Spaces," *Imago Mundi* 48 (1996): 5–24.
20   Claudio Saunt, *Unworthy Republic: The Dispossession of Native Americans and the Road to Indian Territory* (New York: W. W. Norton, 2020).
21   Jordan Branch, "Mapping the Sovereign State: Technology, Authority, and Systemic Change," *International Organization* 65, no. 1 (2011): 2.

postcolonial theorist Edward Said argues that "at some very
basic level, imperialism means thinking about, settling on, and
controlling land that you do not possess, that is distant, that is
lived on and often involves untold misery for others."[23]
Extending this connection further, he notes that imperialism is
the theoretical lens while colonialism is the physical act
of transforming seemingly "empty" territories into those more
beneficial to colonial forces.[24] In the United States, imperial
ambition manifests through settler colonialism, a process that is,
as anthropologist Patrick Wolfe states, "a structure," and therefore present in every aspect of society.[25] In this way, the continual
assertion of the United States as a sovereign state is dependent
on facilitating and upholding settler colonialism. Defined by
Potawatomi philosopher Kyle Whyte, settler colonialism is the
"complex social processes in which at least one society seeks to
move permanently onto the terrestrial, aquatic, and aerial places
lived in by one or more other societies who derive economic
vitality, cultural flourishing, and political self-determination from
the relationships they have established with the plants, animals,
physical entities, and ecosystems of those places."[26] Settler colonialism is thus inherently spatial, dependent on gaining control
over both people and environments. This logic of conquest relies
on mapping, measuring, parceling, and, especially, owning
land.[27] Land, in the settler colonial context, is property. Legal
scholar Brenna Bhandar argues that "the physical occupation and
use of the land as basis of ownership has been defined quite
narrowly by an ideology of improvement in settler colonial
contexts."[28] And more specifically, in the context of the desert
lands of the United States, settlers transform territories occupied

22   Danika Cooper, "Legacies of Violence: Citizenship and Sovereignty on Contested
        Lands," in *Landscape Citizenships*, ed. Tim Waterman, Jane Wolff, and Ed Wall (New
        York: Routledge, 2021), 225–252.
23   Edward Said, *Culture and Imperialism* (New York: Alfred A. Knopf, 1993), 7, quoted in
        Nicholas Blomley, "Law, Property, and the Geography of Violence: The Frontier, the
        Survey, and the Grid," *Annals of the Association of American Geographers* 93, no. 1
        (March 2003): 128.
24   Said, *Culture and Imperialism*, 9.
25   Patrick Wolfe, "Settler Colonialism and the Elimination of the Native," *Journal
        of Genocide Research* 8, no. 4 (December 2006): 388; Lorenzo Veracini, *The Settler
        Colonial Present* (New York: Palgrave Macmillan, 2015).
26   Kyle Powys Whyte, "The Dakota Access Pipeline, Environmental Injustice, and US
        Settler Colonialism," in *The Nature of Hope*, ed. Char Miller and Jeff Crane (Boulder:
        University Press of Colorado, 2019), 323–324. The Potawatomi Nation was located
        originally in the Wabash River Valley in what is now the state of Indiana. Under
        the Indian Removal Act of 1830, the Potawatomi peoples were forced to march to a
        reservation in Kansas, in what is known as the Potawatomi Trail of Death.
27   Katherine McKittrick, *Demonic Grounds: Black Women And The Cartographies Of
        Struggle* (Minneapolis: University of Minnesota Press, 2006).
28   Brenna Bhandar, *Colonial Lives of Property: Law, Land, and Racial Regimes of
        Ownership* (Durham, NC: Duke University Press Books, 2018), 34.

In the nineteenth century, Warren's map, *Map of the Territory of the United States from the Mississippi to the Pacific Ocean*, was considered the most authoritative and comprehensive map of the western territory. In it, the desert is presented as a literal black, empty space, straddled by surrounding topography; through representations as vacant, flat, and expansive, the desert landscape was imagined as an effective location for the construction of railroad networks that would transport settlers, cargo, and goods between the two coasts of the United States. Maps like this one, that visualized emptiness, reinforced dominant narratives of the desert's potential for transformation and incentivized settlers to imagine it as a landscape ripe for economic growth and opportunity. Gouverneur Kemble Warren, *Map of the Territory of the United States from the Mississippi to the Pacific Ocean*, 1858. Courtesy of Cartography Associates via Creative Commons and the University of Denver Penrose Library.

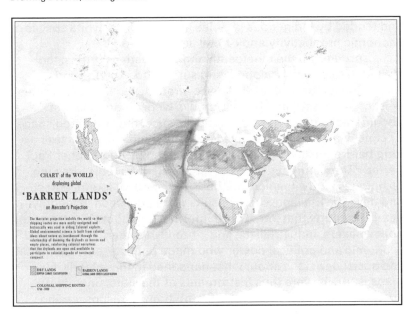

The legacy of the emptiness myth has persisted in current environmental and geographic science. Today, most of the world uses the Moderate Resolution Imaging Spectroradiometer (MODIS) Land Cover classification system to measure and analyze the Earth's surface and climatic conditions through satellite imagery. MODIS Land Cover categorizes desert ecologies under the heading of "barren." When the MODIS dataset is overlaid with the Köppen Global Climate Classification dataset, nearly all global territories that are classified as "barren" are also classified as "dry." Barren landscapes are defined as "land with limited ability to support life." The dataset is universally accepted as accurate and today is used by nearly every country in the world to make a broad range of assessments about land. Land Cover categorization systems like the one produced by MODIS imagery directly correlate economic productivity with vegetation and frame the value of "barren" geographies as primarily a consequence of their ability to be physically manipulated and repurposed into other, more economically productive land uses. The idea that landscapes are valuable based on their economic potential is a persistent and pervasive colonial interpretation of nature. Danika Cooper, *Chart of the World Displaying Global "Barren Lands" on Mercator's Projection*, 2021. Courtesy of the author.

and tended by Indigenous peoples into exclusive, white spaces of economic productivity and capital accumulation.[29]

Throughout the nineteenth and twentieth centuries, the United States commissioned land surveys to examine and record the features of newly "discovered" lands in the territories west of the Mississippi River. Surveys were among the first documents of these territories and, as such, they rendered space a "conceivable object, an object that the mind could possess long before the lowing herds," as reasoned by geographer Paul Carter.[30] These surveys used the latest scientific tools, drawing techniques, and analytical methods to record, diagram, parcel, and describe the landscape. Results were published in lengthy, detailed reports that introduced information about US deserts to policymakers, industrialists, and citizens in eastern centers of US economic and political power who made political, environmental, and social decisions about what happened in these lands. Like maps, surveys were thus instruments of the state, unambiguously entangled with broader US ambitions of dispossessing Indigenous peoples of their lands, building settlements for white settlers, and establishing private property as the only legitimate avenue for occupying land.

After the Treaty of Paris (1783)—which ended the American Revolutionary War and established the United States as a sovereign entity—and the subsequent Louisiana Purchase (1803)—which resulted in the US's acquisition of nearly 1,000,000 square miles of land west of the Mississippi River—geographic expeditions were deployed by the federal government to affirm new and shifting national boundaries. Throughout the nineteenth century, the federal government sponsored many multiyear missions to survey the western territories in search of suitable sites for white settlement, trade and transportation routes, and resource extraction. These expeditions worked to uphold US settler colonial objectives and reiterated the myth that these lands were not only geographically empty but also empty of value and meaning, such that they might be reinvented in the white cultural imaginary as spaces in need of transformation to channel profit to the nation-state. Geographer Nicholas Blomley has asserted that the survey helped to abstract space into an empty site so that it only had meaning within the logic of private

29   Winona LaDuke, *All Our Relations: Native Struggles for Land and Life* (Cambridge, MA: South End Press, 1999).
30   Paul Carter, *The Road to Botany Bay: An Exploration of Landscape and History* (Minneapolis: University of Minnesota Press, 1987), 113, quoted in Roger J. P. Kain and Elizabeth Baigent, *The Cadastral Map in the Service of the State: A History of Property Mapping* (Chicago: University of Chicago Press, 1992), 329.

property.[31] In her discussion on usefulness, feminist scholar
Sara Ahmed asserts that when a colonizer (or settler colonizer)
establishes land as unused, its transformation into something to
be used or that is useful to colonial agendas justifies the colonizing force.[32] Following this logic, the survey renders the desert
empty and unused as means for justifying its transformation into
parcels of private property.

When US President Thomas Jefferson deployed Meriwether
Lewis and William Clark on their famed survey expedition (1803–
1806), he instructed them to identify and survey "the most direct
and practicable water communication across this continent
for the purpose of commerce."[33] The resulting survey not only
expanded the territorial reach and economic range of the United
States, but it also revealed a social agenda: the expedition
presented the desert as *empty* of people and value while
simultaneously *full* of socioeconomic opportunity. For instance,
during their travels, Lewis and Clark encountered and depended
on many Indigenous people as interpreters and guides, none
more than Sacagawea, a Lemhi Shoshone woman; but William
Clark's famous 1814 map of the expedition relegates the presence
of Indigenous peoples to a small, almost hidden label marking
their territories in favor of emphasizing topographic features,
potential overland trade routes, and promising sites for white
settlement.[34] The marginalization of Indigenous peoples from
surveys represents "the imposition of a new economic and
spatial order on 'new territory'" that organized, controlled, and
divided "empty" lands into parcels of private property.[35] Within
a few short decades, surveys helped to fundamentally transform
the desert landscape into a geography of private property by
violently removing various Indigenous peoples from their
ancestral lands and forcibly confining them to reservations. Once
"land" was established as "private property," it became a mechanism of disciplinary power by the state to define who could and
could not occupy colonized US lands.[36]

Another kind of survey, the geological survey, became
central to the US economy when, in the 1850s, minerals were

31   Blomley, "Law, Property, and the Geography of Violence," 129.
32   Sara Ahmed, *What's the Use?: On the Uses of Use* (Durham, NC: Duke University Press, 2019), 48.
33   Blackhawk, *Violence over the Land*, 151.
34   Blackhawk, *Violence over the Land*, 149–158. Dorceta E. Taylor, *The Rise of the Conservation Movement: Power, Privilege, and Environmental Protection* (Durham, NC: Duke University Press, 2016), 110–112.
35   Kain and Baigent, *The Cadastral Map in the Service of the State*, 329.
36   Cole Harris, "The Lower Mainland, 1820–81," in *Vancouver and Its Region*, ed. Graeme Wynn and T. R. Oke (Vancouver: UBC Press, 1992), 67.

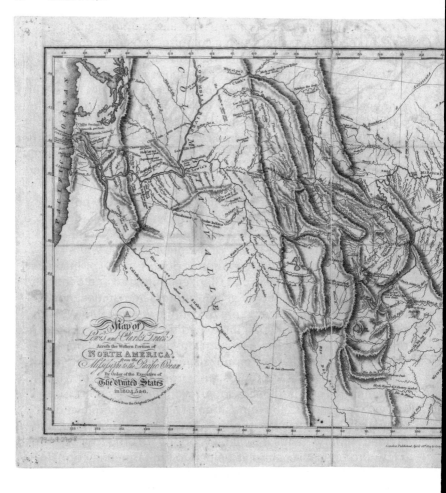

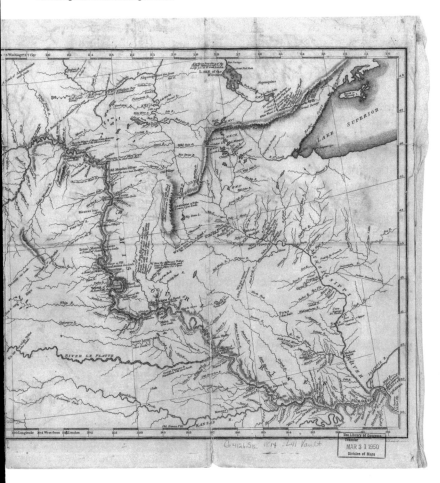

Emptiness was legitimized as a geographic category through early nineteenth-century maps made of the United States' western frontier. In this 1814 map of Lewis and Clark's expedition, emptiness was drawn through a deliberate erasure of Indigenous peoples who they encountered on their journey. The image shows in detail topographic landforms, maps watercourses, tracks overland migration routes, and notably, largely leaves out any defining characteristics of the presence of Indigenous communities. Through their inclusions and omissions, maps were politically strategic in presenting the landscape as an instrument to fulfill the political and economic agendas of the federal government. In this case, the territory devoid of people provided opportunity for United States settlers to move into the region and reinvent it for their own benefit without having to address the displacement and dispossession of those already there. William Clark, *A Map of Lewis and Clark's Track Across the Western Portion of North America, from the Mississippi to the Pacific Ocean*, 1814. Courtesy of Library of Congress.

discovered below the surface of the United States' desert lands. The discovery of gold, silver, iron, lead, and uranium shifted the significance of the Great Basin, Mojave, Sonoran, and Chichuahuan Deserts dramatically. Mining gave the desert new value. With the emergence of a growing national interest in the geological composition of desert lands, the federal government saw the need for a general geological survey to ensure that minerals were identified and effectively extracted. Between 1860 and 1879, the United States sponsored four major geographical expeditions, together named the Great Surveys of the West, to assemble and document the geological potential of large swaths of land west of the Mississippi River.[37] Unlike other land surveys, these drawings made what was below the surface visible, and by bringing into view the verticality of the desert, they reterritorialized the desert as a site full of opportunity for wealth and profit. These cross-sectional drawings worked at the intersection of science, development, and capital to exploit the most from these newly legible spaces.[38]

Though the settlement of desert regions in the United States had been in process for decades by the mid-nineteenth century, the prospect of striking it rich enticed a new and hopeful population of amateur miners and settlers from the eastern parts of the United States to its western desert regions despite the environment's perceived drawbacks. In conjunction with the geological surveys, federal mining laws—the Lode Mining Law of 1866 and the General Mining Law of 1872—gave US citizens the right to mine on colonized, federal lands with little to no regulation. As a result, the geological survey brought, as geographer Brian Braun has astutely recognized, "the qualities of the state's territory into the domain of political rationality, and in turn into proximity with other bodies of knowledge so as to put the state's resources to their most full and profitable use."[39] The geological surveys along with legislation accelerated the rate and pace of development in the desert by presenting it as abundant, and certainly not-empty. Mineral resource extraction encouraged the migration of US settlers to landscapes they had never been

37   These four geological surveys were sponsored by the United States Department of War, and they documented landforms, geology, botany, and cultural interactions. The Geological Exploration of the Fortieth Parallel was led by Clarence King from 1867 to 1869. The United States Geographical Surveys West of the One Hundredth Meridian was led by George M. Wheeler from 1872 to 1879. The Hayden Surveys, or the United States Geological Survey of the Territories, was led by Ferdinand Hayden from 1871 to 1878. The Powell Surveys, or the Geological Survey of the Rocky Mountain Region, was led by John Wesley Powell from 1869 to 1879.
38   Bruce Braun, "Producing Vertical Territory: Geology and Governmentality in Late Victorian Canada," ECUMENE 7, no. 1 (January 2000): 28.
39   Braun, "Producing Vertical Territory," 28.

to before, and these fast-growing settlements produced needs for other industries, transportation networks, and development patterns to follow.[40] Braun argues that geology remade territory into vertical space, and to optimize its verticality, the state required that its inhabitants become "geological subjects" whose property regimes include "the internal architecture of the earth."[41] The geological survey was thus part of a state apparatus to ensure that every aspect of the desert lands contributed to a capitalist, imperial agenda sponsored by the United States; it guaranteed that no part of the desert was immune from the transformations of capital, power, and social control.[42]

Visions of Abundance

As the mining industry accelerated in the second half of the nineteenth century, US settlers began to believe the desert could be an even more productive landscape than had been previously thought, and this shift in perspective contributed to the growth of settlements across the US's desert regions. Federal land policies further enticed eastern settlers to migrate west by offering free land—passed in 1877, the Desert Land Act allotted settlers 640 acres of public land in exchange for settling, irrigating, and cultivating the desert. As a political strategy, this land law helped to facilitate a radical socio-spatial transformation of the desert: hundreds of thousands of Indigenous peoples were violently displaced and dispossessed of their homelands to make way for settlers;[43] desert ecology was overturned through hydraulic infrastructure that redistributed water to saturate the region; and

40   Patricia Nelson Limerick, *The Legacy of Conquest: The Unbroken Past of the American West* (New York: W. W. Norton, 1987), 99.
41   Braun, "Producing Vertical Territory," 29 and 34.
42   The idea that capitalism has transformed every aspect of the planet is extensively examined through Neil Smith's seminal work, *Uneven Development: Nature, Capital, and the Production of Space* (Athens: University of Georgia Press, 1984).
43   We don't know exactly how many Indigenous people were displaced or killed in the desert regions of the United States, and if there were official numbers, they would likely be inaccurate and lower than reality. What we do know is that, in most regions throughout the nineteenth and early twentieth centuries, there were state and local policies that legalized and encouraged the removal of Indigenous peoples from lands desired by settlers (often by any means necessary). California's first governor, Peter Burnett, for example, announced in 1851 that the state would be at war with Indigenous communities "until the Indian race becomes extinct." In June 2019, California's current governor, Gavin Newsom issued a formal apology for the genocide perpetrated on California's Indigenous communities, though today many of these same communities still remain unrecognized by the federal government as sovereign, have not been allotted any lands of their own in the state of California, and continue to be disenfranchised by inadequate access to health care, clean water, and food security and intensifying disparities in wealth between Indigenous and settler populations. Jill Cowan, "'It's Called Genocide': Newsom Apologizes to the State's Native Americans," *The New York Times*, June 19, 2019, https://www.nytimes.com/2019/06/19/us/newsom-native-american-apology.html.

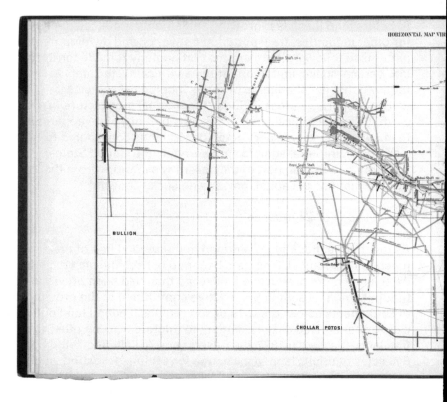

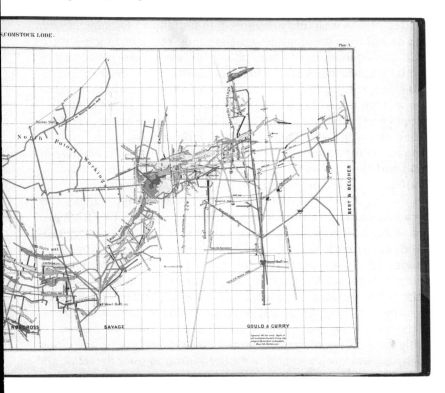

As part of an emerging national identity of progress, productivity, and control over nature, nineteenth-century geological surveys played an important role in the quest for knowledge about the American West. When the Comstock Lode was discovered in the drylands of the Nevada territory in 1859, it sparked a silver rush that flooded prospectors to the area. As mining became more industrial, investors wanted precise and measured appraisals of the landscape before committing large sums of money for mining operations. As part of the Geological Exploration of the Fortieth Parallel (1867–1869), Clarence King and a group of natural scientists produced impressive and revolutionary geological drawings of the Comstock Lode that visualized the geological composition below the surface through sections, providing a roadmap for advanced technologies of extraction using deep tunnels. Today, these kinds of geological sections and survey drawings are still used to guide extractive activities within the drylands of the United States and beyond. Clarence King, *Plate 7: Longitudinal Elevation, and Plate 4: Horizontal Map, Virginia Mines, Comstock Lode*, 1870. Courtesy of David Rumsey Map Collection.

the desert was violently reinvented, materially and imaginatively, into an agrarian empire that enriched the national economy.[44]

In conjunction with land policy, local boosters, civic leaders, and land speculators strove to attract settlers west to their towns and cities. Throughout the nineteenth century, printmakers were commissioned to create images of US towns and cities to attract people and industry to the western lands.[45] These mass-produced urban portraits were often published in newspapers and magazines that circulated widely throughout the nation: between 1840 and 1890, an estimated 4,000 lithographs of as many as 2,400 places were produced, making them ubiquitous in the North American cultural imagination.[46] Drawn from the bird's eye perspective, these lithographs visualized the geography from an imagined, oblique viewpoint high above the town, depicting its buildings, streets, open spaces, and surrounding areas. These images advertised the landscape as sites of viable, attractive, and profitable settlements and helped to "reflect a new land and a new attitude toward the land."[47] This aerial perspective allowed the viewer to simultaneously envision the overall organization of the landscape and imagine how their lives might be if they settled there. The images presented these desert towns and cities as idyllic, pastoral, and highly modern through their depictions of lush greenery and sophisticated technologies and infrastructures, as well as their deployment of the Jeffersonian grid, and thus transformed the public's perception of the desert from a place stripped of life to one "that could, with the correct deployment of technological expertise or proper stewardship, be (re)made hospitable to life."[48]

Early on, homesteaders recognized that access to water was of highest priority as it was a limiting factor for reaping the benefits offered by westward migration. Americans took pride in conquering dry ecology and overcoming its constraints through

For more about the genocide in California, see Brendan C. Lindsay, *Murder State: California's Native American Genocide, 1846–1873* (Lincoln: University of Nebraska Press, 2015).

44   Cooper, "Legacies of Violence."
45   Many of the lithographers who made these prints began as anonymous assistants to other artists or as agents in the sale of lithographs before becoming artists in their own right. See John W. Reps, *Views and Viewmakers of Urban America: Lithographs of Towns and Cities in the United States and Canada, Notes on the Artists and Publishers, and a Union Catalog of Their Work, 1825–1925* (Columbia: University of Missouri Press, 1984), 3–16.
46   John W. Reps, *Bird's Eye Views: Historic Lithographs of North American Cities* (New York: Princeton Architectural Press, 1998), 12; Reps, *Views and Viewmakers of Urban America*, 3.
47   Donald H. Karshan, "American Printmaking, 1670–1968," *Art in America* 56 (April 1968): 27.
48   Elizabeth A. Povinelli, *Geontologies: A Requiem to Late Liberalism*, illustrated edition (Durham, NC: Duke University Press Books, 2016), 16.

hydraulic infrastructures—canals, ditches, aqueducts, dams, and reservoirs—which were imperative to the success of agricultural industries, as they provided steady sources of water.[49] As demand for agricultural productivity increased, more intensive infrastructures were needed, ones that required large sums of money and governmental assistance. In 1888, the US government authorized an irrigation survey led by John Wesley Powell, the director of the US Geological Survey (USGS) to identify water sources in the arid regions of New Mexico, Colorado, Nevada, and Montana.[50] Irrigationists believed that by directing water toward settlement and agricultural fields, the desert's water, no matter how scant, could be used more productively and efficiently. By the following year, Powell's survey had identified 150 sites for water reservoirs and 30,500,000 acres of desert land suitable for irrigated agriculture and development.[51] In 1900, William Smythe, journalist and first chairman of the National Irrigation Congress, published *The Conquest of Arid America*, in which he claimed that hydraulic engineering could "drive the desert back inch by inch" and that homesteaders would "translate [the desert's] gray barrenness into green fields and gardens."[52] He crusaded for irrigation becoming part of a national agenda for the West, writing, "When Uncle Sam puts his hand to a task, we know it will be done. When he waves his hand toward the desert and says, *'Let there be water!'* we know that the stream will obey his command."[53] Smythe's proposal that the desert could be engineered out of its scarcity and reconstructed as a place of abundance through hydraulic infrastructure was an idea championed by many politicians and supported by westerners and easterners alike.

When the National Reclamation Act of 1902 created a federal irrigation fund, President Theodore Roosevelt proclaimed that reclamation—the act of cultivating desert land through the implementation of hydraulic infrastructure—was "one of

49   P. Hirt, A. Gustafson, and K. Larson, "The Mirage in the Valley of the Sun,"
      Environmental History 13, no. 3 (July 2008): 482–514.
50   Scott Kirsch, "John Wesley Powell and the Mapping of the Colorado Plateau, 1869–
      1879: Survey Science, Geographical Solutions, and the Economy of Environmental
      Values," *Annals of the Association of American Geographers* 92, no. 3 (2002): 548–
      572; Everett W. Sterling, "The Powell Irrigation Survey, 1888–1893," *The Mississippi
      Valley Historical Review* 27, no. 3 (1940): 421–434, https://doi.org/10.2307/1896085.
51   Donald Worster, *A River Running West: The Life of John Wesley Powell* (New York:
      Oxford University Press, 2001); Donald J. Pisani, *To Reclaim a Divided West: Water,
      Law, and Public Policy, 1848–1902* (Albuquerque: University of New Mexico Press,
      1992); "John Wesley Powell's Undertakings," PBS, last modified May 23, 2019, https://
      www.pbs.org/wgbh/americanexperience/features/john-wesley-powell-undertakings.
52   Patricia Nelson Limerick, *Desert Passages: Encounters with the American Deserts*
      (Albuquerque: University of New Mexico Press, 1985), 88.
53   William E. Smythe, *The Conquest of Arid America*, 2nd ed. (New York: Harper, 1905;
      Seattle: University of Washington Press, 1970), xxvii, quoted in Limerick, *Desert
      Passages*, 83. Emphasis in the original.

the great steps not only in the forward progress of the United States but of all mankind."[54] Roosevelt's explicit association between infrastructure and society's advancement was shared by many irrigationists who believed that overturning arid lands was imperative to the success of the nation. The era of irrigation not only produced visual representations of a newly conceived *abundant* desert, but it also helped propagate the perception of the arid West as a place of economic opportunity—the bird's eye lithographs made of these desert settlements and circulated through the eastern states often explicitly highlighted these water technologies and their effectiveness in producing lush and verdant agricultural fields through vignettes inset on the corners of the composition.[55] These illustrations deliberately constructed new visions of the desert as landscapes tamed through infrastructure and teeming with potential for profit. Further, these images supported new systems of power that depended on the dispossession of Indigenous peoples from their lands and produced social and environmental systems dependent on more water than naturally available, an incompatibility that continues to be unsustainable and deeply tenuous both today and for the future. These infrastructures, no matter how massive and technologically sophisticated, have never been able to keep up with the demands of settler society for water; instead, these infrastructural interventions are more often responsible for exacerbating the incompatibilities between supply and demand than resolving them.[56]

Hybridity, or How to Make New Desert Worlds

The desert exists at the complex intersection of nature, history, and power, though too often it has been imagined and imaged flatly: reduced to an instrument of the state that upholds political

54   Telegram from Theodore Roosevelt to National Irrigation Congress, September 15, 1903, in F. H. Newell, comp., *Proceedings of the First Conference of Engineers of the Reclamation Service* (Washington, DC: Government Printing Office, 1904), 121, quoted in Donald C. Jackson, "Engineering in the Progressive Era: A New Look at Frederick Haynes Newell and the U.S. Reclamation Service," *Technology and Culture* 34, no. 3 (July 1993): 539.
55   John W. Reps, "Settling the Last Frontier; Cities of the West, Plains, and Rockies," in *Bird's Eye Views: Historic Lithographs of North American Cities* (New York: Princeton Architectural Press, 1998), 80–115.
56   Danika Cooper, "The Canal and the Pool: Infrastructures of Abundance and the Invention of the Modern Desert," research article, *Landscape Research* (2021), https://doi.org/10.1080/01426397.2021.1958308; Danika Cooper, "Waters Resist: Modernity, Aridity, and the Fight Over the Orme Dam," *Journal of Architectural Education* 74, no. 1 (Spring 2020): 37–47; Danika Cooper, "Waving the Magic Wand: An Argument for Reorganizing the Aridlands around Watersheds," *Plan Journal* 5, no. 1 (2020): 163–184.

and economic power structures. Thinking more expansively about deserts requires a shift to epistemological and ontological frameworks that honor and prioritize a future for dry environments that is anti-colonial, socially and environmentally just, and multidimensional. Building from journalist Charles Bowden's conception of the desert "as an environment demanding a radical change in the cultural and economic concepts underlying Anglo-American modes of appropriating space," the desert thus must be redrawn, and therefore imagined, as a world of rich and complex ecologies and sociopolitical conditions.[57] This requires the difficult and profound task of destabilizing deeply engrained Western understandings of nature and replacing them with ones that are dynamic and relational. To this end, hybrid drawing offers a methodological opportunity to visualize and actively engage the desert as a site of multiple, capacious, and intertwined social, epistemological, and political worlds.

Hybridity, as both a conceptual framework and a representational technique, is a counterstrategy to the pervasive trope of "emptiness" that dominates environmental science and Euro-American visual culture in the desert. It acknowledges the desert as a multidimensional, pluralistic landscape. Drawing this kind of hybrid landscape builds from linguist Mikhail Bakhtin's notion of "intentional hybridity," a process that occurs when "two points of view are not mixed but set against each other dialogically" such that an authoritative worldview is disrupted and transfigured.[58] Intentional hybridity, postcolonial theorist Robert J.C. Young argues further, "enables a constestatory activity, a politicized setting of cultural differences against each other dialogically," in order to emphasize new worldviews that depend on a multiplicity of cultural contexts, meanings, and languages.[59] Like intentional hybridity, hybrid drawing prioritizes the emplacement of multiple historiographic and sociopolitical ontological frameworks to upset the dominance of colonial representations of space by "depriving the imposed imperialist culture, not only of the authority that it has for so long imposed politically, often through violence, but even of its own claims to authenticity."[60] Hybridity

57   Catrin Gersdorf, The Poetics and Politics of the Desert: Landscape and the Construction of America (Amsterdam: Rodopi, 2009), 20. In this passage, Gersdorf is describing Bowden's approach to the desert in his book Killing the Hidden Waters: The Slow Destruction of the Water Resources of the American West (Austin: University of Texas Press, 1977).
58   Mikhail Mikhailovich Bakhtin, "Discourse in the Novel," in The Dialogic Imagination: Four Essays, trans. Caryl Emerson and Michael Holquist, ed. Michael Holquist (Austin: University of Texas Press, 1981), 360.
59   Robert J.C. Young, Colonial Desire: Hybridity in Theory, Culture and Race (London: Routledge, 1995), 22.
60   Young, Colonial Desire, 23.

Urban viewmakers traveled across North America during the mid-nineteenth century creating bird's eye lithographs of colonial settlements. These promotional materials were distributed by local politicians, boosters, and land speculators in the hopes of enticing others to migrate and settle in the western lands. As this image shows, Phoenix was divided into 98 blocks, each 300 square feet. The town is drawn with a wash of green tone alluding to the potential of the site as a lush paradise of agricultural potential. The top corners of the image highlight the presence of the Arizona Canal, a major hydraulic artery through the city, emphasizing to the image's viewers that the town had access to ample water. The description at the bottom right corner emphasizes Phoenix's potential for agricultural

productivity. It reads: "Phoenix is the center of an extensive and fertile valley almost 50 miles in length by 10 in width, and containing 300,000 acres. Every variety of grain, grasses, fruits and vegetable give a prolific yield." The description, which continues, highlights the town's manufacturing mills for textiles, flour production, and ice. The lithograph is persuasive in presenting Phoenix as a site of immense abundance, where the desert climate and ecology has been overcome through advancements in irrigation technology. C.J. Dyer, *Bird's Eye View of Phoenix, Arizona*, Schmidt Label & Litho Co, 1885. Courtesy of Library of Congress.

opens up the potential to conceptually overlay multiple ways of knowing, being, and engagement with the environment into one drawing of the desert. In the context of US deserts, hybridity can adopt an anti-colonial approach by centering Indigenous worldviews, assertions for sovereignty, and historical and contemporary engagements with territory, all of which have been rendered invisible or undermined by the dominant Euro-Western paradigm of capital, progress, and growth.

In tactical terms, hybridity as a drawing technique necessitates visualizing the desert through a combination of multiple drawing types, views, temporalities, and media such that they interact on the drawing plane to create a more pluralistic image of the desert. In other words, drawing can work toward producing, in the words of anthropologist Arturo Escobar, a "dissenting imagination" of the desert.[61] Hybrid drawings use the technique of collage—assembling, overlapping, and recombining different parts—to create this pluralistic, multifaceted reading of the landscape, which does not prioritize one point of view over another but instead fuses together multiple temporal, spatial, political, epistemological, and geographic contexts. Collage has been used by many artists, cartographers, and spatial designers to counter colonial narratives and affirm liberatory ones, though there is much opportunity to explore this technique in the context of desert landscapes.[62]

Drawing the desert in its multiplicity thus renders it as "meshwork," a term coined by social anthropologist Tim Ingold to describe a world in which many worlds exist that are plural, overlapping, and relational.[63] This many-worlds episteme is in direct opposition to the Euro-American one because it unsettles the notion that there is only one valid mode of knowledge

61   Escobar, *Designs for the Pluriverse*, 89.
62   For instance, artist and water rights activist Mealaaloha Bishop's mixed-media oil painting *Kalo Pa'a o Waiāhole* (2018) layers visual imagery to tell stories about how the Kanaka Maoli (Native Hawaiian) community has fought to protect their lands and waterways against mounting pressures from landowners and developers on the island of Oahu. For more about the work of Mealaaloha Bishops, see Candace Fujikane, "Mo'o'āina Cascades in Waiāhole and He'eia: A Cartography of Hau(mea)," in *Mapping Abundance for a Planetary Future: Kanaka Maoli and Critical Settler Cartographies in Hawai'i* (Durham, NC: Duke University Press Books, 2021), 174–207. In recounting histories of inland exploration of Canada in the seventeenth century, cartographer Margaret Pearce and Michael Hermann collage field notes from Samuel de Champlain's colonial expedition with those of the Indigenous nations he encountered in *They Would Not Take Me There* (2008). Through the juxtaposition of these two kinds of voices, Pearce and Hermann reveal the conflicting narratives of those told by colonial settlers and those told by Indigenous people. Michael Hermann and Margaret Pearce, "'They Would Not Take Me There': People, Places, and Stories from Champlain's Travels in Canada 1603–1616," *Cartographic Perspectives* 66 (2010): 41–46, 66.
63   Tim Ingold, *Being Alive: Essays on Movement, Knowledge and Description* (London: Routledge, 2011), 68.

production and engagement with the environment. By contrast, the many-worlds worldview highlights the power of alternative methods to open up new possibilities for desert worlds that are unburdened by modernist views of ecology, progress, and power. In drawing deserts from this pluralistic perspective, the literal collaging of multiple worldviews and viewsheds reveals how various ways of knowing the desert produce altogether new engagements with it. This hybridity does not, as anthropologists Reade Davis and Laura Zanotti argue, "simply constitute different perspectives on a common material world, but [is], in fact, constitutive of different worlds and make possible different kinds of relationships between humans and non-humans."[64] In other words, hybrid drawings of the desert can not only expose the uneven and unequal actions inflicted on the desert and those who live in it but also prompt wholly new worlds that unsettle and repair the historic and present injustices.

A just future for the desert requires a socionatural dynamic that is resilient and relational, non-exclusionary and non-extractive, a practice which Indigenous scholars and activists are already leading. Within the United States and beyond, Indigenous people have long contested settler colonial and extractive development through their embodied and practiced caretaking of Earth. Through these practices, they have repeatedly exposed how state-sponsored environmental management is directly tied to settler colonialism and capitalism, the very systems that have caused and exacerbated the crisis they purport to help solve. As a result of this relationship, the need to find alternatives for climate adaptation that do not reproduce the pitfalls of the past within the contemporary is mandatory and urgent. Winona LaDuke (Anishinaabe) works to resist infrastructural projects that are socially and environmentally harmful, offering alternative infrastructural systems that are alimentary and life-giving.[65] Zoe Todd (Métis), alongside her Freshwater Fish Futures collective, is working to imagine an anti-colonial, pluralistic future that prioritizes a multi-species planet.[66] The O'odham Anti-Border Collective, a group of land and water defenders from the Tohono O'odham Nation, has been actively protesting the US-Mexico border wall, which continues to threaten their sovereignty and

64   Reade Davis and Laura Zanotti, introduction to "Hybrid Landscapes: Science, Conservation, and the Production of Nature," special issue, *Anthropological Quarterly* 87, no. 3 (Summer 2014): 603.
65   Winona LaDuke, *All Our Relations: Struggles for Land and Life* (Cambridge, MA: South End Press, 1999); and Winona LaDuke and Deborah Cowen, "Beyond Wiindigo Infrastructure," *South Atlantic Quarterly* 119, no. 2 (2020): 243–268.
66   See more about the Freshwater Fish Futures collective at https://freshwaterfish futures.ca.

produce environmental harm to their sacred lands.[67] The Red Nation, a collective of Indigenous scholars and activists, recently published an alternative to the Green New Deal that presents a plan for climate action that explicitly overturns colonialism and capitalism to make way for more liberatory and life-affirming practices.[68] As the climate crisis forces a reckoning with the ways that settler societies occupy the planet, hybrid drawing opens realms for active resistance to the dominant modes of place-making by imagining a world that is relational, dynamic, and resilient. In this way, hybrid drawing is a tool for reparative justice that acknowledges the desert's past while simultaneously focusing on its future.

67   See more about the O'odham Anti Border Collective here: https://www.facebook. com/AntiBorderCollective.

68   The Red Nation, *The Red Deal: Indigenous Action to Save Our Earth* (Brooklyn: Common Notions, 2021); Nick Estes, "The Red Nation: All Relatives Forever," The Red Nation, http://therednation.org.

{ TAKING }

{ MAKING }

Hybrid drawing—or the combination of multiple drawing types and/or alternative ways of telling stories through an image—engages multiple points of view simultaneously and renders visible the erasures present in images that prioritize singular or dominant readings of the landscape. How one chooses to map and visualize the creation of the current boundaries of the United States shapes the reading of its history. Positioning the territorial United States as the result of systematic and violent land grabs (taking), rather than through stories of passive land cessions and acquisitions (making), makes North American history accountable to past injustices and gives voice to alternative historical narratives. Danika Cooper, {Taking} Indigenous Lands / {Making} United States, 2020. Courtesy of the author.

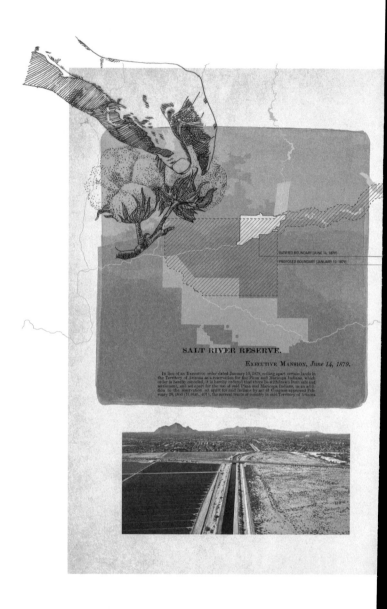

Layering multiple drawing types and media into the same hybrid drawing acknowledges that landscape is dynamic, continually shifting in response to changing cultural perceptions, policies, and technologies. The Sonoran Desert in Arizona has been subject to the forces of settler colonialism, agricultural production, and Indigenous dispossession; as a result, hybridizing images of the Sonoran landscape with federal policies, photographs, and maps presents the desert as a site of complex relationships over time and space. Salt River Pima Maricopa Indian Community's reservation lands, in the Sonoran Desert, have experienced

46,627
acres

Earth Magician shapes the world;
  Behold what he can do!
Round and smooth he molds it.
  Behold what he can do!
Earth Magician makes the mountains.
  Heed what he has to say!
He it is that makes the mesas.
  Heed what he has to say.
Earth Magician shapes the world;
  Earth Magician makes its mountains;
Makes all larger, larger, larger.
  Into the earth the Magician glances,
Into its mountains he may see.

this complexity. At the beginning of 1879, the Pima and Maricopa Indigenous groups were promised nearly 680,000 acres by President Rutherford B. Hayes, although a few months later, their lands were reduced to just 46,000 acres. The unallotted lands became the foundation for Phoenix's settlement and agriculture, both which required intensive hydraulic infrastructure. Pima poem, "Earth Magician shapes the world," in A. Grove Day, *The Sky Clears: Poetry of the American Indians* (Lincoln, NE: Bison Books, 1964). Danika Cooper, *Hybridizing the Sonoran Desert*, 2021. Courtesy of the author.

Ariella Aïsha Azoulay is professor of Modern Culture and Media and comparative literature at Brown University, as well as a film essayist and curator of archives and exhibitions. Her books include *Potential History—Unlearning Imperialism* (Verso, 2019), *Civil Imagination: The Political Ontology of Photography* (Verso, 2012), *The Civil Contract of Photography* (Zone Books, 2008), and *From Palestine to Israel: A Photographic Record of Destruction and State Formation, 1947–1950* (Pluto Press, 2011). Among her films are *Undocumented: Unlearning Imperial Plunder* (2019), and *Civil Alliances, Palestine, 47–48* (2012). Among her exhibitions are *Errata* (Fundació Tàpies, 2019, HKW, Berlin, 2020), and *Enough! The Natural Violence of New World Order* (f/stop Photography Festival, Leipzig, 2016).

ARIELLA AÏSHA AZOULAY

IMPERIAL DESERT EFFECT—PALESTINE IS THERE, WHERE IT HAD ALWAYS BEEN

Dear Samia,

I tried, but I could not find a poem that conveys the meaning of the imperial desert as I understand it. I was reminded, however, that when you first invited me to participate in the Preston Thomas Memorial Lecture Series, "Into the Desert: Questions of Coloniality and Toxicity," I had returned to *Khirbet Khizeh*, a short novel that was published in 1949, a few months after the declaration of the state of Israel, when everything started to be qualified as "Israeli."[1] The book was authored by S. Yizhar, an "Israeli" soldier who was among those who expelled Palestinians from their homeland and who became a well-known writer in Israel. I picked up an excerpt from his novel and broke it into separate sentences, creating an inventory of plunder. If it echoes a poem, that is because, under the imperial condition, plunder gives rise to the Republic of Letters. The novel introduces readers to what I mean when I say the production of the "imperial desert effect": an enterprise that turns worlds into desert sites in which different actors are permitted to partake in the process of making the desert bloom. The production of the desert is an industrial enterprise that requires the participation of many actors who don different hats.

1   The 2020 Preston Thomas Memorial Lecture Series, titled "Into the Desert: Questions of Coloniality and Toxicity," were convened by Samia Henni between October and November 2020 at the Department of Architecture, Cornell University. See https://aap.cornell.edu/news-events/desert-questions-coloniality-and-toxicity.

To make things bloom within these manufactured deserts is not a metaphor but an industrial operation, a narrative structure, a historical *plot* of settler colonialism. I could not find the text from which I gave my initial lecture, but I found a fable instead. Sometimes texts get lost in order for fables to emerge, to convey the moral of a genocidal story that was told too many times over decades. The dormant memories I inherited from my ancestors still buried in Algeria confirm that this fable was not so different than the one that describes the conquering of Algeria. I tried to not forget the many characters involved. The order in which they appear does not reflect their importance. As often in fables, proper names are unnecessary. One's individuality ought to be understood as somewhat secondary to their position, occupation, and training, even when it may have shaped the nature of their positions and the course of their training. The visual depictions included alongside this fable emphasize that these positions could also have been inhabited by others. Their silhouettes reside in photographs and needed only some permanent ink to take clearer form.

I share this fable with you in the following pages.

Yours,
Aïsha

A Fable in Several Acts
The Characters:

Militant Zionists
Guardians of worldly sovereignty
National architect
Prime minister
Photographer
Ministers
Literary writer
"Infiltrators"
Water engineers
British policemen
Settlers
Strikers
Neighbors
Enemies
Inhabitants
Warriors
Soldiers
Destroyers
School children
Palestinian returnees
Informed citizen
Voice of the state
Engineers
Citizen-perpetrators
Newborn Israelis
Newly proclaimed Israeli-Jews
Custodian of Absentee Property
Guardians of this piece of earth
Refugees
Subjects
Racial capitalists
Expellees
Descendants of expellees
International imperial actors
Conquerors
Authorized signatories
Extras
State actors
Cultural agents
Museumified subjects
Anti-partition Arab-Jewish activists

The huts appeared to have been uninhabited for
a very long time...

We kicked in the wicket in the big wooden gate in the
clay walls and entered a square courtyard with a hut
on one flank and another hut on the other...

Another kick and a casual glance into an abandoned
home, and a storage room where the dust of crops
coated cobwebs both tattered and greasy-looking.

Walls that had been attentively decorated
with whatever was at hand;

a home lined with plaster and a molding
painted blue and red;

little ornaments that hang on the walls, testifying to a
loving care whose foundations had
not been eradicated;

traces of female-wisdom-hath-builded-her-house,
paying close attention to myriad details

whose time now had passed;

an order intelligible to someone and a disorder in which somebody at his convenience had found his way; remnants of pots and pans that had been collected in a haphazard fashion, as need arose, touched by very private joys and woes that a stranger could not understand; tatters that made sense to someone who was used to them—a way of life whose meaning was lost, diligence that had reached its negation, and a great, very deep muteness had settled upon the love, the bustle, the bother, the hopes, and the good and less-good times, so many unburied corpses.

But we were already tired of seeing things like this, we had no more interest in such things.

—S. Yizhar, *Khirbet Khizeh*[2]

The Arena

Though **militant Zionists** wielded a scary power in 1948, seeking to destroy Palestine and neutralizing Palestinian resistance in order to impose a state by and for the Jews in Palestine, they didn't act in a vacuum. Against the forces that sought to produce out of Palestine a desert made to bloom—an enterprise praised in a document known as the "Declaration of Independence" discussed later—Palestinians didn't stop striking, participating in what is now a more-than-seventy-years-long Great March of Return.

Among the different meanings of "desert," one of its verb forms refers to a withdrawal from military service—*to desert.* Not surprisingly, the dictionary describes the action as illegal, since dictionaries were made to teach people that destruction is essential to establishing sovereignty, imperial actions are bounding, and wars are necessary. The fable inscribed here, transmitted by **guardians of worldly sovereignty** (distinct from the imperial kind), ascribes illegality to imperial military campaigns rather than to the instinct and commitment to desert from them.[3] As much as this fable is about the desert, it is also an amplification

2   S. Yizhar, *Khirbet Khizeh*, trans. Nicholas de Lange and Yaacob Dweck (Jerusalem: Ibis Editions, 2008), 41–42.
3   In *Potential History: Unlearning Imperialism*, I distinguish worldly sovereignty from imperial sovereignty: "Worldly sovereignty refers to the persisting and repressed forms and formations of being in the world, shaped by and through intimate

of calls to desert the imperial project of the desert, to stymie the
imperial desert effect. The production of the imperial desert effect
transformed Palestine into an onto-epistemological challenge, a
geographical quandary. This quandary is the result of constant
attempts to bend Palestine's geography and to depict it as Israel's
"other"—as in the "Israeli-Palestinian conflict." Those who relate
to this place under this two-sided paradigm enact and entrap
themselves within this onto-epistemological challenge since
Palestine exists where it has always been, neither elsewhere nor
"in" the past. Though it was proclaimed a bygone, relegated to
a past and putatively succeeded by an imposed Israel, it persists
and resists in the very same place. The imperial desert effect
creates a buffer zone between the existence and persistence of
Palestine and its peoples and the Zionist enterprise of violence,
which strives to remove the former from their homeland and
prevent them from interfering in the project of "making the
desert bloom." This imperial desert effect is also what enabled the
destruction of worldly sovereignty in Palestine and ushered in its
replacement by an imperial one, one indexed by a single ethnos.

The National Plan

Destruction alone doesn't produce the imperial desert effect.
The effect is produced when the soil of flattened worlds is also
produced as "ready to be made to bloom." Such a transformation
requires planners. In this fable, shortly after the new state was
proclaimed, a **national architect** was commissioned to prepare
a national plan for Israel by the man who was made its **prime
minister.**[4] **Militant Zionists** were in the midst of expelling
Palestinians from their land by the time the **national architect**
started studying and surveying different areas—the desert being
one of them—in Palestine-turned-Israel. This type of study that
strips a place of everything except its material and climatic
qualities, and that removes the people who live there, their
knowledge, and modes of life, is already an act of producing the
desert. The imperial desert effect produced throughout Palestine

knowledge of the world and its secrets, of its multiple natural, spiritual, political, and
cosmological taxonomies preserved and transmitted over generations and shared
among those entitled and invested to protect them. Imperial sovereignty consists of
the massive expropriation of people's skills so as to transform them into governable
subjects in a differential body politic. Worldly sovereignty consists of care for the
common world in which one's place among others is part of the world's texture."
Ariella Aïsha Azoulay, *Potential History: Unlearning Imperialism* (London: Verso,
2019), 388.

4   The first National Outline Plan, designed by then-head of the Government Planning
Department Arieh Sharon, was approved in 1951. See the iterations of the National
Outline Plan in 1951 here: https://www.ariehsharon.org/NewLand/TheNationalPlan.

created a buffer zone between the undeniable Palestinian presence and the Jewish protagonists who partook in the genocidal state violence of destroying one world and superseding it with another manufactured by certain architects.

The general national plan for Israel included schemes to disperse the Jewish population across different localities, paying special attention to the Naqab (Negev in Hebrew) and the Galilee, where Palestinian presence was not fully removed and where **returnees** refused to accept their fate as **expellees**. From the point of view of an expert in architecture, drafting such a plan was a prestigious job. Yet no level of prestige could conceal the fact that these experts were complicit in crimes in the order of "crimes against humanity," which, as Hannah Arendt explains in her report from the Eichmann trial in Jerusalem, consist of an attack on the diversity of people who share the world.[5] The destruction of Palestine and the attempt to eradicate the diverse forms of life there through the establishment of an ethno-state should not be discussed through the bi-national terms ("Israel-Palestine") imposed on it by leaders with international support. Even as it is part of a campaign of destruction, within a so-called "bi-national" conflict, imperial violence is not recognized as crime. Employing the category of "crimes against humanity" prevents one from relating to Palestinians as members of a "conflicting side" and attributing the genocidal violences exercised against them to an economy of conflict. Rather it enables one to recognize these violences as crimes in their own right—that is, as crimes against humanity, that are not defined by the national or ethnic identity of the victims targeted by them. This type of crime further evinces the onto-epistemological challenge created by the state insofar as such crimes cannot be brought to a closure without the abolition of the law that maintains the state and that ordains it as one where such crimes are unrecognizable as crimes. In other words, the crimes against Palestine and Palestinians are not committed elsewhere, but in the very place where the state of Israel is and under the very law that defines the state of Israel. Under this law, preassigned roles dictate who is a perpetrator and predetermine what is a crime.

5   In the epilogue, Arendt emphasizes the attack on human diversity as the major trait of crimes against humanity, and argues that it differs from others "not only in degree of seriousness but in essence": "It was when the Nazi regime declared that the German people not only were unwilling to have any Jews in Germany but wished to make the entire Jewish people disappear from the face of the earth that the new crime, the crime against humanity—in the sense of a crime 'against the human status' or against the very nature of humankind—appeared." Hannah Arendt, *Eichmann in Jerusalem: A Report on the Banality of Evil* (New York: Penguin Classics, 2006), 267–268.

The production of the imperial desert effect on a state scale requires the operation of many technologies by experts who, through their training, manage to dis-implicate themselves from the very crimes in which they partake. The **photographer** whose photographs are printed as part of the publication of the national plan was commissioned to take photographs of different regions, including the desert.[6] We don't know the **photographer's** name, and we don't know if they were explicitly instructed to capture the desert without people or to not capture the expulsion of people from the desert. The **national architect's** plan seemingly required "clean" images of the desert itself, a dry and barren land. In these surveys, Palestine is already discarded. The imperial practices of environmental taxonomy are useful in seeing beyond Palestine or in not seeing it at all. The experts, as these photographs and plans convey, saw the Naqab in its material forms, flows, and substances:

> In the heart of the Negev, south of the huge [Ramon] crater, limestone with remnants of volcanic eruptions in the shape of basalt hills. In the Ramon Crater itself — acute alluvial forms due to sudden rains and strong fluctuations in temperature during the day. After the rains, the valleys are covered with poor grass. The area is on the border between the wilderness and the pastures frequented only by a few Bedouins.[7]

Before the expulsion, these "few Bedouins" counted 90,000 — 15 percent of the Jewish population in all of Palestine at the time (which was less then 600,000).[8] The Northern Naqab was also represented with a people-free image:

> The soil adheres to rainwater and after drying becomes an impermeable crust that facilitates the rapid flow of additional rainwater to the wadi channels. Purposeful tillage can ensure its fertility. The amount of rainfall (250–300 mm per year) is not enough to grow barley

6   Sharon's National Outline Plan was published as *Tikhnun fisi be-Yisrael* (Jerusalem: Government Printing Press and Survey of Israel Press, 1951), with an English translation, published as a booklet under the title *Physical Planning in Israel*, included as an insert. The photographs included can be found in the digital archive of Arieh Sharon, a website maintained by Sharon's daughter and grandson, https://www.ariehsharon.org/Archive/Physical-Planning-in-Israel/Land-and-Landscape.
7   Sharon, *Tikhnun fisi be-Yisrael*, vi.
8   See UN Special Committee on Palestine, Report to the General Assembly, A/364 (September 3, 1947), https://unispal.un.org/unispal.nsf/0/07175de9fa2de563852568d3006e10f3.

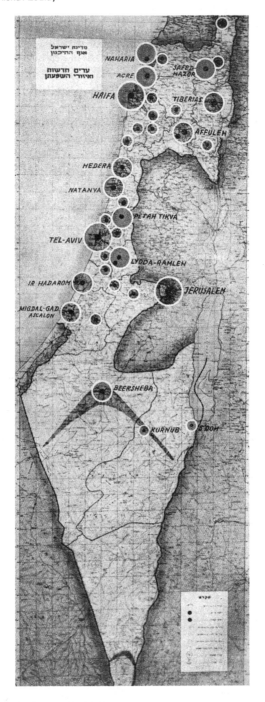

"Dispersion of Population." An iteration of the National Plan for Israel by Arieh Sharon, 1951.

נוף באזור הר הנגב

בלב הנגב, דרומית, מן המכתש הענק רמון (ואדי־רמון). אבני גיר מתקיפת הקרטון עם
שרידים של החתך־צורית וולקניות בצורת גבעות בולת. במכתש רמון עצמו — צורות־נוף
חריפות בעקבות גשמים פתאומיים בורדים והנידות טמפרטורה חזקות כמשך הימימה.
העמקים מכוסים צרורות ה+פרורות. ואחד־י הגשמים — עשב זל, האזור הוא גובל בין
הישימון ובין שטחי המרעה הנפקדים על ידי בידואים מעטים.

"Landscape in the Negev [Naqab] Mountain." The National Plan for Israel by Arieh Sharon, 1951.

without further irrigation. And the drought here is a normal phenomenon. By irrigating, the area will be able to become one of the richest agricultural areas in Israel. The climate is healthy.[9]

Anyone could tell that it was not the Naqab desert that was being studied and represented but rather its speculative abstraction, an image of what it could become if the world that it is was only a removable obstacle. It may be that for the different protagonists involved, this world did not appear to them as such. The **national architect** was not required to deal with the obstacles that human presence posed to their plans. This was the job of other armed agents. The **national architect** needed only concern themself with the topographical and climatic challenges posed to the prospect of Judaification. The desert was no exception, except maybe in that it had to become a rich agricultural area, which it was not. The study of the desert against—that is, in neglect of—its inhabitants was already an imperial endeavor, regardless of the imperial nature of the **national architect**'s solutions.

The Declaration

The newly self-appointed **prime minister** didn't wait for the plan before praising its success. In May 1948, in a ceremony known at the time as "the Declaration of the Establishment of the State of Israel," he described the achievements of Zionists using this idiom:

> ...they made deserts bloom... built villages and towns, and created a thriving community... bringing the blessings of progress to all the country's inhabitants.[10]

Against existing worlds, documents and plans were drafted proclaiming progress and triumph and their fictions executed.[11] In imperial worlds, the power to proclaim a place as desert and to authorize actors to "make it bloom" (i.e., to destroy it) is

---

9   Sharon, *Tikhnun fisi be-Yisrael*, IX.
10   Minhelet HaAm [People's Administration], "Declaration of the Establishment of the State of Israel," May 14, 1948, https://www.jewishvirtuallibrary.org/the-declaration-of-the-establishment-of-the-state-of-israel. The anniversary of the Declaration on 5 Iyar in the Hebrew calendar is celebrated as the Israeli Independence Day; the Declaration of the Establishment of the State of Israel is also referred to both colloquially and in official government records and communications as the "Declaration of Independence": see, for example, its listing on the website of the Knesset, Israel's legislative body, https://main.knesset.gov.il/en/about/pages/declaration.aspx.

enshrined in pieces of paper like this. These documents simultaneously proclaim the existence of the state of Israel and the inexistence of Palestine. By the time of the Declaration of Independence, **militant Zionists** had expelled 250,000 of the 750,000 Palestinians they would eventually expel by 1950.[12] The **prime minister** and other **ministers** were preoccupied with bringing Jewish migrants first from Europe and then from Muslim countries/or North Africa and the Middle East/or the Arab World to labor in this enterprise—schematizing their dispersal across Palestine so that all of Palestine would become Jewish.[13] New **inhabitants** were intended to impede the return of **expellees**. Palestinians who sought to return to their homes were doomed to appear as **"infiltrators"** in the newly designed eyes of "Israelis," the **inhabitants** of the newly declared state whose identity was manufactured and defined by the Zionist project.

Denying Return

There is only one way to describe **"infiltrators"**: from the point of view of these Israeli eyes, since the designation of people who were expelled from their homes as **"infiltrators"** is predicated on the very existence of those eyes.[14] We encounter these eyes in the **literary writer**, whose quasi poem begins this fable—the **literary writer**, whose intellectual development coincided with military service, with an order to expel Palestinians from their lands and deny their return. The **literary writer**, sharing with the reader of his novel the wording of such an order, actually recalls a real one: "Operational order number 40, purpose: expulsion of the Arab **refugees** from these villages and preventing their return by destroying the villages."[15] In this real order, Palestinians are already referred to as **"refugees"** before being expelled. Yizhar cannot deny that they were **"inhabitants"** and this is how

11   Studying the Zionist planning of Israel, Zvi Efrat writes: "Not a random improvisation in laying the foundations, no lack of professional culture, no speculative initiatives, certainly no organic or spontaneous development created it [the Israeli space]—but rather a great intention, and success, in running one of the most comprehensive and controlled architectural experiments in the modern age." See Zvi Efrat, *The Israeli Project: Building and Architecture 1948–1973* (Tel Aviv: Tel Aviv Museum of Art, 2004), 991.

12   See Wikipedia, s.v. "1948 Palestinian exodus," last modified October 1, 2021, https://en.wikipedia.org/wiki/1948_Palestinian_exodus.

13   On the Jewish migrants see Gil Eyal, *The Disenchantment of the Orient: Expertise in Arab Affairs and the Israeli State* (Stanford: Stanford University Press, 2006).

14   On the invention of the "infiltrator," see Ariella Azoulay, "The Imperial Condition of Photography in Palestine: Archives, Looting, and the Figure of the Infiltrator," *Visual Anthropology Review* 33, no. 1 (Spring 2017): 5–17.

15   The military order was published in Hebrew on a website dedicated to S. Yizhar: see lusiml, "The Deportation Involves Gravel," *S. Yizhar Returns*, November 18, 2019.

I covered all the figures who attended the Declaration of the Establishment of the State of Israel on May 14, 1948, with ink, in order to foreground the document at the center of this ceremony. Image altered by the author.

A Palestinian, his son, and a donkey are stopped by soldiers while attempting to return to their home shortly after being expelled. Image altered by the author.

he recalls the order they received: "also the subsequent and even more noteworthy clause, which explicitly stated, 'assemble the inhabitants of the area extending from point X (see attached map) to point Y (see same map)—load them onto transports and convey them across our lines; blow up the stone house and burn the huts.'"[16] Given that they were never **"infiltrators"** but rather **returnees**—and under the international law **"refugees"**—Palestinians continued to return; they continued to try to reach home, to find refuge elsewhere in Palestine, to cultivate their land, and to transgress the Israeli law that was imposed on their land. Even when they failed, they refused to recognize themselves in the roles assigned to them by the state—roles that claimed that they are no longer *of* Palestine, that their presence in Palestine is an external threat, that their displacement (even within Palestine) reinforces the buffer zone that prevents "incompatible entities" or "antagonistic people" from coming in contact with one another beyond the roles assigned to them by the **soldier**'s novel.

Engineering the Future

With military orders, documents of declaration, and plans, time was inversed—deceiving those whose sensorium was attuned to the land. Blooming is always preceded by producing a desert "made to bloom." The **militant Zionists** hadn't yet made *the* desert—the Naqab—bloom when the declaration was proclaimed in May 1948. Zionists had only built nineteen tiny settlements of approximately fifteen to thirty people each when the partition plan resolution was announced in 1947—the total Jewish population in the desert was fewer than 2,665.[17] In building new settlements, the Zionists needed and relied upon Palestinian knowledge and labor to navigate and cultivate a land they conceived as infertile and difficult to inhabit. In order to survive, they extracted desert knowledge and then betrayed this local knowledge in a similar way that they betrayed the people who taught them.[18] Rather than learning how to live in the Naqab—to

16   Yizhar, *Khirbet Khizeh*, 8–9.
17   In 1946 there were even fewer Jews in the Naqab—only 510. In response to the Morrison-Grady Plan (1946), which suggested that the Naqab should be under direct British control, the Zionists organized a quasi-military campaign, occupying eleven areas in the Naqab to increase the Jewish presence there. The map of the eleven Jewish settlements from 1946 can be seen at Wikipedia, s.v. "11 Points in the Negev," last modified September 9, 2021, https://en.wikipedia.org/wiki/11_points_in_the_ Negev. On the issues of land ownership and the Jewish and Bedouin populations in the Naqab, see Ruth Kark and Seth J. Frantzman, "The Negev: Land, Settlement, the Bedouin and Ottoman and British Policy 1871–1948," *British Journal of Middle Eastern Studies* 39, no. 1 (2012): 53–77.

inhabit the desert as a desert—**water engineers** were asked to build a pipeline to connect and provide different localities with water. A company was established to realize the **prime minister**'s vision for the Naqab and to seek solutions. **Water engineers** strove to determine how to live in the desert while disregarding its condition. "Making the desert bloom" was a political project. This is no secret. It is still proudly stated on the homepage of the national water engineering company's website:

> Mekorot's activities for sustaining life and agriculture in the Negev began in 1943 with the discovery of water in drillings conducted on a hill in the Nir Am area. The amount of water found in boreholes in the Nir Am area allowed the establishment of the first water plant in the Negev. The plant contained a pumping station and a 1000 cubic meters pool, and *it played an important role in the struggle for setting the boundaries of the western Negev.*[19]

The Partition Plan

Each Jewish locality built in the lead-up to 1948 was established to create a "fact on the ground": a "post" to be counted as a Jewish settlement in any partition plan to come. The goal was to stretch Jewish presence in Palestine across a seemingly even side on the map, provisionally establishing the coordinates of the future division of Palestine. In 1945, Jews occupied only 5 percent of the land, and Palestinians were the majority, but these facts didn't count once imperial actors got their hands on scissors.[20] The Naqab was allocated to the Jewish state.[21]

The partition plan is a curse. It was and continues to be used as an imperial tool that further divides the fabrics of shared life and yields long-lasting disasters. The details of the partition plan confirm how it misapprehends the reality on the ground, in

18   See the newsreel "Jewish Squatters in Palestine," filmed in 1946 in one of these eleven new settlements, which were established instantly nearby Arab localities: British Movietone News, October 17, 1946, 00:57, AP Archive, http://www.aparchive.com/metadata/youtube/7c9f0ba053594bc5b74a592d9438f1c6.

19   Emphasis by the author. "Water to the Negev," Mekorot, last modified October 12, 2020, https://wold.mekorot.co.il/Eng/newsite/WaterManagementandSupply/Pages/WatertotheNegev.aspx.

20   See "Vanishing Palestine," Palestine Remix, interactive map, 2015, https://interactive.aljazeera.com/aje/palestineremix/maps_main.html. By the time the UN welcomed Israel as a member state in 1949, that 5 percent had grown to 78 percent, following the forceful expulsion of at least 750,000 Palestinians.

21   Some of the concrete destructive consequences of this decision are seen in sedentarization policies toward the nomadic population, attempts at integrating it while keeping these villages unrecognized or under constant threat of destruction.

light of the so-called "facts" on the ground. Allocating the Naqab to the Jewish state is proof—if proof is needed. The numbers have already been stated: at the time of the partition plan's proposal in 1947, the Jews numbered fewer than 3,000 in all of their twenty localities. The decision about Palestine was made not by its **inhabitants** but rather by imperial states, which had already, in 1916 with the Sykes-Picot Agreement, partitioned the Middle East between England and France. Since the beginning of the British mandate, the British were obsessed with the partitioning of Palestine, and following World War II the United Nations chaperoned this process led mainly by Anglo-American forces. For years, these states invested in crafting and dividing "the Middle East," while also imposing imperial infrastructures that enabled them to control it under various configurations.[22] Albeit a tiny minority in the Naqab, with the help of **water engineers**, the Zionists imposed on the Naqab the invasive infrastructure of a pipeline, which earned them the reputation of harbingers of progress as well as the desert. The disregard shown by imperial powers toward the 19,000 Bedouins living in the Naqab recurs on different scales and in different places, including on the scale of the partition plan in toto. In 1948, 400,000 Palestinians—almost half of the Palestinian population in all of Palestine—lived on land that was allocated to the Jews.[23] The plan divided Palestinians and turned them into a "minority" in a newly established state built in their homeland.

Going on Strike

The Palestinians refused to collaborate with the 1946 Anglo-American Committee of Inquiry in the destruction of their homeland. A decade earlier in 1936, Palestinians went on general strike for three years against the partition of their land and

The existing forty-five unrecognized villages in the Naqab are organized under the Regional Council of Unrecognized Villages (RCUV). See *Off the Map: Land and Housing Rights Violations in Israel's Unrecognized Bedouin Villages*, report prepared by Human Rights Watch, March 2008, https://www.hrw.org/sites/default/files/reports/iopt0308webwcover.pdf. On the more than 118 times that the village of Al-Arakeeb was destroyed, see Patrick Strickland, "Negev: Israel Razes Palestinian Village for 113th Time," *Al Jazeera*, May 18, 2017, https://www.aljazeera.com/news/2017/5/18/negev-israel-razes-palestinian-village-for-113th-time; on the history of the sedentarization in the Naqab, see Ghazi Farah, "Israeli State Policy toward Bedouin Sedentarization in the Negev," *Journal of Palestine Studies* 18, no. 2 (Winter 1989): 71–91.

22   See Jacob Norris, *Land of Progress: Palestine in the Age of Colonial Development, 1905–1948* (Oxford: Oxford University Press, 2013).

23   See Wikipedia, s.v. "United Nations Partition Plan for Palestine," last modified February 24, 2022, https://en.wikipedia.org/wiki/United_Nations_Partition_Plan_for_Palestine.

against Britain's promises to turn their homeland into a national home for the Jews. This general strike was harshly suppressed by **British policemen** and has yet to receive the attention it deserves as a **strikers'** campaign against a **settlers'** enterprise that sought not only to steal land but also to destroy the equilibrium of local ecosystems and land knowledge.[24] Palestinians went on strike against their dispossession. It was an act of care for their homeland in the face of accelerated expansion, gentrification, and resource exhaustion.

In a reversed mirror image, Zionist groups invested in the destruction of Palestine, building settlements with the sole goal of seizing as much land as possible. Similar to other colonial projects, the British were invested in imposing the divide-and-rule model in Palestine. Thus, while they supported the Zionist project, they also imposed restrictions on its expansion. Against the British restrictions on building new settlements, the Zionists invented "instant settlements" called "Tower and Stockade."[25] Prefabricated and prepared in advance, a settlement could be imposed as a "fact on the ground" in less than twenty-four hours.[26] Fifty settlements were built in three years; most were adjacent to Palestinian villages. Take, for example, Beit Afa in the Naqab, which shared its name with its corresponding Arab locality but with a different spelling. After a year, settlers changed its name to Negba, which means "moving toward the Negev." Pre-1948, the proximity between small Zionist settlements and Arab villages in Palestine could still yield different types of non-antagonistic relations. But from the moment the **prime minister** proclaimed the existence of the state, **neighbors** were proclaimed **enemies, inhabitant warriors**, and **soldiers**.

The term "desert" takes on additional meaning in this context: the **soldiers**, as we saw in the excerpt from the novel, were allowed to produce the desert condition, to lay waste and to destroy; at the same time, they could desert their **neighbors**, abandoning them with no intention to return. In other words, the proclamation of the state generated a desert effect on a state scale: Palestinians were expelled, their villages deserted and

---

24   See Ghassan Kanafani, *The 1936–39 Revolt in Palestine* (New York: Committee for a Democratic Palestine, 1972), http://pflp-documents.org/documents/PFLP-Kanafani3639.pdf.

25   On the British opposition to Zionist land acquisition in the Naqab, see Ruth Kark, "Jewish Frontier Settlement in the Negev, 1880–1948: Perception and Realization," *Middle Eastern Studies* 17, no. 3 (July 1981): 334–356.

26   See the interview with Shlomo Gur, the architect of Tower and Stockade: "We were not strong, but we overlooked," by Ariella Aïsha Azoulay, in Azoulay, *Ekh zeh nir'eh lekha?: 25 siḥot, 44 tatslumim* (How does it look to you?) (Tel Aviv: Bavel, 1999) (in Hebrew).

This was Umm-Khalid, 1948. Image altered by the author.

Imperial desert soil, not included in the National Plan.

School children are sent to clear the rubble of what they are being told are "Abandoned Arab villages," 1949. Image altered by the author.

Building Netanya on Umm-Khalid lands, 1950. Image altered by the author.

ready to be made to bloom by their **neighbors**-turned-**enemies**, i.e., the Zionists who deserted them, literally betraying them and their pre-existing relationships.

The Soil of the Imperial Desert

The taxonomy of desert soils is missing one. Without this soil, it is impossible to understand the enterprise of the imperial desert effect. Hubris. This type of soil testifies to the fact that a worldly life, worldly sovereignty, was targeted. It is a soil produced by the **destroyers**. Special companies removed the bigger chunks of rubble; others recycled them in landscapes of all sorts. **School children** were brought from all over the country to clear the land of rubble and turn it fertile, sowing a new sense of attachment to it. The production of the rubbly desert soil is an orchestrated enterprise that calls upon people from the humanities and liberal arts to participate and intervene. This rubbly soil functions as a buffer between Palestinian presence-even-when-absent and the triumphal project of state construction.

When one looks for images from the establishment of Netanya, for example, the city where I grew up, one finds sand dunes that point to the putative "nothingness" from which the city emerged. These "historical" images of Netanya are actually of the Arab village Umm Khalid. Did I already say that Palestine is there, where it had always been? In the late 1920s, Netanya was built on lands purchased from the neighboring village Umm Khalid. In other words, Netanya was not built out of nothing, but was part of Umm Khalid. The Arab villagers and Jewish immigrants shared certain things: common spaces, weather, services, etc. With the declaration of the state of Israel, Umm Khalid was produced as a desert, abandoned of its world so that it could be incorporated into the history of Netanya. Here and there, some Palestinian houses survived the production of the desert. They were salvaged as "historical" ruins, but they are integrated into the Zionist-created space as completely ahistorical—floating in urban space, not as evidence of the systematic destruction of Palestine, but as semi-museumified relics that the Jewish **inhabitants** are invited to encounter as left there from an unknown past. On the crowd-sourced Palestinian website Palestine Remembered, they are being identified and contextualized. The Palestinian villages of which they were a part are still being reclaimed by **Palestinian returnees** across the diaspora who use Palestine Remembered to upload, search, and annotate photographs from Palestine.[27] They refuse to allow for Palestine to disappear from the photographic record, challenging the desert effect that was produced to do exactly this.

The Conquest of the Desert

Executing the imperial desert effect on the state scale became the state's flagship project: its source of national pride, its object of exhibition, and a kind of knowledge it could export to other places. Signing a document that replaces *what is* with a vision of *what will* be is a common imperial procedure that enables an imperial power to impose ownership over stolen lands and to normalize imperially obtained possessions. In 1948, shortly after the **prime minister** signed the document that proclaimed Palestine inexistent and legitimized the desert effect across all the lands that the newly created state had conquered—including those that were beyond what was allocated to it by the partition plan—he signed another document. This one announced the erection of an International Convention Center.[28] Obviously, **architects** and **engineers** were called upon to draft a plan that would ratify what was also declared with that document: that the Arab village Sheikh Bader, on whose lands it was built, was no more. But it is there, in the same place it has always existed. The **inhabitants** had to be notified about its disappearance in plain sight, and by recognizing the disappearance as an established fact they actualized the citizenship bestowed on them by the settler colonial state. The **informed citizen** is attuned to the **voice of the state** as it is spoken by **architects** and **engineers**, experts who are formed as **citizen-perpetrators** at the same time that the land is being transformed to physically echo those crafted plans. For the **newborn Israelis**, there was nothing more factual than the Israeliness of everything that surrounded them. From their particularly assigned positions, those **newly proclaimed Israeli-Jews**, regardless of if they were Zionists before the Nakba, would have to regard the project of "making the desert bloom" as their own and partake in it.

In front of the sign publicly announcing the creation of the International Convention Center stands a citizen learning to look at a map or plan of the **new state**, a legitimate substitute for what

27   Palestine Remembered, https://www.palestineremembered.com.
28   The decision to establish the International Convention Center deliberately replicated the ceremony of the Declaration of the Establishment of the State of Israel. A charter (*megilah*) was signed by the prime minister, the president, different ministers, members of the Knesset, and some of the Jewish Agency administrators. See "Mira Altman Fulfilled Ben Gurion's Vison," *Walla*, January 5, 2021 (in Hebrew), https://finance.walla.co.il/item/3409661.

The informed citizen. Image altered by the author.

An entrance ticket to the exhibition "The Conquest of the Desert," International Convention Center, Jerusalem, 1953.

is simultaneously being robbed of others: lands and properties proclaimed by the Israeli **Custodian of Absentee Property** as "abandoned property." Palestinians, **guardians of this piece of earth** for centuries, were forced to become **refugees** when the Zionists forced them beyond the newly erected borders of what they proclaimed to be "their state"; the Palestinians who found ways to resist their expulsion were nevertheless **subject** to military rule that ended only in 1966, one year before Israel conquered the West Bank and Gaza and transferred its military rule to these parts of Palestine. The care that **guardians of this piece of earth** had once shown was replaced by the logic of **racial capitalists** who saw in this piece of earth inexhaustible resources. The **informed citizen** in the image is trained not to see what was left of Sheikh Bader, which, until 1948, was a thriving neighborhood in Jerusalem. Even if nothing will be left of it, Sheikh Bader is there, where it had always been, and its **expellees** and their **descendants** will return.

The production of the imperial desert effect is inseparable from the production of people who could recognize these places as desert. Again, desert not in the climatic or topographic sense but as a condition of malleability that imperial citizens, under their different capacities and professions, are granted rights to transform, i.e., to till, and to make bloom, etc. Making the desert bloom should be understood as the arena in which a set of rights that is definitively antagonistic to others—their land, possessions, and survival—is permitted. The General Assembly of the Bureau International des Expositions— an intergovernmental organization founded in 1928 that is in charge of overseeing and regulating World Expos—recognized the eligibility of Israel to host an exhibition on the topic of the desert, held in Jerusalem in 1953, which would generate insights about "ways to beat back the desert for food and living place in an increasingly populated world."[29] With the creation of the state of Israel and its International Convention Center, Israel became a kind of expert in exporting its imperial knowledge, its how-to of making a desert bloom. Thirteen states (mainly European and the US) and international organizations such as UNESCO and the World Health Organization participated in this

---

29   According to the Bureau International des Expositions (BIE), "The 1953 Conquest of the Desert exhibition in Jerusalem, recognised by the 28th General Assembly of the BIE on 13 November 1951, entailed a discussion about the reclamation and population of desert areas. It was the first major international exhibition to take place in the newly created state." See "Expo 1953 Jerusalem," Bureau International des Expositions, published January 29, 2016, https://www.bie-paris.org/site/en/1953-jerusalem.

exhibition, whose title yields the nature of the project: "The Conquest of the Desert."[30]

Palestinians' long tradition of strike can also be understood as a strike against the racial-capitalist ideal of "productivity" that Zionists imposed upon the land through its conscription of all of its citizens into the process of transforming the land into a desert to be made to bloom. The strike of 1936–1939 was not only against British colonialism and the Jewish immigration it facilitated, but also against the deserting of their country and its further opening to international entrepreneurs, as these Euro-American forces had acted in other places. Such concerns motivated their strike against and refusal to communicate with the Anglo-American Committee of Enquiry, charged by **international imperial actors** to bring a "solution" to the problems caused by Europe's longstanding interventions in the area. The **conquerors** of the land were soon recognized as its **sovereigns**, and later recognized as **authorized signatories** of international agreements of ceasefire and peace. Palestinians were forced to become **extras** in different international arenas in which decisions about them were made externally and against their interests, as international law continues to determine that such decisions and agreements may only be made between **state actors**.

The Ongoing Strike against Partition

This fable ends with an image from Bir al-Saba (currently Beer Sheva), which is considered in Israel to be the "capital of the Negev." Most of the thriving city of Bir al-Saba was destroyed, except for some precious architectural structures, like the Grand Mosque, which different **cultural agents** have, unsurprisingly, aimed to turn into a museum for Islamic and Near Eastern Cultures. The museum was never a cultural institution but an imperial technology used to house and facilitate the operation of other imperial technologies whose violences are less camouflaged. Palestinians again are going on strike, this time as **unmuseumified *subjects*.** They are here, where a museum was erected to proclaim their "pastness"; they are here, opposing this imperial temporality by their continuous presence. They gather in the plaza in front of the museum—their former mosque— performing their existence in the present, opposing, as their

30   On the exhibition and the participating countries and organizations see Wikipedia, s.v. "Conquest of the Desert (exhibition)," last modified May 20, 2021, https://en. wikipedia.org/wiki/Conquest_of_the_Desert_(exhibition).

ancestors did for decades, the partitioning of their country. The fact that this brutal plan and its distorted realization resulted not in two states but in one state of apartheid, doesn't mean that the same "old" struggle is over. Striking against the blooming of the imperial desert is not a lost cause.

It is only from the logic of the **settlers'** state that the opposition to partition was shaped as the exclusive cause of Palestinians. That Arab Jews in the neighboring countries were forced to become "Jews" (shorn of their Arabness) and "Israelis" reveals how the partition of Palestine impacted their world too.

Here is a call written by Siril Shirizi, one of the founders of the Jewish Anti-Zionist League, a group of **Anti-partition Arab-Jewish activists**, in May 1947:

> Jewish Men! Jewish Women!
>
> Zionism wants to throw us into a dangerous and hopeless adventure. Zionism contributes to making Palestine uninhabitable. Zionism wants to isolate us from the Egyptian people. Zionism is the enemy of the Jewish people.
>
> Down with Zionism! Long live the brotherhood of Jews and Arabs!
>
> Long live the Egyptian people![31]

Going on strike against partition today means dwelling in this repressed struggle that precedes the state of Israel's creation. It means persevering until its abusive state apparatuses are dismantled, the destruction of Palestine is repaired, reparations to the Palestinian **expellees** are prioritized, and objects regain the power they have in many local fables to disenchant the people who've remained captive to their designated roles. Going on strike against partition today is also going on strike against further destroying the earth. It means deserting the imperial project of the desert.

31   Jewish Anti-Zionist League, "Appeal to the Jews of Egypt," May 1947, included in
      a report by the World Zionist Organization Political Department, Central Zionist
      Archives, Jerusalem, quoted in Gudrun Krämer, *The Jews in Modern Egypt 1914–
      1952* (Seattle: University of Washington Press, 1989), 180. For another statement by
      the Jewish Anti-Zionist League, written in June of the same year, see Marsil
      Shirizi, "Anti-Zionism for the Sake of Jews and the Sake of Egypt," in *Modern Middle
      Eastern Jewish Thought: Writings on Identity, Politics & Culture, 1893–1958*, ed.
      Moshe Behar and Zvi Ben-Dor Benite (Waltham, MA: Brandeis University Press,
      2013), 164–173.

Saphiya Abu Al-Maati is an architect and researcher interested in the intersection of policy, conflict, and the built environment. She obtained her MArch from Columbia University and a Bachelor of Peace and Conflict Studies specializing in Human Security from UC Berkeley. Saphiya has served as an Advisor to the Hareer and Boubyan Development Agency and the Kuwait Council of Ministers, consulting on national urban projects. She was awarded the Science Po and Kuwait Foundation for the Advancement of Science's grant for "On the Stakes of War and Peace: Diplomacy, Anthropology, Climate, and Conflict" and has co-taught design studio courses at Barnard College and Columbia University GSAPP. Her research on the influence of regional political parties on the physical development of Kuwait has been a part of multiple conferences, including the UNESCO World Heritage Conference (Bahrain) and the International Association for the Study of Traditional Environments Conference (Portugal).

Asaiel Al Saeed is a practicing architect who obtained her professional BArch from Kuwait University in 2019. She works between architectural design and research, and co-taught several courses at Kuwait University from 2019 to 2021, including the undergraduate architecture thesis studio. Her research interests revolve around resource planning, contested sites, and the policies that produce conflicted spatial conditions. In 2021, her research project titled "Agriculture as a Territorial Mark" was recognized for Excellence in Architecture, Planning & Housing by the Kuwait Ministry of State for Youth Affairs. She was appointed as one of four co-curators of the Kuwait National Pavilion at the 17th Venice Architecture Biennale (2021).

Aseel AlYaqoub holds a BA from Chelsea College of Art and Design in London and an MFA from Pratt Institute in New York. AlYaqoub was a co-curator of the Kuwait National Pavilion at the 17th Venice Architecture Biennale (2021) and was awarded the Art Jameel Commission in collaboration with Alia Farid (2018). Her work has been exhibited at the Museum of Humour and Satire, Gabrovo; Edge of Arabia, London; Pierogi Gallery, New York; Art Claims Impulse, Berlin; Foreman Art Gallery, Sherbrooke, Quebec; Sultan Gallery, Kuwait; Museum of Modern Art, Kuwait; and The Contemporary Art Platform, Kuwait. Her research has been presented at symposiums such as Abu Dhabi Art; Nuqat Conference, Kuwait; and The National Museum of Qatar, Doha.

Yousef Awaad Hussein is an architect and practicing urban designer. He holds an MArch from Harvard University Graduate School of Design and a BArch with distinction from McGill University. He is the recipient of Harvard University's Penny White Project Fund for a proposal titled "Kuwait's Urban Landscape: An Aerial View" and the Centre for Geographic Analysis' Fisher Prize for a study titled "Territory, Survey, Cartography—South China Sea." His research has been published and presented at a number of symposiums, including the ISOCARP World Planning Congress and the International Association for the Study of Traditional Environments. Yousef is currently the Project Manager for the 4th Kuwait Master Plan and holds a position as Senior Urban Designer at Perkins&Will, working on projects across London, Riyadh, and New York.

SPACE WARS: AN INVESTIGATION INTO KUWAIT'S HINTERLAND

A CONVERSATION WITH SAPHIYA ABU AL-MAATI, ASAIEL AL SAEED, ASEEL ALYAQOUB, AND YOUSEF AWAAD HUSSEIN

Samia Henni (SH):

> As curators of the Kuwait Pavilion at the 17th Venice Architecture Biennale, you responded to the proposed theme, "How will we live together?," by interpreting and projecting Kuwait's desert landscapes and histories. You titled the pavilion *Space Wars: An Investigation into Kuwait's Hinterland*. Could you tell us about the genesis of this exhibition project?

Yousef Awaad Hussein (YAH):

> When the commissioner of the pavilion, Zahra Ali Baba, first brought the four of us together, our approach was to weave our independent research into an encompassing project representing Kuwait at the Biennale. So, the topic was born out of our individual interests and potential synergies, at the scales of Kuwait, the Gulf region, and the design disciplines. However, the catalyst was the 1991 Gulf War moniker: the "First Space War." Why was it given that name? How did it change the course of our history? What tools were involved? Is this relevant today? Where did it take place? We asked these questions to unpack and investigate what we believe to be an underrepresented part of our national discourse.
>
> The consensus was that, before we could answer "How will we live together?," we first needed to understand how we lived together historically and how we live together currently. This collective conclusion ultimately meant that only in discovering our past could we understand the present and, in turn, project our future.

Aseel AlYaqoub (AAY):

> Because much of the existing architectural discourse in Kuwait focuses on the metropolitan area, we steered

away from the city and began touring the remaining national landscape. At first glance and at a distance, most of the hinterland appeared to be vast and unoccupied, confirming cringey Orientalist definitions of the desert. However, as we began zooming in and flying through Google Earth, we encountered fascinating spatial conditions.

On the ground, access to many of the sites we found was limited due to their functions as military sites, oil fields, and nature reserves. From above, they became semi-accessible. The aerial view allowed for a more scrutinized reading of the edge conditions, infrastructural decisions, and new planning strategies. As a result, we began addressing our questions with even more questions, mesmerized and dumbfounded by some of these spatial conditions.

Asaiel Al Saeed (AAS):

We were interested in the city-to-desert ratio that defined Kuwait's landscapes. Knowing that the metropolitan area makes up only 20 percent of Kuwait's total land, it was important for this project to draw attention to the potential embedded within the remaining and seemingly unoccupied 80 percent of national land—which essentially provides and supports the city through its natural resources, environmental operations, and industrial processes.

Saphiya Abu Al-Maati (SAA):

The scope of the project has grown since we first began. Initially, we focused on investigating the spatial conditions we observed, "spatial wars"—programmatic or functional spaces that exist in awkward or problematic adjacencies to one another—outside of the metropolitan area. Over time, and through more in-depth discussions, the project expanded to cover the role of the hinterland across art, architecture, economics, politics. It's become much more comprehensive, and it's definitely better because of that.

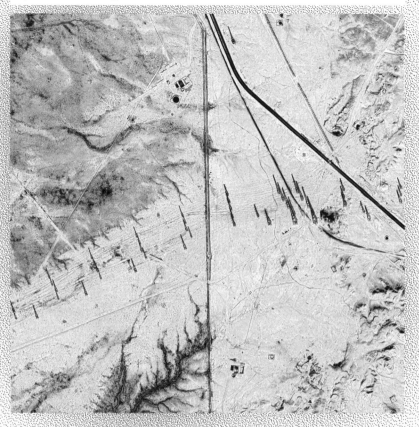

Nature Reserve and Oil Field. Courtesy of Atlas of Places. © Space Wars.

SH: Could you describe some of the characteristics of
            that 80 percent of national land before the war?
            How did it relate to the city-state?

SAA: In the years immediately leading up to the invasion, this
        landscape functioned much like it does today. It was a
        space logistically and economically tied to the metropol-
        itan area, a space of production and business. Camping
        was also popular then, though it was done with much
        more care and sensitivity towards the environment than
        it is today.

        If we look back even earlier than that, however, the rela-
        tionship of these spaces to the metropolitan area was
        more reciprocal. Historically speaking, the desert land-
        scape was not considered foreign to the lifestyle of
        settled individuals. It was a natural part of living that
        was acknowledged as necessary for the exchange of
        goods, tribal migration, and the expansion of territory.
        The dichotomy of city versus desert could be argued
        as a construction of imported knowledge and self-
        Orientalism.

        As Kuwait City and subsequent neighborhoods were
        built during the mid- to late 1900s, the hinterland quickly
        became seen as a space for those unable or unwill-
        ing to adapt to new social norms. Life revolved around
        the newly constructed city, designed to encourage and
        support a very different, more European lifestyle than
        the traditional way of living, and the spaces and people
        outside of this came to represent a past that Kuwait was
        trying to leave behind.

        While today there is a movement within Kuwait, and the
        Gulf region as a whole, to center awareness and appreci-
        ation for traditional culture and heritage, the hinterland
        remains removed from many of these discussions. I
        think this is exacerbated by the fact that the majority of
        Kuwait's metropolitan area exists along the coast, there-
        fore maintaining more of a distinct separation than one
        might find in other countries with similar environments.

AAS: It is equally important to note that the pre-oil coastal city was once protected by three mud walls that were built between 1760 and 1920. Although the walls mainly served defensive purposes, they essentially defined the city borders and distinguished it from the remaining hinterland. While this emphasized a sense of physical separation between the two, it also introduced interesting meeting points that allowed for social and cultural exchange, which later paved the way for the post-oil urban planning practices that came to define modern Kuwait.

AAY: There's also the question of which war. During the 1920s, Kuwait was attacked multiple times by neighboring tribes, specifically at the Fort of Jahra. Although disconnected from the port-city in the north, Jahra was an important agricultural area that served the Kuwaiti population. As Kuwait was a protectorate of the British Empire at the time, the attacks were continuously thwarted. However, frustrated by the ongoing territorial disputes, the British sat around a map of Asia (at a scale of 1:1,000,000) to redefine the boundaries and buffer areas of not only Kuwait but also Iraq and Najd.

As a result, Kuwait lost two-thirds of its hinterland territory and the landscape was politicized; its spatial conditions and narratives were transformed into treaties and lines. Thus, the "80 percent" national landscape that we are accustomed to today is the result of a war. The once open desert was an important sociopolitical and economic landscape, clumsily defined into neutral zones and boundaries. The top-down mapping and planning of Kuwait's borders ultimately led to more territorial disputes such as the Gulf War, further solidifying the outline of Kuwait into the nation's psyche.

This may be why the urban symbol continues to serve as the primary geographic scope. The walls that Asaiel mentioned, now demolished, continue to echo a geospatial divide between the city and the remaining landscape. Kuwait's consignment to that history repeatedly focuses on its urban geography, perceiving the remaining hinterland as culturally and geographically distinct.

SH: How did the 1991 Gulf War affect what you call Kuwait's hinterland? What are the major transformations that the war engendered?

AAY: The Gulf War's most significant impact on the environment was the scorched earth method—a common war tactic used throughout much of recorded history. It is an ominous military strategy that aims to obliterate anything that might be useful to the enemy: transport vehicles, industrial resources, food stores, agricultural areas, water sources. As Kuwait heavily depends on its oil resources, the Iraqi forces were ordered to use the scorched earth policy during their retreat from Kuwait in 1991 in order to create an obstacle for advancing forces, as well as to deprive the population of their most valuable asset.

The progression and modernization of industry and warfare produced long-lasting effects. This can be seen in the haunting documentation of over 700 oil wells burning throughout the desert during the liberation of Kuwait. The visual and auditory results of this catastrophe dominated environmental discourse due to its chronic effects on a global scale.

Constant images of the fires, replayed over and over across multiple media outlets, may have saturated the event. This is evident in Werner Herzog's film *Lessons of Darkness* (1992) and Sophie Ristelhueber's photobook and photographic series entitled *Aftermath* (1992). Both representations have a sense of objectiveness, as though the catastrophe was perceived and documented by an alien observer more fascinated by the aesthetics of disaster than by the disaster itself. The footage and the photographs capture an admittedly awkward yet terrible beauty, given the subject's gravity.

We wanted to revisit the Gulf War after thirty years to remind the world that there are still remnants to this day and that its side effects do not only pertain to the oil fires. The digging of trenches, extensive use of landmines, and the barrage of tanks by liberation forces also impacted the hinterland. Many of these areas of the desert remain perilous—they are still fenced off for rehabilitation or require permission and guides to access and explore.

YAH: Parallel to the environmental effects, how the hinterland was viewed and navigated had global repercussions in media and technology. The Gulf War was the first war to be seen and covered in real time from above, from airplanes and satellites. This aerial perspective defined both the war and the desert. The resulting images came to characterize the conflict's illustrative legacy and Kuwait's hinterland. After the war, the news media collectively concluded that continuous coverage of major global events, like war, was profitable—especially when shown at a distance, through the rapid succession of stills obtained from cameras placed on smart bombs and through satellite imagery, detached from the actuality of combat.

Likewise, GPS technology was first introduced to the global public during the war. The newly utilized tech allowed the foreign coalition army to traverse an otherwise difficult-to-navigate landscape with ease and precision. Many soldiers wrote home asking loved ones to purchase and send spare equipment. In one such letter, a solider wrote: "Mom and Dad, please send GPS."

The methods and technology introduced during the 42-day war earned it the moniker, the "First Space War." Coverage of the war was like an advertisement for new tech, and both would become ubiquitous additions to modern consumer-based life. Ultimately, Kuwait's hinterland was presented to a global audience through the smoke of war, providing, perhaps, a less-than-accurate view of the desert's true geographical, cultural, and historical significance.

SH: Is Kuwait's hinterland a desert? If so, why did you use the term "hinterland" instead of "desert"? How would you define the desert?

AAS: The term "desert," which originated from Latin *desertus*, means "left waste." Its Arabic equivalent is صحراء (*sahraa*), signifying vast lands where water is scarce. "Hinterland" on the other hand means "behind land," which translates to Arabic as بر (*barr*), meaning the opposite of a body of water.

Although both words have been widely used to describe Kuwait's landscape, our process of unpacking the layers and conditions that make up this space entailed properly understanding and utilizing the language and names given to it by people who previously occupied it and currently interact with it. We were interested in comparing how different words frame the different perspectives, how language sets up ways of understanding and perceiving environments.

YAH: Kuwait's hinterland is in part a desert, but not wholly one. The terms are sometimes used interchangeably to label the vast territory. The scientific meaning of "hinterland" leans towards living conditions that appear remote and hostile to plant and animal life, like high temperatures and infrequent precipitation. But these attributes activate a unique ecological setting for native species. The monotony and flatness of maps also work to designate this space as an unproductive, empty territory. Yet Kuwait's "desert" is anything but that. It is very functional and home to resources that support both the metropolitan area and native species.

"Hinterland" widens the scope as an alternative reading that includes the desert as part of its definition—rather than simply characterizing the landscape as a natural and geographic condition.

SH: What is the curatorial project of *Space Wars: An Investigation into Kuwait's Hinterland*?

Saddam Road and Sand Extraction. Courtesy of Atlas of Places. © Space Wars.

AAY: It is really a co-authored and cooperative project focused on initiating a discourse around Kuwait's hinterland by engaging various disciplines. While we began by cataloging sites across the hinterland to grasp their impact, influence, and spatial relationships at multiple scales, we opened this research up to collaborators and contributors working across and around nature, geography, architecture, urban planning, landscape architecture, and the military, and began to think through questions of political, environmental, and economic sustainability in relation to the city's expansion. As a result, the project assembles a diverse, inquisitive, critical, and imaginative set of concerns. They are a vital extension of our research, enabling new juxtapositions and connections.

Inevitably, the curatorial project's goal is the exhibition, which is overwhelming in the context of the biennale structure. There is much to consider in mega exhibitions that promote national representations, such as scale, temporality, and thematic programs. Forced to adapt to the obstacles posed by COVID-19, our roles as curators shifted. It became less about mediating works and more about curating as a creative activity. It was a process of self-reflection. We wanted to enable discourse rather than become it, and to bring histories, spaces, and interpretations of the hinterland into the collective consciousness. The project also consists of a publication, which served as a framework to arrange, disconnect, and categorize the content, as a guide for how the exhibition would materialize, and as a case study through which other hinterlands could be read.

YAH: Our national pavilion sits in the Artigliere Arsenale. It presents a series of works, one of which is a three-piece 7.2 x 3.2 meter carpet. The carpet—which emerges from an interview we conducted with Kuwaiti Lieutenant General Abdulaziz AlJassim, who described the landscape "as though it were a carpet"—offers a past, present, and future. It allows one to trace the layering of uses and histories that has made up Kuwait's hinterland over the years. The carpet is abstracted over a fixed geographical mapping of the national territory,

Space Wars: An Investigation into Kuwait's Hinterland. Kuwait Pavilion at the 17th Venice Architecture Biennale, in the Artigliere Arsenale, Venice, Italy, August 29–November 21, 2021. Courtesy of Report Arch and Andrea Ferro Photography.

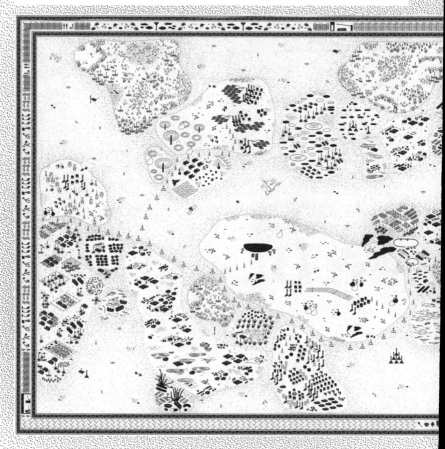

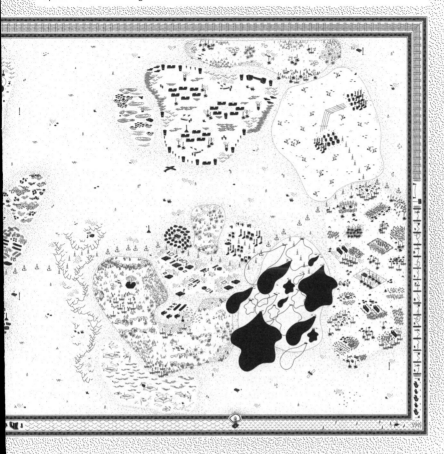

Hand-drawn carpet of the Kuwait hinterland. Triptych, 7.2 x 3.2 m. Courtesy of the Curators. © Space Wars.

loosely aligning with the reality on the ground. It constitutes a field of activity, with nested programs populated alongside distinct moments in time.

The left-most section depicts the historical nature of occupying the desert. For example, large plumes represent the 1991 oil fires, and the density of activity illustrated in industrial lands are low, as oil extraction was limited pre-1950. Military sites are presented as historical walled forts from the 1920s, and archaeological tumuli graves are mapped out from the Early/Middle Bronze Age. The central section illustrates how one relates to the landscape today, with spatial frictions made apparent as uses rub against each other surrounding the metropolitan area—waste, military, industry, agriculture, oil, stables, and reserves. Here, extraction is directly tied to oil spills both within fields and across their formal boundaries. A similar parallel is the remnants of camping—toilets, water tanks, tires, and furniture—scattering across the landscape. Sheep and camels occupy the lower half of the carpet, as grazing is unregulated, leading to desertification. The density of plant species increases within nature reserves as they become one of the only spaces for native species to survive. Finally, the rightmost section layers futures and proposals put forward by contributors onto the existing territory.

Across the carpet, the flora and fauna species evolve. Camping and remote housing densities vary. Types of resources develop—all over time. The carpet's border represents the national border of Kuwait today, including the United Nations Iraq-Kuwait Observation Mission (UNIKOM), shared oil extraction in the southern neutral zone with Saudi Arabia, military fences, and border patrol.

The spaces, adjacencies, and activities uncovered and discussed throughout the process are weaved together to form three vignettes of past perceptions, present discernments, and future conceptions. In this way, the carpet remaps the desert, reframing the existing narrative and countering earlier discourse by overlaying or chronologically rearranging historical evidence, to provide an alternative viewpoint that questions assertive sociospatial relations.

SAA: Adjacent to the carpet is a series of projections showcasing archival footage, satellite imagery, and proposals for sites that build a comprehensive narrative of the hinterland. Alongside these projections are two handcrafted benches welded by local craftsmen using recycled steel from waste sites in the desert, acting as a central display that physically manifests the content of our research. Finally, there is a حلفا (halfa), Pennisetum in Latin, which is a plant species previously found in the southern desert. Due to urban expansion it no longer naturally occurs there—what remains in its place is the neighborhood أبو حليفة (Abu Halifa), translated to "Father of the Pennisetum."

AAY: The archival footage is one of the project's bookends, as it visually threads the history of Kuwait's hinterland transformation. The video loop begins with grainy black-and-white footage of the wall that divides the port-city from the desert. The perspective fluctuates between aerial and ground views, gradually transforming into color. The footage registers the geospatial divide, but also a thriving ecosystem. The desert transforms into a functional staging ground as more operational landscapes are introduced, such as oil fields, infrastructure, agricultural lands, housing projects, etc.

The projection displaying the satellite imagery presents the accumulation of all these sites as they are today. It's an aerial tour similar to the one we embarked on via Google Earth at the beginning of the project. The viewer travels above campsites that litter the desert, across the blackened earth of an oil field to a solar farm, over highways that eventually end at the base of an archaeological site.

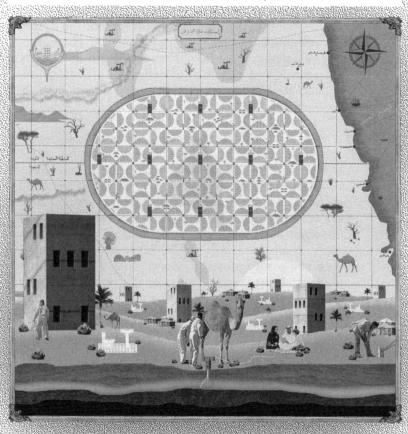

The Open Workshop, "Staking the Land," 2020. Courtesy of The Open Workshop.
© Space Wars.

As they are different lengths, the looping projections converge and diverge between the past, present, and contributors' work. There are moments when the screens coincide in terms of content, and other times when they create interesting juxtapositions and contradictions. It's a new experience each time it's viewed, leaving room for visual interpretation rather than didactic analysis.

SH: How did the invited participants react to your call? What are the different responses to/interpretations of your brief? Could you provide some examples of these submissions?

SAA: It was interesting to see how much the topic seemed to resonate with individuals working across very different fields. When you put forward a proposal or a piece of work your team has authored, you always hope that it will be of value to others, but you never know. In this case, the responses were even more enthusiastic than, I think, any of us had expected. I'd attribute that partly to its broad nature and the room it created for contributors to explore their own interests, but also to the fact that, by design, it's a research topic that can be applied globally. We are all dealing with the consequences of environmental neglect, and we are all tied to cultural or natural legacies across the landscapes in which we reside. By framing Kuwait as only a case study for this line of research, rather than the end point of it, we were able to include individuals who we otherwise might not have had the opportunity to learn from.

In doing so, the interpretations of the brief varied greatly, and the research became much richer. Even in responses that unexpectedly focused on similar themes, the approaches were still quite unique. This is most evident in the publication that accompanies the pavilion and provides a compilation of all the research and contributions collected throughout the project. The publication has served as an archive of sorts, allowing us to not only showcase the work of invited artists, historians, architects, and ecologists, but also put them in greater conversation with one another. The elements of the pavilion that Aseel and Yousef described are also present throughout the publication, but they are presented in a different format, taking the form of architectural proposals, historical essays, research projects, and artistic interpretations. While the pavilion ends up being a relatively short-lived physical component of the project, the publication enables the work to have a much longer lifespan.

YAH: The publication is divided into four sections—"The Gulf War," "Cultural Production," "Planning," and "Nature"— which offer a selection of theoretical, research-based, projective frameworks for understanding each section. The first section begins with LCLA Office's research project "A Model of the Desert, the Desert as Model," positioned as a continuation of the practices of Marcel Duchamp and Man Ray, as well as of Sophie Ristelhueber's long-distance photographic conversations. This is followed by Dani Ploeger's essay on the proliferation of GPS-based navigation in the civilian domain after the Gulf War. He responds with a temporary land art installation created using a GPS-guided bulldozer. The bulldozer erases the remnants of warfare, creating a monument signifying how the landscape overcame this moment in time. Your contribution, Samia, comes next, with a practical understanding of the relationships between violent conflict, archives, and the environment. It shows the lasting scars of warfare and the human-made toxification of the desert. Jawad Altabtabai's proposal reflects upon this toxification, using memories of burning oil wells to preserve polluted and contaminated grounds across the country with the consolidation of the dispersed oil lakes dotting the desert. The section concludes with a conversation with a retired Kuwaiti Lieutenant General who witnessed the changes of the national landscape from his fighter jet's perspective. He offers thrilling stories of the Gulf War from above and memories of what the hinterland once was.

The publication accompanying *Space Wars: An Investigation into Kuwait's Hinterland*. Courtesy of TB.D Studio. Photograph by Mohammad Ashkanani.

The publication accompanying *Space Wars: An Investigation into Kuwait's Hinterland.*
Courtesy of TB.D Studio. Photograph by Mohammad Ashkanani.

SAA: The rest of the publication follows the same logic throughout its additional three sections—with each section composed of various approaches to similar topics. Within "Cultural Production," projects span from an in-depth history of the desert truffle and its significance in regional heritage to possibilities of reimagining camping as a cultural phenomenon. The "Planning" section covers work that looks at the potential role of archaeology in infrastructural development, in conversation with projects that tackle the future of oil production and the spaces it will eventually leave behind. The section on "Nature" brings together various perspectives on local flora and fauna, a wonderful exploration of the complexities of living within thriving desert ecosystems. Concluding the publication is a series of aerial satellite photographs completed in collaboration with Atlas of Places that bring us full circle in our exploration of tools and methodologies utilized both historically and present-day to plan, access, and understand the spaces in question.

Regardless of the avenue of research that each contribution has chosen to engage with, across all of the contributions is a very obvious concern and care for these spaces that encourage us to continue this pursuit. While the project has a distinct starting point, there is no real end. We hope this project will continue to grow and develop as the hinterland itself continues to evolve and change over time.

Paulo Tavares is an architect, researcher, and educator. His work has been featured in various exhibitions and publications worldwide, including *Harvard Design Magazine*, the Oslo Architecture Triennale, the Istanbul Design Biennale, and the São Paulo Biennale. He is the author of *Forest Law* (Eli and Edythe Broad Art Museum, 2014), *Des-Habitat* (K. Verlag, 2019), *Memória da terra* (Ministério Público Federal Brasília, 2020), and *Lucio Costa era racista?* (N-1 Edições, 2022) and was cocurator of the 2019 Chicago Architecture Biennial. He teaches spatial and visual cultures at the University of Brasília in Brazil and leads the spatial agency autonoma.

PAULO TAVARES

THE COLONIAL-MODERN POLITICS OF DESERTIFICATION

...sabemos dos sertões pouco mais além da sua etimologia rebarbativa, *desertus*, e, a exemplo dos cartógrafos medievos, ao idealizarem a África portentosa, podíamos escrever alguns trechos dos nossos mapas a nossa ignorância e o nosso espanto: hic habent leones... Não admiram o incolor, o inexpressivo, o incaracterístico, o tolhiço e o inviável de nossa arte e das nossas iniciativas...

—Euclides da Cunha

...We know of the *sertões* little more than its rough etymology, *desertus*, and, like medieval cartographers when idealizing a portentous Africa, we could write our ignorance and our astonishment in some parts of our maps: *hic habent leones*... No wonder the colorless, the inexpressive, the uncharacteristic, the defective, the unviable of our art and our initiatives...
    —Euclides da Cunha[1]

---

1   Euclides da Cunha, *Obra Completa* (Rio de Janeiro: Editora Nova Aguilar, 1995), 158. Euclides da Cunha is considered one of the most important writers of Brazil's First Republic (1889–1930). He is the author of the canonical book *Os Sertões*, published in 1902, which constructed a new imagination of the Brazilian hinterlands and the national racial formation.

Since far-right president Jair Bolsonaro took office in early 2019, we have seen Brazil's Amazon burn at unprecedented rates. Satellite data gathered in October 2020 by the national space agency INPE (Instituto Nacional de Pesquisas Espaciais) showed a 61 percent rise in fire hotspots, leading to the rainforest's worst dry season in a decade.[2] In just two years, deforestation in the Amazon has increased by 48 percent.[3] We have also seen the ways that Bolsonaro's protofascist regime, which believes climate change is a plot by "cultural Marxists," is not concerned with this escalating devastation. To the contrary, his militarized cabinet is actively intensifying deforestation by weakening environmental protections and Indigenous land rights.[4] Bolsonaro attempted to transfer the custody of Indigenous territories from the Ministry of Justice to the Ministry of Agriculture, thus subjecting Indigenous

2   Reuters, "Brazil's Amazon Rainforest Suffers Worst Fires in a Decade," *Guardian*, October 1, 2020, https://www.theguardian.com/environment/2020/oct/01/brazil-amazon-rainforest-worst-fires-in-decade.
3   See the recent study by the environmental advocacy NGO Instituto Socioambiental, Alana Almeida de Souza, Cícero Augusto, and Willian Pereira, *Desmatamento em 2020: Amazônia legal e suas áreas protegidas (unidades de conservação e terras indígenas)* (São Paulo: Instituto Socioambiental, 2021), https://www.socioambiental.org/sites/blog.socioambiental.org/files/nsa/arquivos/nt_desmatamento_2020_prodes_consolidado.docx_1.pdf.
4   Jonathan Watts, "Brazil's New Foreign Minister Believes Climate Change Is a Marxist Plot," *Guardian*, November 15, 2018, https://www.theguardian.com/world/2018/nov/15/brazil-foreign-minister-ernesto-araujo-climate-change-marxist-plot.

peoples and their lands to the interests of Brazil's powerful agribusiness lobby. At the United Nations, he blamed Indigenous peoples for the fires, and he has also declared that Indigenous communities should be "integrated" into national society, reinstating the anti-Indigenous discourse that marked the country's military regime (1964–1984).[5]

The Bolsonaro government has ambitious plans for implementing a large-scale neocolonial project to "occupy" the Amazon.[6] These predatory plans were made public in August 2019 in a set of leaked documents detailing the construction of numerous infrastructures such as highways, dams, and waterways to enhance resource exploration and attract non-Indigenous migrants to settle in the region. According to General Maynard Santa Rosa, Bolsonaro's former Special Secretary for Strategic Affairs, "development" is essential to assert national sovereignty and integrate so-called "desert areas" of the Amazon.[7] The vision that the Amazon forest needs to be "integrated," "occupied," and "developed" correlates to its definition as a "desert" by military strategies and planners, "an immense green desert," in the words of General Santa Rosa.[8]

How can the tropical forestlands of the Amazon, the most biodiverse region on Earth, be considered a "desert"? And what is the notion of desert being employed here? This piece delves into the long and ongoing history of the "desertification" of the Amazon, exploring how the concept of desert, beyond an environmental condition, is a political construct whose origins are set in racial-ized colonial geographies and imaginaries. The scorching of the Amazon forest—which in turn warms the global climate—is fueled by the resilience of these colonial ideologies, as well as by the ways in which myths of the frontier came to be defined as Brazil's manifest destiny.

5   Anthony Boadle, "Brazil's Bolsonaro Blames Indigenous People for Amazon Fires in UN Speech," *Reuters*, September 22, 2020, https://www.reuters.com/article/un-assembly-brazil/brazils-bolsonaro-blames-indigenous-people-for-amazon-fires-in-u-n-speech-idINKCN26E0AM.

6   Manuella Libardi, "Leaked Documents Show Brazil's Bolsonaro Has Grave Plans for Amazon Rainforest," *openDemocracy*, August 21, 2019, https://www.opendemocracy.net/en/democraciaabierta/leaked-documents-show-brazil-bolsonaro-has-grave-plans-for-amazon-rainforest.

7   Tatiana Dias, "Movido a Paranoia," *The Intercept Brasil*, September 19, 2019, https://theintercept.com/2019/09/19/plano-bolsonaro-paranoia-amazonia.

8   Maynard Marques de Santa Rosa, "A Esfinge Amazônica: Problema E Solução," *DefesaNet*, April 22, 2021, https://www.defesanet.com.br/tfbr/noticia/40425/TFBR---TOA---A-Esfinge-Amazonica--Problema-e-Solucao.

São Paulo's sky on August 19, 2019, darkened at noon due to smoke plumes coming from the so-called "Day of Fire," when president Jair Bolsonaro's supporters orchestrated criminal burnings across the Amazon in deforestation efforts. Photograph by Andre Lucas/picture alliance. Courtesy of Getty Images.

NASA's Aqua satellite image captures the "fire season" in the southern regions of the Amazon basin, a global hub of soybean and beef production. Smoke clouds from hundreds of burning sites cover the entire area. In the top-right corner of the image, the vast conserved green area completely engulfed by spots of fire is the Xingu Indigenous Park. There is growing evidence that the southeastern regions of the Amazon basin, the Arc of Fire zone, where deforestation has massively altered the environment, is in transition from a forest ecosystem to a savannah, desert-like ecosystem. Courtesy of NASA via the MODIS Rapid Response Team, Goddard Space Flight Center.

Desertões

Portuguese colonizers referred to Brazil's vast hinterlands as *sertão*, short for *desertão*, that is, desert. "Looking at the *sertão*, seen from the sea, it seems very large, because as far as we looked we could not see anything apart from lands filled with trees," wrote Pêro Vaz de Caminha in 1500 in his report to the Portuguese king on the "finding of your new land."[9] Etymologically *sertão* or *desertão* refer to an "uncultivated place, far from villages and cultivated lands, far from the coast."[10] The term *sertão* in eighteenth- and nineteenth-century dictionaries carries this meaning, denoting an inner territory that it is neither urban nor rural, but wild: "the point or site most far from the cultivated terrains, bushes or forests far away from the coast."[11] *Sertão* therefore describes not only a physical geography in opposition to the shore, but also a social geography outside the bounds of culture, a "wilderness" landscape dominated by forests and "savages." The coast, on the otherhand, is the territory of cultivated lands, villages, and cities—that is, the space of "civilization."

The construction of this *imaginative geography*, to borrow a term from Edward Said, is derived from the spatial rationale of the colonial project implemented by the Portuguese Empire in Brazil.[12] Mercantile doctrine meant colonization was predominantly directed at extracting natural products as commodities for the European market (wood, minerals, sugar, cotton, rubber, coffee), so the colonial government sought to concentrate occupation along Brazil's continental shoreline to prevent foreign incursions and secure monopoly over trade. *Sertão* then came to be defined in opposition to the coastal space of the colony, demarcating to the colonizers a frontier to unknown lands beyond the reach of the State and Christianity. By the nineteenth century this opposition between interior (*sertão*) and coast (colony) was aligned with the dichotomy of "primitive" and

9   Pêro Vaz de Caminha to Manuel I of Portugal, 1500, Biblioteca Nacional, digital archive, http://objdigital.bn.br/Acervo_Digital/livros_eletronicos/carta.pdf.
10   Maria Elisa Noronha de Sá Mäder, "O vazio: o sertão no imagináríoda colônia nos séculos XVI e XVII," (master's thesis, Pontifícia Universidade Católica do Rio de Janeiro, 1995), 2.
11   Francisco Julio de Caldas Aulete, *Dicionário Contemporâneo da Língua Portuguesa* (Lisbon: Parceria António Maria Pereira, 1881), s.v. "sertão." In the *Dicionário da Língua Portuguesa* written by Rafael Bluteau in 1789, *sertão* is similarly described as "the interior, the heartland, opposed to the maritime and the coast." See de Sá Mäder, "O vazio," 2.
12   Edward Said, *Orientalism* (New York: Vintage Books, 1979), 49. In the passage "Imaginative Geography and Its Representations," Said unfolds how the representation of the oriental "other" by Western knowledge implicates geographic projections and representations.

"civilized" that informed racial thought and racialized scientific theories developed in Europe. Clarifying his use of *sertão*, Augustin Saint-Hilaire, a French naturalist who conducted several expeditions to the Brazilian hinterlands in the early nineteenth century, noted that "when I say depopulated I am referring, of course, to the civilized inhabitants, since gentiles and wild animals are even overpopulated."[13] This association between desert and Indigenous territories was also registered in colonial maps, such as in the map of the Brazilian interior designed by Francisco Tosi Colombina in 1751, where the term *sertão* is used to designate the lands of the Xavante.

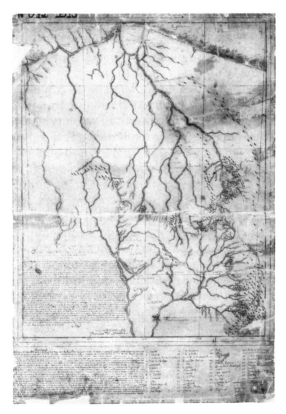

"Mapa Geral dos Limites da Capitania de Goiás" (General Map of the Limits of the Capitania of Goiás), elaborated in 1751 by the Italian cartographer and military engineer Francisco Tosi Colombina. The detail shows the areas marked "Sertão of the Xavante Gentile" and "Sertão of the Acraa Gentile." Courtesy of Arquivo Público do Distrito Federal.

13 Augustin Saint-Hilaire, *Voyage aux sources du Rio de S. Francisco et dans la province de Goyaz* (Paris: A. Bertrand, 1847–1848), published in Brazil as *Viagem às nascentes do Rio São Francisco e pela província de Goiás*, trans. Clado Ribeiro de Lessa (São Paulo: Companhia Editora Nacional, 1937).

Sertão does not describe natural conditions, but rather denotes a socio-spatial construction that defines Europe's racial and cultural other, delineating the frontiers of the "uncivilized," the "wild," and the "uncultivated." This epistemic framework enables the concept to be applied to hinterland territories as ecologically diverse as the arid backlands of northeast Brazil and the humid forests of the Amazon. Not only was this imagined geography central to the ways in which Europe defined itself as the locus of progress and modernity, but it also functioned as an ideological legitimation for Empire's self-assigned "civilizing mission." Consider, for instance, the imperial role of nineteenth-century climate determinism, which conflated racialized categories such as "uncivilized" and "primitive" with descriptions of the environment like "tropical," "torrid," and "wild."[14] Forged at the intersection of racial thought and natural science, this image of *sertão* came to signify something beyond the natural environment: a *terra-nullius* to be conquered and civilized. It was above all a political frontier to imperial expansion, regardless of whether that frontier was dry or humid.

More than a natural environment, *sertão* is a political landscape rooted in colonial geographies and imaginaries. Thus, it is important to *de-naturalize* the idea of the desert and along with it a set of correlative constructions such as "empty," "void," "wild," "uncultivated," "primitive," and so on. For beyond physical descriptions of nature, these terms are impregnated with racist dimensions that enabled and legitimized colonialism. To *de-naturalize* the desert, to understand it as a cultural, political, and racialized landscape, is all the more significant because it is precisely through a process of "naturalization" that the notion of desert continues to function as a powerful colonial tool. We see this in operation today when representatives of Bolsonaro's protofascist regime legitimate their colonial policies by resorting to militarized images of the Amazon as an "immense green desert."

Frontier Mythology

Sertão was redefined in the first decades of the twentieth century by a new generation of modern intellectuals, writers, and artists in Brazil concerned with ascribing national meaning to the

14   One example of nineteenth-century climate determinism is Henry Thomas Buckle, *History of Civilization in England* (London: Longmans, Green, and Co., 1878). On the way this discourse was applied to Brazil, see Thomas E. Skidmore, *Preto no Branco: raça e nacionalidade no pensamento brasileiro* (Paz e Terra: Rio de Janeiro, 1976).

hinterlands. "Dazzled by the opulent coastline and the mirages of a civilization that we receive packed inside transatlantic liners," writes Euclides da Cunha, "we forgot the vast interior from where the real physical basis of our nationality is unleashed."[15] The quest for an independent form of national expression meant pivoting from the Atlantic coast to the hinterlands, repositioning the gaze away from Europe, towards the interior of the country.

The cultural valorization of the backland *sertões* was entangled with the recuperation of a colonial movement called *bandeiras* (literally flag-carrying) as a myth of Brazilian national foundation. The *bandeiras* were large civilian paramilitary colonial expeditions that, from the late sixteenth century onwards, penetrated the Brazilian hinterlands with the aim of capturing and enslaving Indigenous peoples.[16] Through their long incursions and militia wars in the backlands *sertões*, the *bandeiras* expanded Portuguese sovereignty over lands controlled by Spain, giving Brazil its continental territory. They were also responsible for opening routes to the gold-rich hinterlands of Minas Gerais, from where most of the wealth of the Portuguese Colonial Empire was extracted in the eighteenth century. In the official narrative of Brazilian history, the *bandeiras* assumed a mythical status, providing ideological material for constructing the ideals of Brazilian national identity and nationhood.

The mythology of the *bandeiras* in Brazil could be compared to the mythologies of the frontier and manifest destiny in the United States, famously represented in the painting *American Progress* (1872) by John Gast. The "conquest of the West" in Brazil became associated with a manifest destiny bound to the nation's past formation and future progress. Unlike the North American colonial tale, however, the "tropical" version of the narrative was centered not on the movement of settler families of farmers colonizing the land, but on the violent conquest of colonial *bandeiras*. This legacy can be attributed to the ways in which political and cultural elites continuously invested in the visual narratives of frontier expansionism through the ideological labor of writers, artists, architects, and intellectuals associated

15   Euclides da Cunha, *Contrastes e Confrontos* in *Obras Completas* (Rio de Janeiro: Editora Nova Aguilar, [1907] 1995), 163.
16   The largest *bandeiras* constituted true paramilitary forces that were also deployed to wage "just wars" against resisting native and maroon communities. For instance, the famous *bandeira* commanded by Manuel Preto and Raposo Tavares in the mid-1620s counted 140 settlers and more than 2,000 Indigenous troops, and was responsible for the destruction of hundreds of Guarani villages and a dozen Jesuit missions. Over two years of operations, they captured and enslaved about 60,000 people. See, for example, John Monteiro, *Negros da terra: índios e bandeirantes nas origens de São Paulo* (São Paulo: Companhia das Letras, 1994).

John Gast, A*merican Progress*, 1872. Oil on canvas, 11 1/2 x 15 3/4 in. Courtesy of the Autry Museum, Los Angeles; 92.126.1.

Oscar Pereira da Silva, *Combate de Botocudos em Mogi das Cruzes* (Fighting Botocudos in Mogi das Cruzes), 1920. Oil on canvas, 100 x 150 cm. A typical heroic representation of the *bandeirante* paramilitary expeditions. Courtesy of Museu Paulista da Universidade de São Paulo.

with the modern movement that formed in Brazil between 1920 and 1950. Looking towards the hinterlands in search of a national spirit, these figures found in the *bandeiras* a typical national motive. The modern movement, as avant-garde Brazilian writer and poet Cassiano Ricardo wrote, was aimed at "opening routes and retaking the West."[17]

The identification of frontier expansionism with national identity and modernity in Brazil was associated with the idea that territorial colonization was a defining element in the formation of Brazil. This is similar to the ways in which the "frontier thesis," as advanced in the nineteenth century by historian Frederick Jackson Turner, came to define mainstream interpretations of national formation and identity in the United States. In his seminal 1893 essay "The Significance of the Frontier in American History," Turner argued that settler colonial expansion towards the "free lands" of the West generated a set of moral values such as individualism, entrepreneurship, and cooperation that constituted the core of North American democracy.[18] As pioneers moved onwards, seizing native land and turning forests into pastures and private property, they developed a feeling of free-dom that gave rise to a dynamic civil society that was distinc-tively American in the sense that it stemmed from the experience of frontier expansionism.[19] Speaking in the United States in 1944, Brazilian sociologist Gilberto Freyre sought to explain the role of the *bandeiras* in the constitution of Brazilian society by drawing on Turner's thesis: "Due to the predominance of this type of exploration of new areas, the colonization of Brazil soon went from being strictly European to becoming a process of auto-colonization: a process that would, after independence, take on a national character." For Freyre, this national process of "auto-colonization" was equivalent to "the phenomenon described by Turner as the mobile frontier."[20]

In that respect the most literal incarnation of the Brazilian frontier ideology is the book *March to the West: The Influence of the Bandeiras in the Social and Political Formation of Brazil*, written in 1940 by the militant modernist Cassiano Ricardo. For Ricardo, as for many intellectuals of this generation, the

17   Cassiano Ricardo, *Viagem no tempo e no espaço: memórias* (Rio de Janeiro: José Olympio, 1970), 39.
18   Frederick J. Turner, "The Significance of the Frontier in American History," in *Annual Report of the American Historical Association for the Year 1893* (Washington, DC: Government Printing Office, 1894), 197–227.
19   For a critical historical view on American frontier mythology, see Greg Grandin, *The End of the Myth: From the Frontier to the Border Wall in the Mind of America* (New York: Metropolitan, 2019).
20   Gilberto Freyre, *Interpretação do Brasil* (São Paulo: Global, 2015), 101.

bandeiras constituted the foundational event of the nation: "When the first *bandeiras* enter the jungle, the history of Portugal ends and the history of Brazil begins." Ricardo defined the *bandeiras* as a force of geographic integration and social "pacification," forging a productive national body while organizing the territory as a homogeneous cultural and political space:

> Every time the aborigines and blacks tried to block the ethnic-democracy of Brazil, the *bandeiras* were the terror of the indians and the maroons... that is, every time that there was a shock between different races, the *bandeira* was the force that reduced ethnic schisms to a common expression, neutralizing the unilateral action of one against the other.[21]

Ricardo's frontier thesis was underpinned by Freyre's theory of "racial democracy."[22] Like Freyre, Ricardo contended that the singular character of Brazilian society was given by the ways in which miscegenation eradicated racial divisions, which he calls "bio-democracy."[23] However, while Freyre based his assertions on the socio-spatial economy of the coastal plantations— interpreting the duality between the master's house and the slave quarters as a microcosm of national formation—Ricardo believed that true "racial democracy" was developed in the mobile frontier space of the *bandeiras*. The racist ideology of "whitening," which directly or indirectly informed visions of "racial democracy" in Brazil, courses through *March to the West*, legitimizing the violence of the *bandeiras* and of slavery: "Biological democracy stemmed in large part from the slavery regime itself... proof that slavery was a necessary evil, even from a bio-democratic or biological point of view."[24]

Similar to Frederick Jackson Turner, Ricardo's frontier thesis grounded national formation in settler colonialism, naturalizing the race-based violence that enabled territorial expansionism.

21   Cassiano Ricardo, *Marcha para oeste: a influência da bandeira na formação social e política do Brasil*, 2 vols. (Rio de Janeiro: José Olympio, 1940), 95. This is a direct translation of the original Portuguese "aborígenes e negros." I have chosen to keep these terms as Ricardo used them to capture the rhetorical and racial violence of the original document, which assuredly saw Indigenous and Black people not as people but rather as obstacles to the Brazilian national program of westward expansion.

22   Though Freyre only used the term "racial democracy" later in his career, he developed the theory in the canonical book *Casa-Grande e Senzala* (Rio de Janeiro: Maia & Grande, 1933). The title literally translates to "Big House and Slave Quarters," which shows the central role that space and, more specifically, architecture played in Freyre's racial and cultural interpretation of national formation.

23   Ricardo, *Marcha para oeste*.

24   Ricardo, *Marcha para oeste*, 14.

But for Ricardo, the Brazilian frontier did not yield a civil society resistant to centralized power, as in the case of Turner's vision of the American frontier. Instead it produced quite the opposite: the *bandeiras* constituted the genesis of a strong and centralized national state whose ultimate manifestation was the dictatorial state implemented by the populist nationalism of the Getúlio Vargas government after the 1930 Revolution.

Auto-Imperialism

After the 1930 Revolution, which brought to power Vargas's fifteen-year rule, the idea that "auto-colonization" constituted a defining process in national formation was transformed into a series of policies and projects of frontier expansionism officially called "March to the West." According to Vargas's vision, this "march" to take control over the western frontier of Brazil would realize a kind of auto-imperialism: "We need to promote this push in order to suppress the demographic vacuums in our territory... Here is our imperialism... We have an expansionism, which is to grow within our own borders."[25] As the dichotomies of coast-interior/colonial space-*sertão* were translated to the dichotomies of "developed-underdeveloped/modern-backward," through the lexicon of planning, the notion of *sertão* as desert came to be synonymous with the concept of "demographic voids." Brazil's modernization was dependent on a neo-*bandeirante* campaign to conquer the interior, a project that could only be carried out by the authoritarian apparatus embodied in Vargas's New State. The colonial policies implemented by the regime came to be understood as a form of "internal imperialism," a process of auto-conquest by which the nation would realize itself.[26]

Needless to say, the Brazilian interior was not a "demo-graphic vacuum" as modern frontier ideology propagated, but a highly diverse social territory inhabited by a myriad of Indigenous nations. This diversity was recorded in a cartographic study by German-Brazilian anthropologist Curt Nimuendajú in 1943–1944, which shows the Brazilian territory as an impressive color-patchwork of sovereign Indigenous lands, cultures, and languages—a reality of the country that, despite the decimation

---

25   Getúlio Vargas, "Cruzada Rumo ao Oeste," in *A Nova Política* 8 (Rio de Janeiro: José Olympio Editora, 1940).

26   As for example in the notion of "intra-border imperialism" presented by sociologist Nelson Werneck Sodré in *Oeste: ensaio sobre a grande propriedade pastoril* (Arquivo do Estado de São Paulo, 1990), 201: "The internal exchange, with the continuous unfolding of markets... will sanction the breadth of this policy of intra-border imperialism, taking it to the poor lands of the West."

State propaganda poster of the "March to the West" campaign, probably printed in 1937, in the context of Getúlio Vargas's New State. The poster reproduces one of Vargas's most emblematic phrases: "The true meaning of Brazilianess is the March to the West." Courtesy of Arquivo Nacional, Rio de Janeiro.

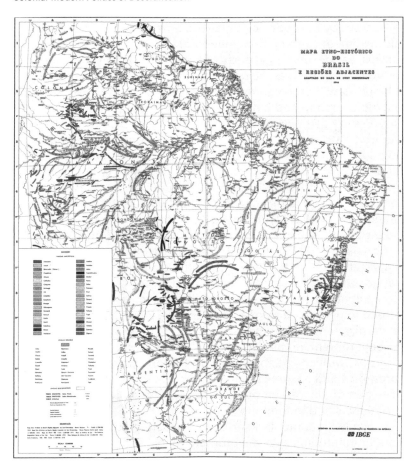

A plurinational territory: ethnohistorical map of Brazil elaborated by Curt Nimuendajú in
1943–1944. Courtesy of Biblioteca Digital Curt Nimuendajú.

carried out by European colonialism, remained true until the
mid-twentieth century. Designation of the Brazilian interior as
sertões, as "desert" regardless of actual terrain and moreover
as "void," thus had less to do with occupation than with the
colonial view that Indigenous peoples were deemed "primitives"
outside the realm of the national-colonial state.

Brazil's self-declared mission of "auto-imperialism" then
required a strategy to deal with the populations whose lands
would be expropriated and colonized. To this end, the Brazilian
State employed an agency exclusively dedicated to governing
Indigenous affairs called Indian Protection Service (Serviço
de Proteção aos Índios), or SPI. Originally named the Service
for Indian Protection and Localization of the National Worker
(Serviço de Proteção aos Índios e Localização de Trabalhadores
Nacionais), or SPILTN, the SPI was responsible for the
"pacification" of Indigenous communities, settling them into
state-controlled outposts so they could be converted into
"emancipated national workers."[27] This neocolonial conquest was
framed under the guise of a patriotic mission of nation-building,
modernization, and humanitarianism. "There is no doubt that
the government, in the same steps that protect, care for, and
save the Brazilian Indian," stated a 1913 internal report of the SPI,
"promotes and ensures the indispensable means to conquer a
large part of the interior of the country, hitherto forbidden both
to nationals and to foreigners."[28]

While Frederick Jackson Turner described the American
frontier in retrospect, at the moment of its historic closing,
the frontier ideology that emerged in the 1920s and 1930s in
Brazil was intended to be a guide for the future: a roadmap for
the "civilizing" and "modernizing" colonial march that would
propel the country "forward" towards development. Forged
through the discourses and imaginaries crafted by the modern
generation, the Brazilian frontier mythology was reappropriated
and refashioned by every subsequent government after Vargas,
democratic and authoritarian, civilian and military. The conquest
of the *sertões* became a state project inasmuch as its appeal
to nationalism and modernity served to legitimate state power
and its violence on the ground. Brazil's future as a nation was

27   This is the term used in various official documents of the SPI, whose main objective
      was to settle and transform Indigenous peoples into national peasants. This was
      inscribed in the agency's mandate as shown by its original name "SPILTN," which
      included the "Localization of the National Worker," alongside "Service for Indian
      Protection."
28   Quoted in Antonio Carlos de Souza Lima, "Um Grande Certo de Paz: Poder Tutelar
      e Indianidade no Brasil," (PhD diss., Rio de Janeiro: Universidade Federal do Rio de
      Janeiro, 1992), 89.

Indigenous Post of the Service for Indian Protection (SPI) established in Mato Grosso, c. 1930. Courtesy of Museu do Índio/FUNAI, Rio de Janeiro.

bound to Freyre's "auto-colonization": a very particular form of colonization that was not only distinctively national but also the very source of Brazilian identity. It was, as Getúlio Vargas said, "*our* imperialism."

One of the most symbolic projects of this colonial-modern ideology was the "ex-nihilo" construction of the modernist capital Brasília in the late 1950s. Located at the center of the national territory, in the backland *sertões*, Brasília was conceived as an extension of the colonial conquest—"a deliberate act of possession," wrote Lucio Costa, the author of the city's masterplan, "a gesture still in the sense of the pioneers, along the lines of the colonial tradition."[29] Another remarkable manifestation of the Brazilian frontier mythology is the public sculpture *Monument to the Bandeiras* designed in 1920 (and constructed in 1953–1954) by the Italo-Brazilian artist Victor Brecheret, who is considered one the most important figures of the Brazilian modern movement. Representing a *bandeirante* troop marching west, the sculpture marks the entrance of the Ibirapuera Park in São Paulo designed in 1953–1954 by modernist architect Oscar Niemeyer—together composing an urban landscape that roots Brazilian national modernity in the colonial frontier. The monument has become a contested site of struggle over what and whose memory is

29   Lucio Costa, *Memória Descritiva do Plano Piloto* (1957), in Lucio Costa, *Registros de uma Vivência* (Rio de Janeiro: Empresa das Artes, 1995), 283. For more on the role of Brasília in the nation's history of modernization, see James Holston, "The Spirit of Brasília: Modernity as Experiment and Risk," in *City/Art: The Urban Scene in Latin America*, ed. Rebecca Biron (Durham, NC: Duke University Press, 2009), 85–114; and the section "Brasília: The High-Modernist City Built—Almost," in James C. Scott, *Seeing Like a State: How Certain Schemes to Improve the Human Condition Have Failed* (New Haven: Yale University Press, 1998), 117–130.

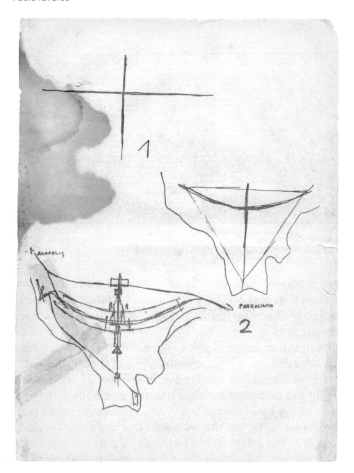

Lucio Costa, conceptual drawing of Brasília's masterplan, 1957. Costa contended that the city emerged from "a deliberate act of possession... a gesture still in the sense of the pioneers, along the lines of the colonial tradition... two axes crossing at right angles, that is, the sign of the cross itself." This is the symbolic-urban foundation of Brasília, the implantation of a colonial-Christian cross as a gesture of conquest of the frontier. It is clearly a gesture impregnated with the violence of colonialism translated into modernization. The metamorphosis of the cross into an airplane flying towards progress, as many interpret it, is one of many symbolic constructions of the relationship between colonialism and modernity in the national formation of Brazil that is so well represented by Brasília. Courtesy of Instituto Antonio Carlos Jobim, Rio de Janeiro.

Victor Brecheret's *Monumento às Bandeiras* (Monument to the Bandeiras) defaced by Indigenous protesters in 2019. © Rovena Rosa/Agência Brasil.

preserved. Every so often Indigenous movements deface the sculpture, which is then promptly cleaned up—a reminder that this national imaginary is grounded in historic violence, land theft, and erasure.

Operation Amazonia

With the US-backed coup of March 1964, which pushed Brazil into two decades of military dictatorship, "auto-colonization" turned into a basin-wide development program called Operation Amazonia. General Golbery do Couto e Silva, the grand strategist behind the operation, delineated "a maneuver for the integration of the national territory... guaranteeing the inviolability of the depopulated interior by closing possible channels of penetration... [that would] under the protection of advanced frontier outposts inundate the Amazon with civilization."[30] This rationale was informed by the enduring legacies of old colonial geographies, an extension of the imperial project to conquer and "civilize" the *sertões*, but now re-framed under the militarized context of the global Cold War and the attendant doctrines of national security implemented across Latin America's dictatorial regimes, including Guatemala, Argentina, and Brazil, among others.

By the early 1970s, while Operation Amazonia was in full swing, world politics were growing increasingly aware of the planetary ecological crisis, as exemplified by the first United Nations Conference on the Human Environment in 1972, arguably a pivotal point in environmental politics. At that time such emergent environmental concerns were largely aligned with concerns over global security due to demographic and economic growth and resource scarcity. This is shown in books such as *The Population Bomb*, written by biologists Paul R. Ehrlich and Anne H. Ehrlich in 1968, and the report *The Limits to Growth*, commissioned by the Club of Rome in 1972. Within the networks of international governance, neo-Malthusian rationales on the global environment informed policies directed at expanding the exploitation of natural resources in order to counter prognoses about deficiencies in the world supply system due to demographic increase, economic growth, scarcity, and the eventual political instabilities these would bring.

30   Golbery do Couto e Silva, *Geopolítica do Brasil* (Rio de Janeiro: José Olympio, 1967).

Operation Amazonia: Dictator General Emílio Garrastazu Médici attends a presentation of the master plan for Amazonia. The following stills are from *A Integração da Amazônia* (1971), a propaganda film made by the Brazilian state-news agency Agência Nacional. Courtesy of Arquivo Nacional, Rio de Janeiro.

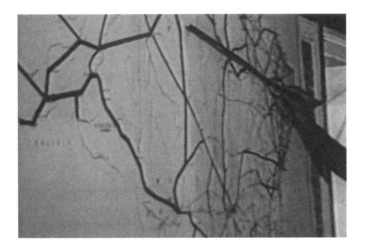

General Golbery's "Maneuver for the Integration of the National Territory," from Golbery do Couto e Silva, *Geopolítica do Brasil* (Rio de Janeiro: Livraria José Olympio Editôra, 1967), 46.

In this context, the Amazon was characterized as a giant land reserve that, once integrated into the world market, could help avert and alleviate these global supply deficiencies. In 1971, the United Nations Food and Agricultural Organization outlined a proposal converting the tropical forests of the Amazon valley into the world's breadbasket through intensive agriculture. The study explained that the global demographic problem was not the "global total," but the abnormal increases in the "low-income/high-fertility" developing world. Among the crowds of the impoverished, where life was precarious, food shortages would lead to further poverty and ecological depletion, and ultimately trigger "social upheaval and political breakdown."[31]

Operation Amazonia followed a similar blueprint, associating the "occupation and integration" of the rainforest with economic development and the quieting of concerns over internal security. In the colonization of the backlands, the generals and their cadre of planners saw the means by which the nation could be propelled to Western modernization. At the same

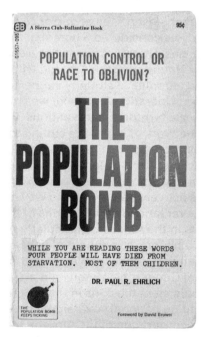

"Population Control or Race to Oblivion?" Cover of Paul R. Ehrlich's *The Population Bomb* (New York: Ballantine Books, 1968).

31   Walter H. Pawley, "In the Year 2070: Thinking Now about the Next Century Has Become Imperative," *Ceres: FAO Review* 4 (July–August 1971): 22–27.

Amazônia **ONTEM, HOJE, AMANHÃ**
PAST, P RESENT, FUTURE

Page of reportage on the military plans to "occupy and integrate" the Amazon, published in the magazine *Manchete* in 1971. Subtitled "Amazon: past, present and future," the illustration makes a connection between the military regime's projects for the Amazon and the colonial *bandeiras* movement. Courtesy of the author.

time, the great "green desert," the *sertão* once seen as the space of "savages," was now considered a potential seedbed for revolutionary insurgencies. Therefore it was necessary to take control over the region by "inundating the Amazon with civilization," as General Golbery's geopolitical strategy suggested.

On the ground Operation Amazonia was materialized into a series of large-scale territorial interventions, including the construction of a network of highways cutting through the entire basin; mega-infrastructures such as dams and artificial lakes; and extraction enclaves, rural colonies, urban settlements, and other projects branded "development poles." This spatial infrastructure was actively employed as a way of controlling political conflicts over land in other regions of the country by resettling peasants in the Amazon, particularly from the troubled northeast region, a historic stronghold of peasant politics. As a prominent Brazilian geographer explained during a summit of the International Geographic Union held in Canada in 1972, "Because of the persistent tensions in the northeast and the necessity of extending national sovereignty over the limits of the territory, the incorporation of the Amazon into the national system is an imperative for the government in that it is capable of offering a joint solution to these two problem-regions."[32]

32   Bertha Becker, "Crescimento Econômico e Estrutura Espacial do Brasil," in *Geopolitica da Amazonia: a nova fronteira de recursos* (Rio de Janeiro: Zahar, 1982), 29.

Highways cutting through the basin were designed as a spatial fix to what president General Emílio Garrastazu Médici, who served between 1969 and 1974, described as two entangled problems: "men without land in the northeast, and land without men in Amazonia."[33] Channeling population westwards would contribute to the occupation and development of "demographic voids" in the forest and, at the same time, "alleviate the economic, social and political tensions" in the northeast.[34]

The last decade of military dictatorship (1974–1984) was marked by the advancement of these so-called "development poles." From the mid-1970s to the mid-1980s, the military government focused on capital-intensive developments in the Amazon: corporate mining complexes, mega-dams, cash-crop plantations, and cattle farms. The basin's southwestern region received land colonization projects financed by the World Bank. At the eastern side, the Great Carajás mining complex established a 4,000 square kilometer, gated enclave with its own private rail system, administrative town, and airport. At the southern edges of the basin, a zone of ecological transition from tropical savannas to humid lowland forests, the military government promoted an ambitious program of colonization by leasing immense territories to private companies.[35]

As the chemical-intensive technologies of the Green Revolution spread through the Amazon, the forest's acid soils were gradually domesticated for large-scale agriculture, and in less than three decades this region was completely transformed into monoculture plantations, chiefly for soy and cotton. Cities were carved out of the jungle overnight, leading to the propagation of numerous satellite settlements and consequent rapid deforestation. Pioneer frontier towns like Alta Floresta and Sinop grew to become the logistical centers of one of the world's largest hubs of soy production, which by the early 2000s was responsible for 60 percent of the Brazilian output.[36]

Operation Amazonia was fueled by the perception that the entire ecology of the rainforest could be geoengineered by means of spatial interventions directed at transforming the "green desert" into a productive agricultural landscape. In the service of global security, modern planning provided not only the

33   Emílio Garrastazu Médici, O Jogo da Verdade (Brasília: Imprensa Nacional, 1970), 79.
34   Becker, "Crescimento Econômico," 29.
35   Like, for example, the Sociedade Imobiliária Noroeste do Paraná (SINOP), a company dedicated to territorial colonization whose acronym is the same as the city of Sinop, one of the most important cities in the region's soy plantation complex.
36   Emídio Rizzo Bonato and Ana Lidia Variani Bonato, A soja no Brasil: história e estatística (Londrina: Empresa Brasileira de Pesquisa Agropecuária, 1987).

The city of Sinop at an early stage of construction. The urban nucleus of the "Development Pole Center-West," implemented by the Sociedade Imobiliária Noroeste do Paraná in the 1970s and 1980s, Sinop became the logistical center of one of the world's largest agribusiness complexes for soy production. Courtesy of the author.

means by which integration and occupation was conceived and implemented on the ground, but also the ideological apparatus that legitimized colonial expansions under narratives of modernization, development, nation-building, and counterinsurgency.

The Politics of Desertification

The projects pursued under Operation Amazonia led to systematic displacement and, in some cases, the near extermination of entire Indigenous communities. As documented in the final report of the Brazilian National Truth Commission published in late 2014, Indigenous peoples were one of the groups most affected by state violence during the military regime. "The Indigenous question became a question of national security," the report affirms, while Indigenous peoples were characterized as "virtual internal enemies" of the state "on the grounds of laying in the way of development projects."[37]

The report situates rights violations perpetrated against Indigenous groups within a broader campaign to "produce demographic voids." The colonial perception that the hinterlands constituted a vast, sparse desert populated by "primitive" tribes was translated into an official state policy designed to empty out native territories and open up land for the settler colonial

37   Comissão Nacional da Verdade (CNV), *Relatório*, vol. 2, *Textos Temáticos* (Brasília, 2014), 205.

project. Compulsory removals and transfers, land expropriations and deforestation, community separations, the denial of health services, and the repression of political activity constituted the means by which this politics was enforced on the ground. "In order to liberate land for colonization and the construction of infrastructural projects," this politics "led not only to formal attempts of denying the existence of certain indigenous peoples in certain regions," the Truth Commission concluded, "but also to means of making this erasure reality."[38] To make this a reality, to turn the forest into "demographic voids," the Amazon has been subjected to a five-hundred-year colonial politics of "desert-ification." Violence against native communities was and continues to be entangled with violence against nature.

The environmental outcome of this militarized neocolonial conquest was widespread deforestation. In 1990, two years before the first UN Earth Summit was convened in Rio de Janeiro—and just months after the first post-dictatorship democratic presidential election of 1989—the National Institute for Space Research (Instituto Nacional de Pesquisas Espaciais, INPE) released the first detailed analysis of deforestation in the Amazon. Using remote sensing technologies, the study reconstructed the deforestation processes that occurred during the twenty years of military dictatorship, mapping the impressive speed and scale of devastation unleashed by Operation Amazonia. Nearly 400,000 square kilometers of the original forest cover had been cleared at an average rate of nearly 22,000 square kilometers per year, resulting in a total deforested area equivalent to the territory of Portugal and Italy combined.[39] Rates of deforestation were so explosive that the study estimated that in less than ten years, if that tendency remained unabated, vast areas of the Amazon would be stripped of forests and turned into drier lands, incurring in a process described today as the "savannization" or "desertification" of the rainforest.[40]

The colonial view that the forest sertões constituted a desert was not simply projection or representation. These imagined geographies carried operative dimensions and concrete consequences at human, social, and environmental levels. This politics operated across discursive, representational, and

38   CNV, Relatório, 205.
39   Philip M. Fearnside, Antonio Tebaldi Tardin, and Luiz Gylvan Meira Filho,
      Deforestation Rate in Brazilian Amazonia (Manaus: INPE, 1990), 1–2. Between 1978
      and 1989, the precise values were 394,722 square kilometers of deforestation at an
      average clearing rate of 21,218 square kilometers per year.
40   Philip M. Fearnside, "Deforestation in Brazilian Amazonia," in The Earth in Transition:
      Patterns and Processes of Biotic Impoverishment, ed. G. M. Woodwell (Cambridge:
      Cambridge University Press, 1990), 211–238.

Satellite images showing before-and-after deforestation patterns at one of the "development poles" in southwestern Amazon, from 1975 to 2001. Patterns of environmental degradation followed the blueprint elaborated by the military regime. Courtesy of the USGS/NASA.

material dimensions, affecting both land and people, displacing Indigenous communities and razing forests to the ground. The potential "savannization" or "desertification" of the forest is the ecological outcome of the colonial politics of producing empty and depopulated "green deserts," a violent process in which forest clearing and ethnic cleansing went hand in hand.

Plantation Deserts

INPE maps demonstrated that environmental destruction followed the spatial interventions and policies designed by the military government and its planning bureaus, moving deeper into the forest along the highways and expanding centrifugally from "development poles." When observed from this cartographic perspective, the geographic footprint of deforestation defines the so-called "Arc of Fire," one of the most enduring and noxious environmental legacies left by the modern planning schemes deployed by the military regime in the Amazon. Formed by a vast logging-and-burn belt that stretches from the border between Bolivia and Brazil up to the Amazon River delta, the "Arc of Fire" follows the blueprint of Operation Amazonia. The apparently chaotic patterns of deforestation plotted on contemporary maps of the Brazilian Amazon are not the collateral product of a lack of government intervention and control, but the result of the opposite. These ruined landscapes are the product of plans fueled by illegal and violent deforestation. They capture the process of *ecocide by design*. The frontier came to operate according to an expansive and destructive territorial economy of its own. First, the biggest and most valuable wood is logged, often by clandestine criminal networks. The remaining forest is then razed and recurrently burned to be turned into pasture. As the frontier advances, more forests are cleared and pastures move further on. What was pasture is then reengineered into high-tech plantations connected to the geometries of the global market, chiefly for soy exports.

Representations of the frontier have been historically associated with labor-intensive, low-tech forms of land exploitation and resource extraction (as in the case of gold, timber, and rubber). In the contemporary Amazon, however, "primitive" forms of capital accumulation, to use a term set by Marx, are articulated by the sophisticated systems of global capitalism. Industrial soy plantations require a process of land engineering that operates across multiple scales, from the manipulation of seeds to the ecological reconfiguration of immense territories.

In the southern regions of the Amazon, one of largest areas of soy production in the world, plantations are highly controlled environments structured by a combination of informational technologies, computerized agricultural machines, drones, and satellite-based surveillance. Nearly automated and requiring virtually no labor force, these empty and sterile ecologies are sustained by the massive application of chemical fertilizers and pesticides produced by transnational corporations such as Monsanto and Syngenta, which are popularly known in the region as "poison."

Plantations, as anthropologist Anna Lowenhaupt Tsing writes, are "ecological simplifications." They configure "machines of replication, ecologies devoted to purification and the production of the same." Plantations engender an entirely new ecology—extracting living beings from their life worlds, transforming them into commodities, and simplifying biological processes in order to discipline the unruly diversity of nature into the monocultural logics of global capitalism. Plantation deserts are not only lifeless, harboring very low biodiversity, but they are also lethal. Apart from being contaminated and toxic, the fabrication of plantation ecology disrupts the lifeworlds of various species, destroying their habitats and leading to extinction.[41]

It is in this region of the Amazon—across the high-tech frontiers of the plantation economy and the lawless burnings at the "Arc of Fire" zone, where massive deforestation and forest degradation are rampant—that the impacts of climate change and global warming are most severely felt. According to recent climate models, the synergetic combinations of extensive land-use conversion, landscape fragmentation, widespread fires, and more severe droughts due to global warming could ignite dramatic and irreversible changes, unleashing the "savannization" of the Amazon.[42] Some scientists believe these prognoses are underestimated. Other models maintain that the interactions between climate change, deforestation, and fire could lead to massive tree dieback and the consequent wholesale

41   Anna Lowenhaupt Tsing, "A Feminist Approach to the Anthropocene: Earth Stalked by Man," lecture, Barnard College, November 10, 2015, New York, NY, video, http:bcrw.barnard.edu/videos/anna-lowenhaupt-tsing-a-feminist-approach-to-the-anthropocene-earth-stalked-by-man. "Thinking though landscape patches, I consider the figure of the Anthropocene through the plantation. By plantation I mean those ecological simplifications, in which living things are transformed into resources, future assets, by removing them from their life-worlds. Plantations are machines of replication, ecologies devoted to purification and the production of the same."

42   Intergovernmental Panel on Climate Change (IPCC), *Climate Change 2014: Impacts, Adaptation, and Vulnerability. Contribution of Working Group II to the Fifth Assessment Report of the Intergovernmental Panel on Climate Change*, ed. Christopher B. Field et al., 2 vols. (Cambridge: Cambridge University Press, 2014).

Giulia Bruno and Armin Linke, rainforest cleared for industrial soybean cultivation, Mato Grosso, Brazil. These photographs capture the development of desertification in the Amazon. They show sequential stages in the process of the forest's conversion into an endless, toxic desert of mono-crop plantations, designed by heavy doses of fertilizers and pesticides produced by the multinational corporations Monsanto iuland Syngenta. © Armin Linke (left) and © Giula Bruno (right).

"desertification" of the rainforest. A major Earth-cooling engine will then be turned off, converting the entire planet into much drier, hotter, less fertile, and inhospitable land.[43]

"If it weren't for deforestation, Brazil would not exist."[44]

As the rainforest burns at ever-increasing rates, we are witnessing the unfolding realization of the colonial view that sees the forest as nothing more than an unproductive desert. The ongoing "desertification" of the Amazon means the ongoing "desertification" of the Earth. This geopolitical order, which materializes a post–climate change planetary condition, has its historical and political origins in the violent world-destroying processes of colonialism. Colonialism is in many different ways a politics of "desertification." It is a mode of power that aims at eliminating diversity and difference—whether that difference be cultural, ethnic, or ecological—and at homogenizing populations and environments in order to control, exploit, and profit from them.

This system relies on violence against communities that is entangled with ecological destruction. Prior to the installation of the plantation states in the Amazon, it was first deemed necessary to clear the land from its original inhabitants and get rid of the forest by logging and burning, calling it a "desert." The production of "demographic voids" laid the ground for these territories to enter into the circuits of the global plantation economy.

Today frontier expansion still follows similar patterns. Political violence and rights violations against local communities are closely associated with forest burnings and the spreading of deforestation. On their own, fires and deforestation constitute a means of exercising political violence, in the same way that eliminating local resistance by assassinating activists is used to open land for farms, mines, and new settlements. The Amazon, the most biodiverse territory on Earth, is one the world's deadliest areas for land and nature rights defenders who are on the frontlines to protect the global environment.

43   Antonio Donato Nobre, *O Futuro Climático da Amazônia: Relatório de Avaliação Científica* (São Paulo: Articulação Regional Amazônica, ARA, 2014).

44   According to a leader of a land-grabbing gang operating in the Amazon. See Simon Romero, "Clashing Visions of Conservation Shake Brazil's Presidential Vote," *The New York Times*, October 3, 2014, https://www.nytimes.com/2014/10/04/world/americas/brazil-rainforest-amazon-conservation-election-rousseff-silva.html?_r=0.

The rise to power of far-right, protofascist president Bolsonaro enabled the escalation of deforestation and violence against local communities and leaders, often enacted by Bolsonaro himself. More than that, his militarized government aims at recuperating the same ideological discourses and planning schemes employed by the late military regime to conquer the "green deserts" of the Amazon. "Our interest in the Amazon is neither the Indian nor the fucking trees," Bolsonaro stated in late 2019, just after great fires devastated the rainforest.[45] We are still fighting the colonial necropolitics of "desertification."

45   Gustavo Uribe, "'Interesse na Amazônia não é no índio nem na porra da árvore,' diz Bolsonaro," *Folha de Sao Paulo*, October 1, 2019, https://www1.folha.uol.com.br/ambiente/2019/10/o-interesse-na-amazonia-nao-e-no-indio-nem-na-porra-da-arvore-diz-bolsonaro.shtml.

XqSu works within the fields of documentary-making, research, and writing. Within the contexts of feminist filmmaking and longer durations of collective research, she is dedicated to addressing the challenges of representation in an increasingly algorithmic world, in which capital, information and environments are enmeshed within regimes of power and control.

XQSU

OVERLAND THERE'S SHORTER TIME TO DREAM: ON THE OCCUPATION OF "XINJIANG"

يىراقىتىلى رىسالەت

تاھىر ھامۇت ئۆزگىل

يىراقتىكى رىسالەت

كۆچمەنلەر بارماقلىرىنى شىشلەتتە يلا

مۇساپىنى ھېسابلايدۇ

ئۇزۇرۇمچىگىچە بولغان

1200 كىلومېتر ئۇزۇرۇلۇقنى پەرەز قىلىپ

ئاپتوبۇس كارىدۇرىنى ئۇزرنى قاناق پاتقوزۇ شنى

يانتۇ بېشى كىتاب ئۇمۇغانا كۆزۇينكسنىڭ ئاقشى قىلىشنى

ئاقتىنى قاناق ئۇ ئالوزۇشنى

يولدا نىمە يىيشنى

نىمەلەرنى خىيال قىلىشنى ئويلاپ

يۇرىكى قاغىدۇ

ئۇزرنى بەزلەپ

سۆيگۈ ئۈچۈن يىراققا كەتتىم ، دەيدۇ

يوتۇنلەي كۆنۈپ قالدىم ، دەيدۇ

قۇمارۇ تولىمۇ ئازەل ، دەيدۇ

مەن يالغۇز ئەمەس ، دەيدۇ

Faraway Risalet
without using her strong fingers
counts the distance
She figures it's twelve hundred kilometers
to Urumchi
and she starts to fret about how to squeeze into
the cot on the bus
the way her glasses will pinch if she lies sideways
how to pass the time
what to eat on the road
what to daydream about
To soothe herself
she says, I make this long journey for love
she says, I am entirely used to it
she says, the desert is so beautiful
she says, I am not alone
she says, people here respect me
but when no one is looking she cries

Now,
she must enjoy long journeys
she must learn to take deep breaths
she must scatter like the sand, harden like a rock
she must flower like a thorn bush, yellow like
a poplar
she must not fear the wide-open land
she must not tire of the sunlight
she must not run from the wind

لېكىن بۇرسەن تىسپ يوشۇدۇڭ يىغلايدۇ

تۆ ئەمدى

كۆزۈڭ سەبزەرگە ئامراق بولۇشنى كېرەك
چولقۇر نەپەس ئېلىشنى تۆكۈشنى كېرەك
قۇمدەك چىچىلىپ، تاشتەك قېتىشنى كېرەك
يانتاقتەك چىچەكلەپ، توغراقتەك سارغىيىشنى كېرەك
كە گرانكىشى قورقماسلىقى كېرەك
ئايتاپتىن زىرىكمە، سەلكى كېرەك
شامالدىن قاچما سەلىقى كېرەك

ئېزىپ قالماس كەسلەپ نجوآلتەك
ياكى
يېپاي كۆزند ۇرۇڭدەن تۆگكدەك
بىراقتىكاي رىسالەت

2015 - يىل مارت، ئۈرۈمچى

Like a lizard that never loses its way
or perhaps
like a camel that's just been broken in
faraway Risalet[1]

1   Tahir Hamut Izgil is one of the foremost poets writing in the Uyghur language.
     He grew up in Kashgar, an ancient city in the southwest of the Uyghur homeland.
     After attending college in Beijing, he returned to the Uyghur region and in the late
     1990s and the 2000s emerged as a prominent film director, best known for the
     groundbreaking drama *The Moon Is a Witness* (1999). His poetry has appeared in
     English translation in *The New York Review of Books, Asymptote, Gulf Coast,
     Berkeley Poetry Review*, and elsewhere. In 2017, as the Chinese state began the
     mass internment of Uyghur intellectuals, Izgil fled with his family to the United
     States. He lives in Washington, DC, where he continues his work as a poet and film
     producer.

     The poem was translated by Joshua L. Freeman. Tahir Hamut Izgil was
     commissioned to handwrite his poem. The translation is courtesy of Joshua L.
     Freeman.

     Parts of the following text first appeared on the online platform *Lausan* in March
     2021, in the midst of the events discussed herein. *Lausan*, which was born out of
     Hong Kong's umbrella movement, has since played an important role in articulating
     intersectional solidarities across various struggles in our crisis-stricken world. The
     initiative is made up of a self-organized and ever-shifting group of young activists
     who sustain the belief that the acts of publishing, writing, translating, remembering,
     and transferring knowledge are in and of themselves political. See "About," *Lausan*,
     2020, lausan.hk/about.

In March of 2021, international clothing companies such as H&M, Nike, and members of the Better Cotton Initiative (including Adidas, New Balance, and Burberry) stopped using Xinjiang cotton. The ban resulted from a cascade of sanctions imposed by the US, EU, and Canada, catalyzed by satellite images, photographs and videos testifying to the forced labor, mass detention, and sterilization of Uyghur, Kazakh, and other Turkic minority groups in the Xinjiang Uyghur Autonomous Region (XUAR).[2] One-fifth of the world's supply of cotton comes out of the XUAR, which encompasses an area bigger than France, Germany, and Spain combined. Sharing borders with Mongolia, Russia, Kazakhstan, Kyrgyzstan, Tajikistan, Afghanistan, and India, XUAR is host to the Taklamakan Desert, the world's second-largest shifting sand desert, bounded by the Kunlun Mountains in the south, Pamir Mountains in the west, Tian Shan

2   While this essay focuses on the incarceration of Uyghurs, the CCP's tactics of mass detention and surveillance affect, no less significantly, many Indigenous comm-unities and and minority ethnic groups in the Xinjiang Uyghur Autonomous Region (XUAR). The region is also known as "Xinjiang," "Northwest China," "East Turkestan," "Uyghuria," "Ghulja," "Tarbagai," "Altay," "Dzungarstan and Altishahr," and/or "Dzungaria and the Tarim Basin Region." A highly contested term, the proper name Xinjiang (新疆) was first used by the eighteenth-century emperor Qianlong, and conferred on the XUAR upon Zuo Zongtang's reoccupation of the region in the late nineteenth century. In Mandarin Chinese, it means "new territory," "new border," or "new frontier."

Mountains in the north, and Gobi Desert to the east.[3] The region is known for providing renewable and clean energy resources internationally.[4] The scale of the XUAR's coerced labor programs, which have imprisoned more than one million Turkic individuals since 2017, made public the complicities of global industries (including renewable energies industries), highlighting how often the imagination of a sustainable future perversely relies on indentured labor.[5]

The Chinese state reacted to the international sanctions with their own.[6] The year 2021 marked the 100th anniversary of the Chinese Communist Party, whose mythologization importantly included the party's fight against Western imperialism during their occupation of China in the 1920s. The sanctions touched a historical nerve. State newspapers condemned the "spread of disinformation and rumors" and denied the realities of enforced labor. Major Chinese pop stars resigned from foreign corporate marketing campaigns while anger swarmed from the state to the public, online and offline. The Chinese state continued to frame Xinjiang as a private affair—an affair that should be managed domestically without foreign intervention—and insisted that its labor programs were developed with care, intended to pull the region out of Islamic extremism and poverty.[7]

Since these incidents in March, many of the international companies who remain heavily dependent on Chinese manufacturing have silently retracted their statements denouncing the enforced labor used in the production of Xinjiang cotton, and instead have opportunistically increased pressure on the US Uyghur Forced Labor Prevention Act to alter and dismantle some of their sanctions.[8] The Chinese state recruitment and employment programs, along with the manufacturers across Xinjiang, continued to frame their management of labor through

3   Wikipedia, s.v., "Taklamakan Desert," last modified October 23, 2021, https://
     en.wikipedia.org/wiki/Taklamakan_Desert.
4   Albert Zhang et al., "Disinformation on Xinjiang," The Xinjiang Data Project,
     Australian Strategic Policy Institute's (ASPI) International Cyber Policy Centre, March
     30, 2021, xjdp.aspi.org.au/explainers/strange-bedfellows-on-xinjiang.
5   William Alan Reinsch and Sean Arrieta-Kenna, "A Dark Spot for the Solar Energy
     Industry: Forced Labor in Xinjiang," Center for Strategic and International Studies,
     April 19, 2021, www.csis.org/analysis/dark-spot-solar-energy-industry-forced-labor-
     xinjiang.
6   AFP, "Chinese TV Stars Cut Ties with Nike and H&M Faces Boycott as Xinjiang
     'Forced Labour' Backlash Builds," Hong Kong Free Press, March 25, 2021,
     hongkongfp.com/2021/03/25/chinese-tv-stars-cut-ties-with-nike-and-hm-faces-
     boycott-as-xinjiang-forced-labour-backlash-builds.
7   Guldana Salimjan, "Naturalized Violence: Affective Politics of China's 'Ecological
     Civilization' in Xinjiang," Human Ecology 49, no. 1 (February 2021): 59–68.
8   Mark Bain, "Who's Trying to Weaken a US Bill Targeting Forced Labor in China?,"
     Quartz, December 18, 2020, https://qz.com/1947334/whos-trying-to-weaken-a-us-bill-
     targeting-forced-labor-in-china.

procedural language, their banal and bureaucratic statements disguising the enforced transfer of over 1.5 million people into prisons, factory floors, and "re-education camps." Instead, it is *through* these mechanisms, which actively bury inherent injustices under the name of business-as-usual and justified state power, that Xinjiang continues to be occupied and colonized.[9] The silent retraction of international manufacturing companies and increasingly strengthened nationalist resentment within China speaks to the urgency of understanding the mechanisms mobilized around widely used anti-imperialist, green, and developmentalist rhetoric—mechanisms that are key to the continual dispossession, exploitation, and erasure of millions of people, and that are anchored within the overlapping projects of settler colonialism and global supply chains. It is also here where the shifting deserts within XUAR have been misrepresented as a passive backdrop to what is otherwise an interplay between these projects and the environmental conditions within which they are realized.

By zooming into the topological and material shifts of Xinjiang outwards, this essay traces the sinews of connections between various sites, histories, geophysical processes, and spatial transformations, and scrutinizes the workings of the larger geopolitical apparatus that needs to be, in many ways, rejected and radically reassessed.

9   Yi Xiaocuo, "Recruiting Loyal Stabilizers: On the Banality of Carceral Colonialism in Xinjiang," *Made in China Journal*, October 25, 2019, madeinchinajournal. com/2019/10/25/recruiting-loyal-stabilisers-on-the-banality-of-carceral-colonialism-in-xinjiang. This procedural violence can be glimpsed in corporate statements regardless of the industry. German car manufacturer Volkswagen has claimed that they "are not aware of and do not believe that forced labour was involved" in their factory located in the capital of the autonomous region. Stephan Wollenstein, head of Volkswagen, continues, "I would say no company could ever make sure [that employees have not been through a camp]. The only thing that we do is we apply procedures. We have a footprint all over the world in different countries where situations are not always to a situation how we would like to have it in Volkswagen. We try to control our company-related processes." John Sudworth, "China Muslims: Volkswagen Says 'No Forced Labour' at Xinjiang Plant," *BBC News*, November 12, 2020, www.bbc.com/news/world-asia-china-54918309.

Solveig Suess, *AAA Cargo*, 2018. *AAA Cargo* is a part-fiction, part-documentary film essay on the New Silk Road. The thirty-four-minute film traces the anticipation of infrastructure and trade on a planetary scale. It follows distribution networks as they expand between China and Europe. Along their routes, geographies are reformatted for logistical purposes. The changing landscapes attract "paralogisticians," a new generation of precarious workers who hack infrastructural spaces through transnational guanxi and long-distance friendships. Desert sands are made restless by westerly winds, disrupting roads and railways, sometimes engulfing whole cities. Through a disorientation of the senses, bodies and landscapes become mobile. Unless otherwise noted, stills courtesy of Solveig Suess.

I.
Dust Storms

Every year during late winter and early spring, atmospheric pressure dips over the Taklamakan Desert in southwest Xinjiang and northwest China, and the Gobi Desert in northeastern China and southern Mongolia, feeding into the strength of the westerly winds.[10] In April and May of 2019, these winds swept across the southwest of XUAR, covering the cities of Aksu, Kashgar, and Hotan in a heavy yellow dust.[11] The storm was disruptive. In some areas, visibility was down to 5 meters. The particulate matter delayed trains traveling along the "Belt and Road" for several days. People were forced to take shelter inside. All flights in and out of Aksu and Kuqa were canceled, and forty-eight flights were canceled in the capital of Beijing. Activities froze as dust threw place into a turbid haze. The dust storm has become an annual occurrence, as compared to half a century ago, when it struck only once every seven or eight years. Each grain of dust carries the potential to travel thousands of kilometers with the storm, riding air currents sometimes as far as California, unbound by jurisdictions.[12] The dust storm is a close reminder of the expanding deserts on the nation-state's peripheries, "Xinjiang" and Inner Mongolia.

10   Matt Telfer, "Beijing's 'Sandstorm' Was Actually a Dust Storm—and That's Much Worse," *The Conversation*, March 18, 2021, theconversation.com/beijings-sandstorm-was-actually-a-dust-storm-and-thats-much-worse-157367.

11   South China Morning Post, "Huge Sandstorm Hits West China's Xinjiang," YouTube, June 30, 2020, 1:10, www.youtube.com/watch?v=IMnE_IwE61E.

12   Gerry Mullany, "Dust Storms Blanket Beijing and Northern China," *The New York Times*, May 5, 2017, www.nytimes.com/2017/05/05/world/asia/dust-storms-northern-china-beijing.html.

A rail line initiated by US tech conglomerate Hewlett-Packard (HP) and built in cooperation with the Chinese state in 2014 traverses the growing deserts of this region—cutting across the typical path of the storm. Despite attempts to optimize the circulation of commodities and to *slow* the desert down by design, the desert expands roughly 2,000 square kilometers a year. These long-distance infrastructures, which span terrains most affected by human-made climate change, need to withstand increasingly erratic weather events. HP's rail line required 500 kilometers of windproof walls to shield its trains against the Gobi's powerful gales.[13] Rows of grass, bush, nets, and stones all form a risk management scheme against the force of wind and the transition of desert into storm.

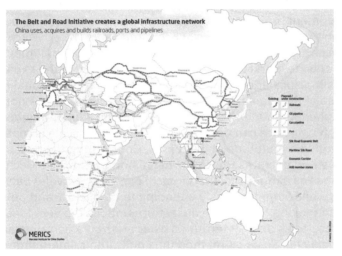

"Mapping the Belt and Road initiative." Courtesy of Merics: Mercator Institute for China Studies, https://merics.org/en/tracker/mapping-belt-and-road-initiative-where-we-stand.

Most of the goods transported along this route are manufactured by multinational IT companies 3,080 kilometers away in Chongqing, central China. The construction of HP's rail line coincided with construction projects by other manufacturers—including Foxconn who supplies devices to Acer, Apple, and Volkswagen—that had shifted their factories towards China's western border as part of the Chinese government–led "Go West" policy campaign inaugurated in 2000. The line marked the

13   Wade Shepard, "These 8 Companies Are Bringing the 'New Silk Road' to Life," *Forbes*, March 12, 2017, https://www.forbes.com/sites/wadeshepard/2017/03/12/8-new-silk-road-companies-that-you-can-invest-in.

beginning of what is now the five-continent, mega-infrastructure project collectively known as the Belt and Road Initiative (BRI), which includes the development of telecommunication cables, railways, dams, and power stations. BRI's massive campaign also provides funds and a labor force to implement these projects predominantly across the Global South, securing more than $340 billion worth of construction contracts in over sixty countries.[14]

A broader framework is needed to understand just how enmeshed states are in this geopolitical project of infrastructural cooperation led by the Chinese government and HP. To register the complex transnational system at work entails an attentiveness at multiple scales: not only in the space that a rail line cuts through but also in the atmospheric stream that flows and interfaces with it; not only on the scale of the frontier, where state-led development projects dot the western Chinese territories, but also on the scale of the Special Economic Zone (SEZ), which produces and is produced by replicable spatial technologies that bring outside markets into state spaces; not only in the expanse of HP's logistical innovations across time and transnational space but also at the global scale of the BRI.[15] The dust storm is not just a phenomenon but also an epistemological phenomenon, through which we can become sensitive to how scale is mobilized within a multitude of processes. Considering the dust storm as a method gestures towards what historian Gabrielle Hecht describes as a multi-scalar approach: one that "move[s] between scales while simultaneously attending to the history and politics of scale-making."[16] Here the dust storm undoes the very idea of these scales as distinct territorial categories on a narrative and material level. Scale-as-method thus pulls into relation times and spaces that have long been kept separate.[17]

14   Lily Kuo and Niko Kommenda, "What Is China's Belt and Road Initiative?," *Guardian*, July 30, 2018, https://www.theguardian.com/cities/ng-interactive/2018/jul/30/what-china-belt-road-initiative-silk-road-explainer.

15   "In the late 1970s, the Four Modernizations program introduced a zoning program in order to open the previously self-contained socialist economy outward in order to engage foreign capital and technology... Deng Xiaoping considered SEZs as both an economic bridge and a political window to the outside world. Different kinds of zones were established in several steps throughout the 1980s and 1990s." Aihwa Ong, "The Chinese Axis: Zoning Technologies and Variegated Sovereignty," *Journal of East Asian Studies* 4, no. 1 (2004): 76.

16   Gabrielle Hecht, "Interscalar Vehicles for an African Anthropocene: On Waste, Temporality, and Violence," *Cultural Anthropology* 33, no. 1 (2018): 114.

17   Hecht, "Interscalar Vehicles."

"Sandstorm in Kumtag Desert near Shanshan (Xinjiang, China) during our dinosaur dig field season 2012," February 18, 2015. Courtesy of Oliver Wings.

II.
The Frontier

Over the past several decades, Chinese state officials have incentivized farmers whose lands fall within the path of these annual dust storms to recultivate their plots of land—converting farmland into forestland. The "Three-North Shelter Forest Program," a civic afforestation initiative aimed at combating "desertification" (or the deterioration of land) and controlling dust storms, enforces the state directive to secure deteriorating soil. The incentivized program offers cash to farmers to plant bushes, trees, and shrubs in more arid areas on their property as a form of windbreak. Also known as the Great Green Wall, the program, which started in 1978, is set to be completed around 2050. Forests now cover more than 500,000 square kilometers of China—the largest artificial forest in the world.[18] The Chinese state has mobilized the political and scientific rhetoric of warfare to justify this monocultural program: "We are now members of People's Commune (Renmin gongshe): we should fight against the natural disaster collectively, and we should not get away from the famine-stricken area when we encounter a few difficulties."[19] Militancy is conveyed through the ambitious scale of the program and the intensity of the response that catalyzed the masses into action. For art historian Asia Bazdyrieva, personifying the changing climate as an enemy is analogous to the othering of populations, like the Uyghurs, Kazakhs, Kyrgyz, in XUAR. Fixating on climate as a rhetorical other—manifesting here as an enemy of the state—is useful for shoring up "in-group" support.[20]

Following the break in political relations between the People's Republic of China (PRC) and the USSR in the 1960s, clashes with the Soviet Union worsened along China's borders. Faced with the possibility of war, Mao Zedong militarized and industrialized the desert regions of Xinjiang. The 1975 film *Spring in the Desert* and the 1965 documentary *Army's Reclamation and Battle Song* chronicle the ambitions of China's Han ethnic majority to build dams and farms across the desert.[21] These

---

18   Jonathan Watts, "China's Loggers down Chainsaws in Attempt to Regrow Forests," *Guardian*, March 11, 2009, https://www.theguardian.com/environment/2009/mar/11/china-forests-deforestation.

19   Zhu Wenshun, dir., *Spring in the Desert (Shamo De Chuntian 沙漠的春天)*, 1975, uploaded by 回忆老电影, YouTube, July 9, 2019, 1:52:20, https://www.youtube.com/watch?v=t3e2-F6Tqf8.

20   Asia Bazdyrieva, in discussion with author, December 23, 2020.

21   Zhu, *Spring in the Desert*; and *Army's Reclamation and Battle Song (Junken Zhan'Ge)*, 1965.

"Xi Calls for Understanding, Protecting Nature when Attending Tree Planting Activity," March 30, 2017. Courtesy of CCTV Video News Agency.

large-scale development projects were carried out by local militia and "educated youth" from China's interior provinces, mobilized by the call to "green the motherland."[22] Huge influxes of ethnic Han migrant workers had moved into the region, consolidating the Party's power at the Sino-Soviet border.[23] The occupation that accompanied the state's modernization and terraformation efforts followed claims by Chinese state ethnologists that the land left by Indigenous herders was "unused."[24] Such grand "greening" projects were implemented in the otherwise "undeveloped" and famine-stricken "remote places" of Xinjiang and Inner Mongolia and, rather than improving the poor conditions, only sidelined

22   Judith Shapiro, *Mao's War against Nature Politics and the Environment in Revolutionary China* (Cambridge: Cambridge University Press, 2001), esp. 159–193. "Green the motherland" ("Lühua Zuguo") was a slogan coined in 1956 by Chairman Mao.
23   Xiaocuo, "Recruiting Loyal Stabilizers."
24   Salimjan, "Naturalized Violence," 60.

the already marginalized local ethnic minorities. From the late 1950s, the Northwest China and Inner Mongolia Autonomous Region Desertification Control Plan outlined a "desertification" governance system whose policies and regulations called on local government departments, communities, and social groups to participate in controlling the desert. Control in this context meant modulating the advancement of the desert, stalling how sand encroached across the region. Sand "does not stop; it only rests."[25] Control was thus the ability to manage the relation between time and distance.

Distinctive patterns of colonialism were encoded within the modernist project of Chinese Communism. Projects, such as the aforementioned Three-North Shelter Forest Program, produced and were produced by the concept of the frontier, where the young settlers' transformation of peripheral landscapes into productive spaces was important in securing the state's influence in China's peripheries. The frontier was crucial in defining the perimeters of national borders, with its power lying in the prospect of extraction and in the material manipulation of its environmental conditions.

Through the sanitized rhetoric of engineering, shaping the physical environment came to provide cover for the colonial dispossession of local populations. This rhetoric caters to extractive forms from cultivation to plantations. As film scholar Cheng Li notes, the dimensions of colonial enclosure—material-ized in the greening of ethnic borderlands—effectively "sinicize" the minorities that inhabit these margins. Cheng uses the term "sinicize" to account for the politics and ethnicities associated with environmental narratives, which were deeply embedded within the greening campaigns of Maoist China: "To sinicize ethnic minorities was to revolutionize and modernize them, given the fact that the Han Chinese people dominated the Communist regime and thought themselves held all the truth of revolution and progress with duties to save ethnic minorities from political, economic and cultural backwardness."[26] Where previously yellow sands covered the landscape, now green waves roll across it like the ocean.

Legitimizing the regime through these projects allowed for the displacement of Indigenous populations—and, very crucially, the dismissal of Indigenous knowledge and forms of relating to

25   Jerry Zee, "Holding Patterns: Sand and Political Time at China's Desert Shores," *Cultural Anthropology* 32, no. 2 (2016): 224.
26   Cheng Li, "Sinification by Greening: Politics, Nature and Ethnic Borderlands in Maoist Ecocinema," *Journal of Chinese Cinemas*, 11, no. 1 (2017): 64n8.

the land—within the political unit of the PRC. Uyghur people had, for millennia, used an extensive network of *karez*, a localized technique to irrigate arid areas. The hydraulic system provided reliable drinking water and distributed snowmelt water from the faraway Tian Shan Mountains toward crops, across what was deemed to be the second lowest point in the world after the Dead Sea. Since the 1950s, and accelerating over the past few decades, Indigenous infrastructures have been replaced by the social-agricultural projects of Maoist socialism—by large-scale forest and farming efforts, by railways and dams. Projects that intended to make "problem" landscapes productive instead created different problems: they caused the region's water tables to rapidly recede, drying out lakes and river beds, intensifying China's annual dust storms.[27]

Atmospheres and geologies continue to be posed as an "engineering problem." Anthropologist Jerry Zee describes Chinese governance as the "programming of unruly more-than-organic machines" that consider the social, botanical, market, aeolian, and political processes as manipulable "components of geo-aerodynamic systems" where the "reprogramming of meteorological and climatic processes appears as the basis for new and experimental configurations of politics."[28] Designing desert spaces into crosshatches of forest relies on a constant toggling between both processes and scales, in numerous "laboratory experiments," computer models, and wind tunnel tests. The results of these experiments, models, and tests, which tend to capture things like erosion and sand sedimentation on a controlled and smaller scale, inform and tweak ongoing larger environmental, social, technical, and economic programs.[29] The engineer-driven methods of reading and registering physical earth systems for the purpose of future projections hinge on what is rendered useful as data. Despite data being a social product—measured by people with specific intentions and practices—longer histories and contexts of colonial dispossession

27   Cui Chunliang et al., "The Karez System in China's Xinjiang Region," Middle East Institute, January 17, 2014, www.mei.edu/publications/karez-system-chinas-xinjiang-region; and Nathan VanderKlippe, "In China's 'Underground Great Wall,' Tunnels Go Dry and Uyghurs Fear for Their Culture," *Globe and Mail*, October 20, 2017, www.theglobeandmail.com/news/world/in-chinas-underground-great-wall-tunnels-go-dry-and-uyghurs-fear-for-their-culture/article36680977.
28   Jerry Zee, "Machine Sky: Social and Terrestrial Engineering in a Chinese Weather System," *American Anthropologist* 122, no. 1 (2020): 9–20.
29   Lorenzo Raffaele, Jeroen van Beeck, and Luca Bruno, "Wind-Sand Tunnel Testing of Surface-Mounted Obstacles: Similarity Requirements and a Case Study on a Sand Mitigation Measure," *Journal of Wind Engineering and Industrial Aerodynamics* 214 (2021), https://www.sciencedirect.com/science/article/pii/S0167610521001379.

Zhu Wenshun, *Spring in the Desert* (Shamo De Chuntian 沙漠的春天), 1975.

are considered superfluous, not relevant, to its production. They are left out of this manageable system.[30] Contexts and histories of colonialism that are relevant, recognized, and calculated as "problems" to be solved end up further legitimizing practices of various forms and structures of settler solutionism and occupation.

The tourism industry has been important in this respect. During the first half of 2019, 310,000 ethnically Han tourists visited state-curated locations in Xinjiang, from the Taklamakan Desert to the Tian Shan Mountains.[31] Chinese state campaigns encourage travelers from the wealthier eastern coast to visit natural attractions not far from sites where they hold local Muslim and Turkic-speaking minorities captive.[32] Glossy images of tourist destinations create a happy veneer, obfuscating the everyday, ongoing realities of mass incarceration, dispossession, and extractive capital perpetrated by the state.[33] At the same time, it is through these images and imaginaries that onlookers and settlers alike absorb cultural-economic justifications to further "open up" the region through massive profit-taking.

The "Go West" campaign encouraged heavy industry and corporate manufacturing to do just that: to "thrust... Great Development" west, moving from the east coast to the low-income regions inland, in search of profits.[34] These regions contain not only the country's largest coal reserves but also a vast reservoir of oil, which provides the foundation for Xinjiang's energy economy. Oil had been surveyed by the Chinese Empire in the region as far back as the Qing period (1644–1911), though it was only after 1917 that a certain "oil fever" spread, as the Russian Empire, later the Soviet Union, funded and designed a Central Asian rail-transport network.[35] The demand for oil surged after the 1990s and accelerated with the "Go West" campaign, in which Chinese state investments totaling $300 billion poured into 685 projects in Xinjiang in 2014 alone.[36]

The notion of "frontier" sustains forms of exploitation. It does this not only by dismissing livelihoods and forms of knowledge deemed unproductive, but also by determining what is valuable and transforming landscapes into sites of value-making.

30   Dee Mack Williams, "The Desert Discourse of Modern China," *Modern China* 23, no. 3 (1997): 328–355.
31   Jessica Zang, "I was in #Xinjiang , #China early this year, and was in love with here, people and food!," Twitter, December 19, 2020, twitter.com/JessicaZ1018/status/1340234318405193730.

32   Agence France-Presse, "China Promotes Xinjiang as Tourist Heaven While Holding
        Muslim Uygurs in Re-Education Camps," *South China Morning Post*, July 18,
        2019, www.scmp.com/lifestyle/travel-leisure/article/3018805/china-promotes-xinjiang-
        tourist-heaven-while-holding.
33   Amy Qin and Edward Wong, "Why Calls to Boycott 'Mulan' Over Concerns about
        China Are Growing," *New York Times*, last updated September 24, 2020, www.
        nytimes.com/2020/09/08/world/asia/china-mulan-xinjiang.html; and Judd C. Kinzley,
        "How Oil Has Shaped Xinjiang," China Dialogue, June 21, 2019, chinadialogue.
        net/en/energy/11031-how-oil-has-shaped-xinjiang.
34   James A. Millward, *Eurasian Crossroads: A History of Xinjiang* (New York: Columbia
        University Press, 2007), 322.
35   Kinzley, "How Oil Has Shaped Xinjiang."
36   Edward Wong, "China Invests in Region Rich in Oil, Coal and Also Strife," *New York
        Times*, December 20, 2014, www.nytimes.com/2014/12/21/world/asia/china-invests-
        in-xinjiang-region-rich-in-oil-coal-and-also-strife.html.

III.
The Zone

The 2014 rail line agreement between HP and the Chinese state was "defined not only according to business logic, but also with certain strategic calculations."[37] The line would, according to HP, save two weeks' worth of transportation time—making it both faster (and less perilous) than ocean-ways and cheaper than airfreight. Beginning in Chongqing, central-west China, the line cuts through Xinjiang into Kazakhstan, Russia, Belarus, and Poland, before reaching its destination in Germany, 11,180 kilometers away. But the geopolitical scale and territorial expansiveness of the BRI and the HP line would not have been possible without China's signature adaptation of SEZs.

Since President Xi Jinping came to power in 2013, the catchphrase used amongst Chinese state planners of the BRI is *youwai zhinei* (由外至内), meaning "bringing the outside in."[38] This logic, brought to life through SEZs, sees the export-process economy driven by transnational capital entering the system of China's state-controlled economy. Environmental and labor deregulation offers legal independence from the domestic laws of the host country through the creation of "zones" in which pools of cheap labor are further entrapped by tax incentives.

The strategies and logistics of zones of exception—that is, the generative and segmented remaking of territory—have become intrinsic to modern statecraft. These "strategies" to boost business through lax labor conditions and tax incentives in the XUAR have proven not only to be unsuccessful in smoothing over regional inequalities but also to exacerbate them, to the continual and disproportionate benefit of the Han ethnic majority.[39] Schemes and benefits for settlers, or Han employees and their family members, include secure jobs and full healthcare, unemployment, and retirement insurance coverage. While the Indigenous populations are dispossessed of their lands, taken up and "re-educated" as bare minimum-wage workers on factory floors, state-led incentives invite settlers to relocate to Xinjiang through systematic, organized employment transfer and

37   Alena Zelenin, "Battle of the Silk Road: Kazakhstan Reformats the Map of Eurasia Logistics," Center for Strategic Assessment and Forecasts, December 21, 2015, http://csef.ru/en/politica-i-geopolitica/326/bitva-za-shyolkovyj-put-kazahstan-pereform atiruet-kartu-logistiki-evrazii-6468.

38   Brian Eyler, "Who's Afraid of China's One Belt One Road Initiative?," *East by Southeast* (blog), April 24, 2015, archived July 31, 2021, https://web.archive.org/web/20210731225910/http://www.eastbysoutheast.com/whos-afraid-of-chinas-one-belt-one-road-initiative.

39   Xiaocuo, "Recruiting Loyal Stabilizers."

land allotment programs.[40] Since 2017, more than one million primarily Uyghur but also other Indigenous peoples and ethnic minorities have been "disappeared" into so-called "re-education camps," and in the following years, a government-led labor transfer scheme has forced prisoners from these "re-education" prison camps *into* the very factories of HP as workers.[41] The cumulative effect has been of raising the region's GDP while retaining the wealth gap between China's east and west, between Han and the Uyghur, Kazakhs, and other Turkic Muslims.

There is a carceral continuum between labor camps and supply chain capitalism. Geographer Deborah Cowen writes that "logistics also drives neoliberal forms of bio-, necro-, and anti-political calculation where cost-benefit analysis and assumptions of market efficiency are embedded into its basic techniques."[42] Time and space are designed with and according to technological efficiency and standardization, eliminating possible political claims and resistances that may rupture the current order. The management and security of the life of the entire supply chain—not just the population it serves—is crucial.

Anthropologist Aihwa Ong's work on the SEZs devised by the Chinese Communist state system frame these zoning technologies as distinctive ways to re-territorialize national socialist space while ensuring the controlled development of capitalism. "Predicated on an astute use of the logic of exception to create economic and political zones that spread economic networks and foster political integration," writes Ong, these technologies redesign and recast geographies of law and violence by rearranging what is inside and outside of state space.[43] Military occupations, land grabs, and dispossessions are all part of this technocratic territorial reconfiguration, violences that have only accelerated since Xi's abolition of presidential term limits in 2018, with Xinjiang being key in developing the spatial technology while further substantiating the state's need to enact racist control in the region.

40   Xiaocuo, "Recruiting Loyal Stabilizers."
41   Vicky Xiuzhong Xu et al., *Uyghurs for Sale: Re-education, Forced Labor, and Surveillance beyond Xinjiang*, Australian Strategic Policy Institute Policy Brief Reports 26 (Barton: ASPI International Cyber Policy Centre, 2020), https://www.aspi.org.au/report/uyghurs-sale.
42   Deborah Cowen, *The Deadly Life of Logistics: Mapping Violence in Global Trade* (Minneapolis: University of Minnesota Press, 2014), 231.
43   Ong, "The Chinese Axis," 92.

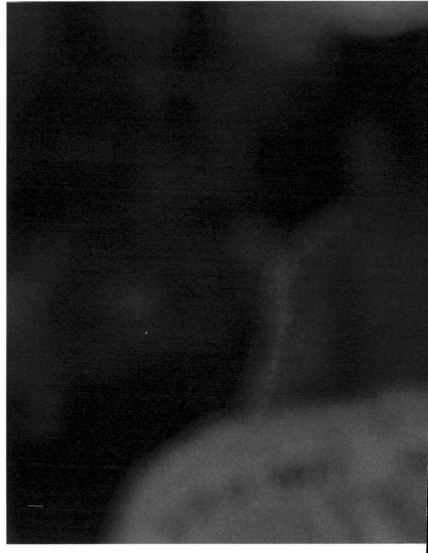

IV.

The Supply Chain

What strategic calculations inform a US tech company's decision to build actual rail lines in the first place? Not concerned solely with the scope of IT infrastructure and with moving commodities, HP's interests include hegemony over the entire transnational distribution route through advanced supply chain management. The beginnings of supply chain management can be found in places previously occupied by US military forces during the Vietnam War (1955–1975) and Korean War (1950–1953).[44] The confluence of US imperialism and these early trials in capitalist supply chain management enabled the surge of transnational supply chains that form the backbone of global capitalism today. By the 1970s, firms in the industrializing Global North were experiencing a downturn in profits due to rising production costs and wages, and sought cheaper alternatives elsewhere. Political scientist Charmaine Chua has argued that firms returned to older, colonial modes of production, in which seeking the extraction of resources and cheap labor internationally allowed for profit to be reaped in the Global North while offshoring production to the Global South.[45]

At the same time, a new type of supply chain management emerged in late 1970s Japan. The Japanese car manufacturer Toyota pioneered moving production outside Japan's sovereign borders, coordinating space and time in a more cost-beneficial manner. As a flexible production technique, just-in-time (JIT) management aimed to shave off expenses, where possible, through various methods of tweaking and "optimization." JIT, in many ways, is a capitalist innovation, developed in the shadow of Japanese imperialism and Japan's new role as a "junior partner" to US empire in the Pacific.[46] Fittingly, HP was the first Western company to incorporate Japan's industrial methods of supply chain management into its corporate machinery.[47]

JIT management operates by rationalizing and calibrating work throughout the whole body of the supply chain. It is a technique that standardizes the production line, with working

---

44   The US military forces still occupy South Korea, where there are still twenty active military installations in the country.
45   Charmaine Chua, in discussion with the author, May 5, 2017.
46   Kim Moody, "How 'Just-in-Time' Capitalism Spread COVID-19: Trade Routes, Transmission, and International Solidarity," *Spectre Journal*, April 8, 2020, spectrejournal.com/how-just-in-time-capitalism-spread-covid-19.
47   Marc A. Weiss and Erica Schoenberger, "Peter Hall and the Western Urban and Regional Collective at the University of California, Berkeley," *Built Environment* 41, no. 1 (2015): 69.

hours that produce a "killing rhythm" of labor, as described by interdisciplinary scholar Stefano Harney.[48] Such a rhythm globalizes an acceptance of working the body at a rate that physically and mentally destroys a person over time.[49]

"Efficiency" is implemented at different scales within the strata of inventory lists to the political-economic agreements along the HP railway. Thousands of laptop computers and accessories are piled neatly in sealed shipping containers to travel across the rail route between Chongqing and Duisburg three times a week. National borders have also transformed: goods are allowed to travel freely along the rail line through Russia, Kazakhstan, and Belarus. By removing impediments such as security checkpoints, HP is able to push neoliberal ambitions of free trade further than ever before.[50]

HP has also negotiated with the Chinese government to implement their own border customs software for processing documents, permitting its containers to remain locked and uninspected at border crossings along the way. Where cargo inspection is necessary en route to Europe, it can now happen at the same time as quarantine and customs clearance.[51] This one-stop service and state-corporate partnership with China, Russia, Kazakhstan, Belarus, Poland, and Germany has installed a new framework of transnational regulation, security, and labor management. As standardized units in digital spreadsheets and inventory lists appear, bodies and environments of distribution disappear across transnational space, producing the capitalist imaginary of a natural, seamless, free flow of things.

One does not have to look far, however, to see that the "free" in this free flow of goods is designed by the market and the state. It is a freedom that entails arresting the movement of certain bodies. Since the development of this rail line across the Taklamakan and Gobi Deserts and the broader BRI,

48 Stefano Harney, *Hapticality in the Undercommons, or From Operations Management to Black Ops*, CuMMA Papers 9 (Helsinki: CuMMA, Aalto University, 2014), 6.
49 Wesley Attewell, in discussion with the author, August 9, 2017.
50 When scrutinizing the politics of financial, corporeal, material movements and how they reorganize social relations with and against profit and power, it becomes clear that "in their drive to quantify and optimize circulation, logistical imaginaries can only enact themselves through the production of space, thereby suturing a form of calculative reason premised on system-wide optimization to the reconfiguration of physical and social landscapes." Charmaine Chua et al., introduction to "Turbulent Circulation: Building a Critical Engagement with Logistics," special issue, *Environment and Planning D: Society and Space* 36, no. 4 (August 2018), 621. The whole special issue is highly recommended to further understand critical logistics.
51 HKTDC Research, "China-Europe Express Trains: On Track to Access Belt and Road Businesses," Hong Kong Means Business, November 1, 2016, hkmb.hktdc.com/en/1X0A7UXL/hktdc-research/China-Europe-Express-Trains-On-Track-to-Access-Belt-and-Road-Businesses.

faster trade through these overland lines has meant increased enforcement of restrictions for local Uyghur, Turkic Muslim, and other Indigenous peoples and ethnic minority groups. In 2016, many from these communities were told to hand in their Chinese passports to local authorities for "examination and management." The region has been heavily policed for forms of "separatist" and "terrorist" activity.[52] This policing ranges from daily identity and mobile phone screenings, WiFi sniffers, and cars with compulsory tracking devices, to 1-meter high-resolution satellite imaging. Xinjiang is currently the key test zone for the entire country's artificial intelligence operations.[53]

Such oppressive fixity is the dark side of logistics.[54] The power that accumulates under the façade of an all-encompassing smooth operator is adept at concealing the fact that it needs friction in order to stay in business. Friction, as anthropologist Anna Lowenhaupt Tsing defines it, is the awkward, unequal, and unstable force that "refuses the lie that global power operates as a well-oiled machine."[55] Understanding these global points of friction is exactly what allows HP to maintain its market dominance, where what is at stake for them involves finding logistical solutions for keeping costs low. Speed, then, is engineered across frictions, traversing between bodies and continents.

It comes as no surprise, then, that HP not only was complicit across its supply chain territories but also actively designed and provided the technology to make the racist population control of colonial occupation in China possible.[56] Similarly, in Israel, HP provides IT infrastructure and support services for the Israeli army and police while also underpinning the system of biometric ID cards, facilitating the militarized settler control and surveillance of the colonized Palestinian population.[57] HP's ambitious control of transnational supply chains thus plays a central role in "technology-enabled racism" within multiple settler colonial and apartheid regimes.

52   "China: Xinjiang Residents Told to Turn in Passports," Al Jazeera, November 25, 2016, www.aljazeera.com/news/2016/11/25/china-xinjiang-residents-told-to-turn-in-passports.
53   Yael Grauer, "Millions of Leaked Police Files Detail Suffocating Surveillance of China's Uyghur Minority," Intercept, January 29, 2021, theintercept.com/2021/01/29/china-uyghur-muslim-surveillance-police.
54   Chua et al., introduction to "Turbulent Circulation."
55   Anna Lowenhaupt Tsing, Friction: An Ethnography of Global Connection (Princeton: Princeton University Press, 2015), 6.
56   Liza Lin and Josh Chin, "U.S. Tech Companies Prop Up China's Vast Surveillance Network," Wall Street Journal, November 26, 2019, www.wsj.com/articles/u-s-tech-companies-prop-up-chinas-vast-surveillance-network-11574786846.
57   "Hewlett-Packard (HP) and the Israeli Occupation," Who Profits from the Occupation, October 2016, www.whoprofits.org/updates/hewlett-packard-hp-and-the-israeli-occupation.

HP's innovations for the BRI aligned with the national interests of the Chinese state because these joint plans assisted the westward movement of industries toward Xinjiang. The consequences of this collaboration are growing ever grimmer, as the state-corporate "mitigation of risks" involves the violent arresting of Uyghur and other Turkic, Indigenous, and ethnic minority populations, along with the increased deterioration of their lands. The implications of these logistical calculations are disturbing ecologies as well as societies, and it is with this urgency that the processes of calculated development and socio-environmental violence need to be seen together as two sides of the same coin.

the bor

V.
Toxic Constellations

As millions of laptops and computer screens wend their way across China toward Western markets, dust storms stubbornly continue eastward. These displaced dusts and sands have too become products themselves, manufactured as an accumulation of soil degradation, labor practices, atmospheric sways, political ideologies, and geological grinds.

The contemporary dust storm moves through a series of chemical transformations, formed when, during its long-range transport, its particles collide with bacteria, gases, and coagulated solid particles. "The dust with pollution aerosols, such as industrial soot, toxic materials, and acidic gases" travels over China's heavily industrialized zones.[58] Particulate matter is then scattered, congealing into a whole new series of constellations, embroiled with manufactured and chemical residue.

These afterlives of unevenly distributed, corporation-led harm ravage the urban remnants of high-carbon industrial practices, extractive economies, and settler colonialism. The dust storms bring a sense of environmental uncanniness; modernity is materially readdressed by the unintentional consequences of its own grand designs. Landscapes remain not backdrops but peripheral deserts alongside the metropolises of Beijing, Seoul, California; frontiers become centered, bringing the outside in. Memories of malpractice, toxic fingerprints, and suspended futures fold into each other and reproduce through toxic constellations.

Calculations of speed and smoothness along corporate supply chains have woven together the state's biopolitical control of the local Uyghur, Indigenous, and ethnic minority populations with its fight against increasingly strange weather. Though this combined control entails the design and engineering of immediate time and space, its long-term, delayed effects form what Rob Nixon would call a temporal disjuncture, a dislocation of causal relations across space.[59] Such geographies of concealment diffuse and obscure the truly global nature of settler colonial dispossession and genocide. Seemingly separate ecological, labor, and Indigenous struggles can be unified in the collective struggle against settler coloniality.

58   Yele Sun et al., "Chemical Composition of Dust Storms in Beijing and Implications for the Mixing of Mineral Aerosol with Pollution Aerosol on the Pathway," *Journal of Geophysical Research: Atmospheres* 110, no. D24 (December 2005), https://doi.org/10.1029/2005JD006054.

"Sandstorm Engulfs Kashi Prefecture in China's Xinjiang," May 31, 2017. Courtesy of CCTV
Video News Agency.

59   Rob Nixon, "Slow Violence, Neoliberalism, and the Environmental Picaresque,"
        Modern Fiction Studies 55, no. 3 (Fall 2009): 449.

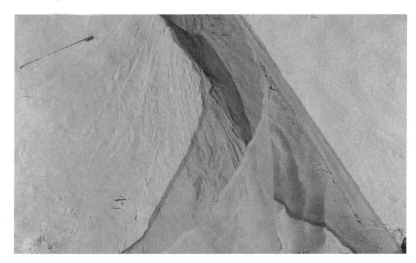

VI.
Naturalized Violence

Even as the BRI cuts through some of the most ecologically fragile places on Earth, the Chinese state aims to have a larger presence in international climate politics, taking on central geopolitical roles in issues of air and water pollution, soil contamination and erosion, and habitat and wildlife loss. At the end of 2019, China's Supreme People's Court made a ground-breaking statement that the BRI should be supported by the judiciary system and that China should "proactively contribute its judicial resources to global environmental governance."[60] This realignment of state judicial resources follows the larger alignment of the BRI with the United Nations' Sustainable Development Goals set up in 2015.[61] "Green" market-driven arrangements made between the Chinese state with other nation-state representatives, international corporations, and the global market in order to manage the climate crisis increasingly occur alongside the continual construction of large-scale infrastructures.

China's future-oriented rhetoric and ambitions to become an "ecological civilization" disguise the settler colonial occupa-tion and dispossession that sustain it, and which constitute, "in Xinjiang particularly, a powerful ruling technique to maintain political stability."[62] Gender studies professor Guldana Salimjan names these ongoing processes as "naturalized violence," where "the construction of a benevolent, caring image of the state further naturalized the violence of displacing" ethnic minorities in the region.[63] The "vacancy" of Xinjiang land persists through exclusion, through the ecotourism and infrastructural projects that replace Indigenous populations as knowledge-keepers and stakeholders in resource management. The top-down labor,

60   Zhang Jingjing , "China's Overseas Investments Face Legal Pushback," interview with Ma Tianjie, *Dialogo Chino*, February 4, 2020, https://dialogochino.net/en/extractive-industries/33346-interview-chinas-overseas-investments-face-legal-pushback.

61   The inclusion of BRI within the UN's 2030 Agenda involves aligning the project with the seventeen Sustainable Development Goals. This would mean prioritizing problems of poverty alleviation, health, education, and employment that constitute "the main concerns of today's global population" under the rubric of the UN. As a project, the BRI is already focused on eight major areas including infrastructure, eco-nomic and trade cooperation, industrial investment, resource development, financial cooperation, cultural exchanges, marine cooperation, and ecological protection. Many of the goals and targets of the 2030 Agenda for Sustainable Development overlap with these eight BRI areas. Donald J. Lewis et al., "Dynamic Synergies be-tween China's Belt and Road Initiative and the UN's Sustainable Development Goals," *Journal of International Business Policy* 4 (2021): 59.

62   Salimjan, "Naturalized Violence," 60.

63   Salimjan, "Naturalized Violence," 60.

"re-education," and counter terrorism programs are dressed in the rehearsed rhetoric of development and class mobility.[64] The toxicity that appears across these processes not only seeps through the heavy industrial and infrastructural projects that so-called "development" entails but also continues through the weaponized state rhetoric that further mobilizes and obfuscates these settler colonial processes.

As sand from the desert protests against the transnational infrastructural and state settler expansion in the form of increasingly frequent dust storms, these storms collude with strong winds and sweep across thousands of kilometers. The collective struggle against settler coloniality must include the interconnected resistance across different deserts, across many stolen homelands, across captive Indigenous populations. It must hold colonial systems accountable—not only oppressive states but also companies like HP and their globally distributed production. But we must also interrogate narratives that prioritize "progress" and economic well-being, as they too often spring from racist and exclusionary ideologies. This interrogation must also go hand in hand with a denaturalization of "green" rhetoric— afforestation, solar power, and clean energy are often complicit in the settler occupation of lands, displacing environmental devastation to some *elsewhere*.[65] Finally, critiques limited by national boundaries will only reinforce the nature of global capitalism's inherent self-concealment by obscuring the transnational reach of dust storms, supply chains, and settler colonial exchange of technology and capital. With the growth of the BRI and its influence, this demands all the more the disentangling of networked processes, especially as they become increasingly obfuscated and difficult to locate.

By registering the dust storm as an epistemological phenomenon and reevaluating each scale that is deployed across this rail route—from the frontier where wars are being waged against growing deserts, to the SEZ where technologies of spatial inversion are bringing outside markets in, to the supply chain where logistical calculations are complicit in creating a carceral continuum—we pierce our modern geographies of concealment and bring into view the lattice of violent relations that sustains the modern state of China and its international markets.

64   Salimjan, "Naturalized Violence."
65   Reinsch and Arrieta-Kenna, "A Dark Spot for the Solar Energy Industry."

Bongani Kona is a writer and the editor of *Our Ghosts Were Once People: Stories on Death and Dying* (Jonathan Ball, 2021). His work has appeared in *Chimurenga*, *The Baffler*, BBC Radio 4, and the collections *Safe House: Explorations in Creative Nonfiction* (Dundurn, 2016) and *The Daily Assortment of Astonishing Things and Other Stories* (Interlink, 2016). He works in the Department of History at the University of the Western Cape and is a co-curator of the *Archive of Forgetfulness* podcast.

ARCHIVE OF
FORGETFULNESS

A CONVERSATION
WITH
BONGANI KONA

Samia Henni (SH):

> During the strict restrictions on mobility that various governments declared to slow down the spread of the COVID-19 virus, you and Huda Tayob co-created and co-curated the podcast series *Conversations with Neighbours*, as part of Archive of Forgetfulness, an archive of mobility and infrastructures. Could you tell us about the genesis of this project?

Bongani Kona (BK):

> Thank you so much for your interest in the podcast series, Samia, and for initiating the conversation. I have to be open with you, though, from the onset about my unease with speaking as a lone voice about a project that by design includes a symphony of voices and holds out this invitation for us to think things through communally. That said, I'll do my best. There is a long backstory to all of this. The Archive of Forgetfulness has its roots, or rather, is built on the foundations laid by an earlier Goethe-Institut project called "Neighbourhood/s." This earlier project—which over a two-year period periodically brought together six brilliant artists, thinkers, curators, and writers from South Africa, Rwanda, Morocco, Egypt, Sudan, and Nigeria—was really propelled by the idea that the "the Sahara does not separate; it connects."[1] It's a theme that also threads through the Archive of Forgetfulness podcast series, *Conversations with Neighbours*. So anyway, the Goethe-Institut reached out to Huda Tayob to ask if she'd be interested in developing the project further. Huda said yes, and, in turn, she asked if I'd be interested in coming on board. I've always held Huda

---

1   The participants were Ali Al Adawy (Egypt), Eric Ngangare (Rwanda), Jumoke Sanwo (Nigeria), Omnia Shawkat (Sudan), Princess Mhlongo (South Africa), and Zoubida Mseffer (Morocco).

in high regard as a scholar and as a person, and so of course I said yes. But by then—I mean when Huda and I started corresponding from our respective homes in Cape Town in 2020—the picture of the world looked vastly different. Empty highways. Closed borders. Police- and military-enforced curfews. It seemed urgent, necessary, to think in that moment of connections between places, peoples, and histories. So, in a very real way the Archive of Forgetfulness picks up on some of the themes explored in the Neighbourhood/s project (Inter-African migrations, for instance), but instead of focusing on the neighborhood as fixed in space and time, we were also interested in how "neighborliness" might enable and engender relationships across borders. And since we are also both interested in political histories and projects that imagine Africa as a "borderless world" and what these mean for our present, we also strived to think of movement and connection beyond their literal definitions. So long story short, this was our starting point.

SH: Could you comment on the choice of the terms "archive" and "forgetfulness" that characterize the premises of your project? What do you mean by these terms? What do they refer to?

BK: The title of the project is inspired by Mahmoud Darwish's prose poem, Memory for Forgetfulness (1987), and I'll quote directly from our website about the project itself:

The Archive of Forgetfulness is an archive of mobility, infrastructure, and story-telling; it holds together acts of remembering, collecting, and gathering stories often untold. The contributions renew lines of connections, resurface forgotten conversations, and establish the beginnings of future collaborations. This project is a space for interrogating the archival gesture, from the bodily and spoken, to the written and performed.[2]

That said, what is inspiring about a collaborative project such as this is how we don't ascribe a fixed meaning to those words, "archive" and "forgetfulness." I'll give an example. In Episode 6 of the podcast, one of the people we spoke to is the Angolan composer Victor Gama, about his long-term research project in the Namib Desert. The project, broadly speaking, traces the arc from Thomas More's book *Utopia* (1516) to apartheid South Africa's nuclear weapons program in the unfinished work of young Angolan anthropologist Augusto Zita. Zita subsequently disappeared during the years of Angola's war with apartheid South Africa, but Victor is in possession of his unpublished research. I mention Victor's documentary project, *Tectonik: TOMBWA*, because, like Augusto Zita, Victor holds to the animist belief that all things are imbued with spiritual matter.[3] The word "archive," then, would take on a different meaning to someone who sees the world in that way. So that has been really enriching, getting access to all of these different perspectives.

SH: You mentioned your interest in political histories that imagined Africa as a "borderless world." Could you elaborate on these imaginaries and imageries? What did they mean then? What do they mean today?

BK: These are questions that I get tremendously excited about, but if we don't set down parameters, we may never stop talking! So, in the interest of everyone's time, I'll draw from the podcast series. I will say though that Achille Mbembe's astonishing essay, "The Idea of a Borderless World," first delivered as a Tanner Lecture on Human Values at Yale University and reproduced in an issue of *Chimurenga*, is worth revisiting, particularly in relation to your question about what these ideas

2   "About," Archive of Forgetfulness, https://archiveofforgetfulness.com/about.
3   Victor Gama, *tectonik: TOMBWA – geografias em colisão* (2013), video documentary, 32:19, https://vimeo.com/61796598.

mean today. One of the arguments he puts forward is that "the western archive does not help us to develop an idea of borderlessness," because "the western archive is premised on the crystallisation of the idea of a border."[4] Like I said, it's an incredibly insightful lecture/essay and one that is worth looking at.

But your questions remind me of Episode 5 of the podcast, which features an interview with the Egyptian filmmaker Jihan el-Tahri. And just to give some background, Jihan used to work as a foreign correspondent covering politics in the Middle East for the British and American press. She walked away from this career in disillusionment, and started making documentary films in the early '90s. Her area of interest is political history, and her films cover large swaths of the second half of the twentieth century in Africa, from the killing of Patrice Lumumba to the Battle of Cuito Cuanavale in Angola, which Nelson Mandela later described as "a turning point in the struggle to free the continent and our country from the scourge of apartheid."[5] In Jihan's own words, she is "obsessed" with liberation movements and, in particular, the question: "What happened to the noble cause of independence and the struggles that were fought to achieve it?" I mention Jihan because her films—*Africa in Pieces: The Tragedy of the Great Lakes* (2000) and *Cuba, An African Odyssey* (2007) are good examples of this—capture the transnational networks of solidarity, across the continent and beyond, that emerged in the fight against colonialism. So, in my mind, her films are both wonderful works of art but also incredibly important historical documents for those reasons. And to answer your question about what these ideas mean for our present, Jihan ends my favorite of her films, *Cuba, An African Odyssey*, with the words:

4   Achille Mbembe, "The Idea of a Borderless World," *Chimurenga*, October 16, 2018, https://chimurengachronic.co.za/the-idea-of-a-borderless-world.

The battle to liberate Africa from colonialism had been won, but the war conducted in the name of real independence is still being fought. Revolutionaries like Che Guevara, Patrice Lumumba, Amilcar Cabral, and Agostinho Neto are today icons all over the continent. Their words still echo in African shantytowns as inspiration to follow if Africans are to change their lot. The means to achieve true independence may be different today but this objective has never changed.[6]

Powerful stuff.

SH: You also mentioned that "the Sahara does not sepa-rate; it connects." Are you referring to the disciplines and people that use the term "Sahara" to separate the north-ern parts of Africa from so-called "sub-Saharan Africa"? How did this constructed "separation" operate? How does Archive of Forgetfulness voice these connections?

BK: There are long-standing connections between the northern parts of the continent and "sub-Saharan Africa." Connections and circulations that exist through language, trade, education, architecture, religion, music, etc., and to underline the point, Episode 8 of the podcast is devoted to tracing the afterlives of the trans-Saharan trade routes of the eighth century. But to answer your question more directly, we have to return again to Episode 5. Jihan el-Tahri, among other provocations, questions the very legitimacy of the term "sub-Saharan Africa." Where does it come from, and is it right that a term that splits the continent into two racialized zones, "Black Africa" and "Arab Africa," is vested with so much authority? Jihan traces the origins of the term to North American foreign policy and really

5   Nelson Mandela, speech at a rally on the occasion of the 38th anniversary of the start of the Cuban Revolution, July 26, 1991, Matanzas, Cuba, transcript, http://db.nelsonmandela.org/speeches/pub_view.asp?pg=item& ItemID=NMS1526.
6   Jihan el-Tahri, dir., *Cuba, An African Odyssey* (France: Temps Noir, 2007).

outlines what is at stake in the continued separation of the north from the south. Why is it, she asks, that we date African Independence to Ghana in 1957 and not Egypt in 1952? What politics is at work in that erasure of Egypt (and the north) in the larger history of liberation on the continent? Why are the terms "Arab" and "African" seen as mutually exclusive? Those are good questions to ponder.

SH: I would add Amazigh people—the West calls them "Berber"—to the constructed division between "Arab" and "Black" Africans, and stress that there are people who are both Arab and Black or Amazigh and Black. This division is also rooted in European colonial practices, which still haunt the continent.

In the *Conversations with Neighbours* that you and Huda conducted, could you recall how your interlocutors described African deserts, their histories, and stories?

BK: I'm actually looking at Emmanuel Iduma's astonishingly brilliant travelogue, *A Stranger's Pose*, which is on my desk. Huda and I were lucky enough to get Emmanuel to read a few extracts from his book in Episode 4, and here he recounts a conversation with a stranger in Bamako, Mali:

When I tell him our mission—overland from Lagos to Sarajevo, along the coast—he says he's happy we aren't travelling through the desert.

There are many burial places in the desert, he begins to aver. We find stones in the desert. We remove the stones and see a decaying corpse. The name on the document remains legible. This is how we recognise the person.

In the desert, death means nothing.[7]

7   Emmanuel Iduma, *A Stranger's Pose* (Abuja: Cassava Republic, 2018), 116.

But again, to answer your question more concretely, we've been talking about the circulation of ideas and culture, and Huda's conversation in Episode 8 with Moshood Jimba, the director of the Centre for Ilorin Manuscripts and Culture at Kwara State University in Nigeria, is one of the most illuminating on the subject. In the episode, he shares how the roots of his interests in manuscripts date back to 2008, following an arduous overland journey from Ilorin in Nigeria to Timbuktu in Mali. Moshood Jimba subsequently wrote an account of his travels, *From Ilorin to Timbuktu: (A Journey across West Africa in Search of the African Past)* (2010). In his travelogue, he recounts in detail how in centuries past (fourteenth through eighteenth), Timbuktu was a cosmopolitan place where different peoples mixed together—traders traveling overland through the desert or by boat via the Niger River—and an esteemed center of scholarship with public libraries stocked with important books and manuscripts. Moshood Jimba also explores, among other things, the longer history of traveling to study in neighboring countries in West and North Africa, and it is really fascinating. But also in that same episode, Moroccan writer and translator Omar Berrada resurfaces the intimate history of slavery (another story of the desert) in Morocco through the silences in his family.

SH: I listened to all the podcast episodes, and I hope that our readers will be inspired by this conversation and will listen to the terrific conversations you and Huda have gathered. Omar Berrada's story and history is fascinating and relevant. Could you please tell that important story of the desert?

BK: Thank you Samia. Omar Berrada is an extraordinary writer, and in an earlier essay I'd like to mention here, he takes umbrage with novelist Tahar Ben Jelloun's assertion that "in Morocco one tends to feel more Arab than African. We're really in the northernmost part of Africa and we have a very different history. Personally, I don't feel at all African. That's not a pejorative or mean statement, but I don't feel African because I have no ties to Africa."[8] To claim that Morocco has no ties to Africa would mean, among other things, erasing the history of the trans-Saharan slave trade. His refusal to forget, I think, is what animates Omar's deeply moving contribution in Episode 8. He probes the silences and collective amnesia around the trans-Saharan slave trade, silences which exist in his own family within the wider society in Morocco. At the center of his reflection is Mmi Aziza, his once enslaved great-great-grandmother, who lived until the 1960s. How recent is that? "My great-great-grandfather bought her on a slave market," Omar says, "and made her his wife." He then asks the question: "How many families in Morocco are keeping their Africanness at bay? Hiding behind an idealized Arabness and the illusion of proximity to Europe? How does that account for the way sub-Saharan migrants are currently treated in our cities?" It's an intimate evocation of a painful history—a history that sits on the skin and travels through bloodlines.

SH: Along with the podcast series, Archive of Forgetfulness includes essays, an online exhibition, and regional projects. Could you tell us more about the singularities and interrelations of these various archives of mobility?

BK: In October 2020, we sent out an open call seeking projects which focus on the things that enable us to move—literally or figuratively—and to guide the process, we asked a set of questions, the same questions which framed some of our podcast conversations:

8   Tahar Ben Jelloun, "Politics and Literature," interview by Thomas Spear, trans. Caren Litherland, in "Post/Colonial Conditions: Exiles, Migrations, and Nomadisms, vol. 2," ed. Françoise Lionnet and Ronnie Scharfman, special issue, *Yale French Studies*, no. 83 (1993): 31.

- How might we trace the afterlives of the trans-Saharan trade routes of the eighth century to surface alternative radical imaginaries of travel and movement?

- How might rethinking the global Swahili worlds reframe our understandings of connections across oceans?
- What personal, political, and cultural histories emerge via infrastructures of mobility?

- What do lines of flight reveal of our shared planetary futures?

- How are larger histories of non-alignment, anti-colonial revolt, and pan-Africanism inscribed into the built environment?

- What remains of political and cultural ideas that imagined the African continent as "the utopia of a borderless world"? How do these dreams of freedom, of other worlds that might have been possible, haunt our ability to move freely or otherwise?

The response we got was really astounding. We received over 300 submissions, and we selected twenty-seven projects, which are featured in the online exhibition. The selected projects include essays, poetry, films, sound works, multimedia, etc., by various practitioners from across the continent and beyond. Then, in addition to the exhibition, six other projects, produced by the regional curators, will be featured on the website at intervals throughout the year. Then, lastly, to circle back to what I'd said at the very beginning, this a collaborative and collective project, and the website reflects that. It includes a symphony of voices and holds out this invitation for us to think things through communally.

Dalal Musaed Alsayer is assistant professor of architecture at Kuwait University. Her research lies at the intersection of architecture, environment, and development in the context of Arabia during the twentieth century. She is the coauthor *of Pan-Arab Modernism 1968–2008: History of Architectural Practice in The Middle East* (Actar, 2021) and is the cofounding editor of *Current: Collective for Architecture History and Environment*. She holds a BArch from Kuwait University; a Master of Science in Architecture and Urban Design from Columbia GSAPP; a Master of Design Studies in Urbanism, Landscape, Ecology from Harvard GSD; and a MS and a PhD in Architecture from the University of Pennsylvania.

DALAL MUSAED ALSAYER

ANYWHERE, USA: ARAMCO'S HOUSING IN SAUDI ARABIA'S DESERT

يا مل عين تسهر الليل ما بات
قزيت من مساي يجنب الجرين

حلفت لو اعطى الرطب والخضروات
وتكثر الارزاق عندي : مآزين
ولوعطوني مع اللبن سبع حاجات
إني على قد الحصية لا شين

ودي بهم لو التمنى خرافات
يا ليتنا مع ضفهم نازلين
لوكان والله ماخبرنا مراحات
لكن طبع الباديه يستوي لي
يا ليتنا يا [ذمير] نمشي مظاهير
في وسط هي دايم الدوم نشهاه
وياليت ماشفنا السواني على البير
ونحيسفهم يا ليتنا ما عرفناه

O weary eye, sleepless at night
I am weary of my stay near the harvests
I swear that even if I am given dates and
    vegetables
And my blessings grow, I will not be well
Even if I am given seven kinds of food with milk,
And as much as I receive, I will be worse.
I long for them, even if wishing is a myth,
I wish we stayed by them in their land
By God we do not give compliments freely
But the way of the desert suits me
Muneer, I wish we were traveling in caravans,
Among the people we always long for.
And I wish we did not see wheels (or water
    extracting structures) over the wells,
And their measuring units, I wish we have never
    known.[1]

---

1   Translated by Sara Saad Alajmi with special thanks to Badriyah AlSalem. Written by
     the female poet ʿAlyaʾ bint Dawī al-Dilbḥī, this two-part poem—which is most often
     shared orally—yearns for the desert. In the first part, the poet responds to a question
     from a fellow tribe member about why her mental health has not yet improved
     after relocating to a city in the Qassim region. In the second part, where she is also
     speaking to her son, Muneer, the poet expresses her desire to roam the desert rather
     than experience the supposedly easier conditions of city life. Ibn Rawās, ʿAbd Allāh
     ibn Muḥammad, Shāʾirāt Min al-Bādiyah (Female Poets from the Desert), eighth
     edition, vol. I (Sharjah, UAE: al-rawy, 2002), 105–106.

In March 1934, a custom US Fairchild 71 airplane arrived in the Eastern Provinces of Saudi Arabia. The airplane was ordered by Standard Oil of California (SoCal) from Kreider-Reisner Aircraft Company to assist its subsidiary, California Arabian Standard Oil Company (CASOC), in its aerial reconnaissance of the Saudi Arabia desert.[2] Just a year before, SoCal signed a concession for oil exploration from the Saudi king, Ibn Saud, granting the company exclusive exploratory rights over 371,263 square miles (961,567 square kilometers) of Saudi Arabia, including all of Ash Sharqīyah (Eastern Province), and parts of Al Ḥudūd ash Shamāliyah (Northern Province) and Ar Riyāḍ (Riyadh).[3] The Fairchild seated only four people; it was equipped with 36 by 18 inch wheels, the largest available on the market at that time, an

2   CASOC was renamed the Arabian American Oil Company (Aramco) on January 31, 1944, to recast the company and its operations in a new light. By using the name Aramco, the company hoped to assuage rising pressures from non-US employees and the Crown Prince. The 1940s were characterized by the Saudi government's continued displeasure with CASOC with regards to its unjust treatment towards its Saudi employees and by the Saudi government's desire to reap the (financial) benefits of the nation's oil. Historian Robert Vitalis calls this strategy, as well as others deployed by the US company, "mythmaking." See Robert Vitalis, *America's Kingdom: Mythmaking on the Saudi Oil Frontier* (Stanford: Stanford University Press, 2007), 77–79.

3   Paul Lunde, "A King and a Concession," *Aramco World*, May/June 1984, https://archive.aramcoworld.com/issue/198403/a.king.and.a.concession.htm. The contract between SoCal and the Kingdom of Saudi Arabia was signed on May 29, 1933.

The US Fairchild 71 over the Arabian desert, Sink, Khaliba, Saudi Arabia, 1934. Photograph by Joseph D. Mountain. Courtesy of Smithsonian National Air and Space Museum (NASM 92-15876).

extra-large tank to increase its flying radius to 350 miles, and a hole in the bottom to allow for aerial photographs.

It was supposedly through this aerial reconnaissance that CASOC had put "Arabia onto paper."[4] Dividing the country into 10-kilometer strips, US pilots Richard C. Kerr and Charley Rocheville, along with CASOC geologists Robert P. Miller and Schuyler B. Henry, began to systematically construct an environmental imaginary of Saudi Arabia and render its desert "legible."[5] The desert's complex histories and narratives, and its particular geomorphology, were illegible to CASOC, and the company never tried to learn and understand these intricacies. Instead, CASOC rendered the desert visible through means and methods exclusively comprehensible to itself. To do this, they "highlighted the visible geology and terrain of the five kilometers on either side of the plane in flight. They located water holes, camel trails, and settlements as well as surface structures. After each flight, a

4   Wallace Stegner, *Discovery!* (Beirut: Middle East Export Press, 1971), 42.
5   On environmental imaginaries in the Middle East, see Diana K. Davis and Edmund Burke III, eds., *Environmental Imaginaries of the Middle East and North Africa, Ecology and History* (Athens: Ohio University Press, 2011). See also Richard Peet and Michael Watts, eds., *Liberation Ecologies: Environment, Development, Social Movement*, 2nd ed. (London: Routledge, 2004); and Julie Cidell, "Sustainable Imaginaries and the Green Roof on Chicago's City Hall," *Geoforum* 86 (November 2017): 169–176. On legibility, see James C. Scott, *Seeing Like A State: How Certain Schemes to Improve the Human Condition Have Failed* (New Haven: Yale University Press, 1998).

traverse map was drawn indicating the plane's route. Especially interesting features were noted and later photographed to be included in mosaic maps."[6]

Seen through the plane's portal and the camera's lens from above, the Saudi desert was rendered flat, beige, empty, and uniform. The desert's intricate histories, social networks, and nuances were compressed into a geological image that was mapped and dissected in the hopes of finding the "black gold" in its depths. Through this systematic mapping of the Saudi desert, CASOC began to assemble an environmental imaginary of the desert in which the environment and all that it contained was cast as backward, archaic, and in dire need of US technological prowess. This environmental image also extended to its inhabitants. CASOC employees also took photographs of people living in Saudi Arabia with the desert set as a desolate background as they posed in awe at the marvels of US technology, which further propagated this environmental imaginary.

Describing their initial experiences of Saudi Arabia's Eastern Provinces in 1936, CASOC employees wrote that, "looking back, it seems that the sand blew more often, with greater velocity and that sandstorms were of far greater frequency than today. That is an assumption because now we have acres and acres of lawns and thousands of shrubs and trees."[7] This assumption

An image of the Saudi desert captured by the US Fairchild 71. Photograph by Joseph D. Mountain. Courtesy of Smithsonian National Air and Space Museum (NASM 9A12496-083).

6   Scott McMurray, *Energy to the World: The Story of Aramco*, vol. 1 (Houston: Aramco Services Company, 2011), 68.

The US Fairchild 71 next to an Arabian tent surrounded by Saudi Arabs. Photograph by Joseph D. Mountain. Courtesy of Smithsonian National Air and Space Museum (NASM 92-15940).

that the sand was unyielding, that it was unnavigable, wild, and needed to be overcome, was a dominant trope in most Western discourses describing the Arabian deserts at the time.[8] It permeated the architectural and urban discourse used by CASOC—and later Arabian American Oil Company (Aramco)—as it developed a sprawling oil empire across the Kingdom of Saudi Arabia, with the company town of Dhahran at its epicenter. With construction beginning in 1934, Dhahran was to exclusively house US employees and their families. The project was never about understanding the Saudi desert, but about transforming it into a typical US suburb. To do this, CASOC worked both

7   "Aramco Communities: Then and Now," *Arabian Sun and Flare*, April 29, 1953, 2.
8   See, for example, L. March Phillipps, *In The Desert* (London: Edward Arnold, 1905); Wilfred Thesiger, *Arabian Sands* (New York: E.P. Dutton, 1959); H.R.P. Dickson, *The Arab of the Desert: A Glimpse into Badawi Life in Kuwait and Sau'di Arabia* (London: Allen & Unwin, 1959); and Ritchie Calder, *Man Against the Desert*, rev. ed. (London: Allen & Unwin, 1959). The desert and the taming of the shifting sands were also extensively covered in Aramco's magazine, *Aramco World*; see "Campaign Against The Shifting Sands," *Aramco World*, February 1962; Graham Chandler, "Desertification and Civilization," *Aramco World*, December 2007, 36–43; Daniel Da Cruz, "How They Find The Oil," *Aramco World*, February 1966; Daniel Da Cruz, "Dry—But Why?," *Aramco World*, August 1967; Daniel Da Cruz, "Convoy To Nowhere," *Aramco World*, June 1969; John Lawton, "Secrets of the Sands," *Aramco World*, February 1988; Robert Lebling, "Dos Passos in the Desert," *Aramco World*, August 1997; Pamela Roberson, "Dunescapes," *Aramco World*, August 1984; "Tracks Across The Desert," *Aramco World*, April 1962; and William Tracy, "The Restless Sands," *Aramco World*, June 1965.

materially and culturally, importing homes, grass, machines, and social customs. From the first imported bungalows in 1936 to the neat cul-de-sacs and little box-shaped houses lining its streets by 1945, the Saudi town of Dhahran became the company town of Dhahran. CASOC/Aramco effectively created an "Anywhere, USA" in the Saudi desert, transforming the desert through imported architecture, practices, and norms.

The Company Town of Dhahran

In 1934, CASOC's acting operation foreman, Fred Davies, suggested "that the company undertake a dramatic housing program—a small town in the desert—far more elaborate than the bare minimum that might be the norm for such camp facilities."[9] In line with other company towns built in the region, such as Abadan, Dhahran was built for practicality and insularity. The decision to build a permanent settlement came in the fall of 1934, when the results of the aerial reconnaissance deemed the area known as Dammam Dome, a geological formation near Dhahran, to have the most potential for underground petroleum. That November, Walter Haenggi, a rig builder and construction foreman from the US who previously oversaw the construction housing for the British-operated concession in Awali, Bahrain, began scouting locations near Dammam Dome to begin construction of the first permanent structures. Davies stated that "the initial community was to consist of living quarters, a cookhouse, a mess hall, and a recreation room. In addition to these living and recreational quarters, an adequate number of offices and a geological laboratory were required. Finally, [CASOC] would also have to drill water wells, install its own plumbing system, and build a power plant."[10] Prior to settling in Dhahran, the early employees of CASOC would move from one expedition site to the next, setting up camp in tents along the way and staying at a head office in the city of Hofuf between expeditions.[11]

---

9   McMurray, *Energy to the World*, 1:73.
10 McMurray, *Energy to the World*, 1:73.
11 These expeditions were nonetheless quite expansive in terms of personnel and equipment. For example, on a typical expedition there were twenty-seven to forty-two people (two US geologists, one interpreter, a cook and his helper, a houseboy, a mechanic and his helper, a car driver, three camel drivers, and somewhere between fifteen and thirty soldiers); three Ford V-8 cars (one touring, one half-ton pick-up, and one 2 3/4-ton express body truck); twelve camels (capable of carrying 400 pounds each); four tents (three 10 x 20 foot "native" tents with grass mat floors and one 16 x 8 foot silk tent); two collapsing tables, chairs, and cots; one short-wave radio; one chronometer; one transit; one portable sketch board; two Brunton compasses; seventeen water storage containers (eight six-gallon water cans; six 6-to-10-gallon water skins; three water bags); in addition to food and miscellaneous

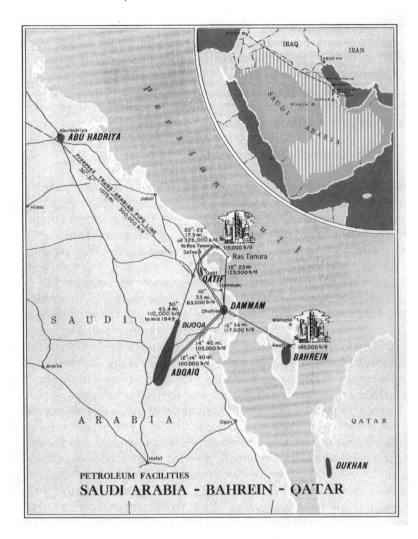

Map of the Eastern Provinces of Saudi Arabia showing the key oil facilities, 1948. Aramco, *Arabian Oil and Its Relation to World Oil Needs* (1948), 22. Courtesy of Aramco.

Most of the CASOC geologists were in their twenties and thirties at the time, recently married or married with children, and living halfway around the world was becoming more challenging. When Reginald Stoner, then-vice president of SoCal, sent a cable in June 1935 that the company would be shipping four prefabricated, air-conditioned, two-bedroom bunkhouses and "some air-conditioned cottages suitable for family living" from the US to Dhahran, many CASOC employees were overjoyed.[12] This move on behalf of SoCal marked a shift in CASOC's operation, from an exploratory enterprise to a more permanent settlement. In the summer of 1936, the first two bunkhouses arrived from the US, and CASOC secured "a 70,000-acre reservation for the permanent camp and its necessary installations" in Dhahran.[13] While it took almost two years for the "discovery" of oil in commercial quantities, the US had already started building the suburb of Dhahran.

On April 14, 1937, the first wives arrived in Dhahran. Both women were white Americans, who were married to two of the white American CASOC employees. A few weeks later, four more cottages arrived. Five months later, four more women and three children arrived—all girls and all uniformly American, white, and Christian.[14] The arrival of these wives, mothers, and daughters was not only symbolic of the permanent nature of the settlement but also emblematic of the type of settlements that CASOC envisioned. Maintaining a specific kind of nuclear family (that is, again, white and Christian), was a central tenet for SoCal, especially as its employees confronted an environment and society vastly different from that to which they were accustomed. US domestic principles were able to remain intact in Dhahran through gridded streets, cul-de-sacs, and little box-shaped houses lining the streets. By February 1940, there were ninety-five cottages, several dormitories, and bachelor quarters for 371 US employees, along with thirty-eight wives and sixteen children sustained by "a force of 3,300 Saudi Arab, Bahraini, Indian and other employees."[15] While CASOC had to downsize its operations during World War II, by July 1945, there were 1,720

equipment. As can be seen from the extensive list, even in expeditions, there was a hierarchy apparent in accommodations and equipment. The three US employees would sleep in the silk tent and eat a typical US diet, but the rest would sleep in the "native tents" with their grass mat floors. For a full list of personnel and equipment, see McMurray, *Energy to the World*, 1:67.

12   Stegner, *Discovery*, 75.
13   Stegner, *Discovery*, 78.
14   McMurray, *Energy to the World*, 1:83. It should be noted that the men who had the highest seniority were joined by their wives and children. Many lower-ranked US employees still lived in bachelor quarters, and non-US employees were not allowed to be joined by their families.

Bachelor housing quarters — Dhahran.

Portable bachelor dormitory — Dhahran.

American family arriving home by taxi — Dhahran.

American schoolchildren at play.

Social gathering — Ras Tanura.

Typical family home — Dhahran.

Spread from *Aramco and World Oil* showing Aramcon Living in Dhahran, Saudi Arabia, c. late 1940s. Roy Lebkicher, *Aramco and World Oil* (New York: Russell F. Moore Company, 1952), 104–105. Courtesy of Aramco.

US citizens living in Dhahran, remaking it into a little piece of the USA.[16]

The 1940s marked a threshold for the Kingdom, Dhahran, and their respective relationships to the US. Not only did SoCal rename CASOC to the Arabian American Oil Company (Aramco) at the suggestion of Herbert Feis, State Department adviser, to recast the Arabian-US relations as a partnership, but James Moose was also assigned as the first full-time Chargé D'Affaires to the Kingdom.[17] At the same time that the Kingdom was becoming geopolitically independent, Dhahran was becoming even more insular. By the late 1940s, Dhahran had a commissary fully stocked with US products, a bakery, K-9 schools that followed the US curriculum, a hospital, a bowling alley, a movie theater, swimming pools, and lush green yards. Aramco also maintained its very own newspaper called the *Arabian Sun and Flare* and a full-fledged social calendar: parades for US holidays, nativity scenes for Christmas, imported turkeys for Thanksgiving, scouting for boys and girls.[18] This Dhahran existed for the US employees of Aramco (who were given the moniker Aramcon by the company), and the Aramcons recreated it in a vision of the US from its architecture to its customs. According to environmental historian Toby C. Jones, "Aramco's homemade, fenced-in town was more American than America."[19] This persistent desire to display Aramco's nationalistic patriotism stemmed from the company's need to remain a US entity, independent from the emerging US-Saudi political relations and the fledgling independent Saudi state.[20] By maintaining its nationalistic US practices,

15   Stegner, *Discovery*, 150; Faisal A. Al-Mubarak, "Oil, Urban Development and Planning in the Eastern Province of Saudi Arabia: The Case of the Arab American Oil Company in the 1930s–1970s," *Journal of Architecture and Planning: King Saud University* 11 (1999): 39.

16   Jack Mahoney, "Editorial," *The Dust Rag*, July 22, 1945.

17   On the US-Saudi relationship during the 1940s, see Barry Rubin, "Anglo-American Relations in Saudi Arabia, 1941–1945," *Journal of Contemporary History* 14, no. 2 (April 1979); 253–267; Douglas Little, "Pipeline Politics: America, TAPLINE, and the Arabs," *The Business History Review* 64, no. 2 (Summer 1990): 255–285; Frank Jungers et al., *American Perspectives of Aramco, the Saudi-Arabian Oil-Producing Company, 1930s to 1980s: Oral History Transcript* (Berkeley: Bancroft Library, Regional Oral History Office, 1995); Irvine H. Anderson, *Aramco the United States and Saudi Arabia: A Study of the Dynamics of Foreign Oil Policy, 1933–1950* (Princeton: Princeton University Press, 2014).

18   *The Dust Rag* was the original name of Aramco's official newspaper. It was renamed *The Oily Bird* for one issue (October 10, 1945), then *Arabian Sun* (October 21, 1945–May 26, 1946), *Arabian Sun and Flare* (June 2, 1945–June 22, 1955), and finally *Sun and Flare* (June 29, 1955–November 11, 1970).

19   Toby Craig Jones, *Desert Kingdom: How Oil and Water Forged Modern Saudi Arabia* (Cambridge, MA: Harvard University Press, 2010), 44; see also Nora Johnson, *You Can Go Home Again: An Intimate Journey* (Garden City, NY: Doubleday, 1982).

20   This nationalist desire can also be attributed to the fact that many US employees still saw their Saudi Arab employees as inferior and subordinate to them. See McMurray, *Energy to the World*, 1:163.

Imported trees and homes on G Street, Dhahran, Saudi Arabia, 1949. Photography by Karl S. Twitchell. Courtesy of Karl S. Twitchell Collection, Special Collections, Fine Arts Library, Harvard University.

the company could continue to operate in an exclusionary manner, bestowing its benefits only to those within the limits of the company town, keeping Saudi Arabia a mere background, somewhere out there beyond the fence.

Racial Hierarchies and Spatial Segregation

When the cottages and women arrived, so did the fence that surrounded the town of Dhahran. For even though Aramco employed Saudi Arabs, Bahraini, Indian, and other employees, it developed a housing strategy that segregated the population along marital and racial lines.[21] These strategies developed by SoCal were aligned with both its earlier operations in Peru and Venezuela, which separated between "native" and "oilman," and with racially driven segregation in the US, as historian Robert Vitalis has explicitly stated:

> Operations in the oil town, Dhahran, rested on a set of exclusionary practices and norms that were themselves legacies of earlier mining booms and market formation in the American West and Southwest. This was a system of privilege and inequality, which we know as Jim Crow

21   Reel R-84, Aramco Folder, IBEC Housing Corporation (IHC): Middle East: Saudi Arabia, Series R: IBEC Microfilm, International Basic Economy Corporation (IBEC) records, Rockefeller Archive Center, Sleepy Hollow, NY, USA (hereafter RAC).

in the United States, as Apartheid in South Africa, and as racism more generally.[22]

At the same time that fully-assembled houses were delivered from the US, UK, and Sweden to house Aramcons, "crews built palm frond–covered *barastis* [huts] for Saudis as well, with several workers living in each dwelling."[23] These temporary shelters for workers were relegated to the margins of the compound, and the only permanent building was a mosque, a gift from the King Ibn Saud, (in)aptly named the Mosque of the Adenese, after the Yemeni laborers who constructed it.[24] The stark reality of this spatial confinement was that

men, separated from their families for up to two or more weeks at a time, ate, socialized, and slept under crude *barastis* of woven palm leaves hung from wooden frames. Water was cooled in large clay pots, toilet facilities were informal, there was no power, and fires caused by candles and stoves were frequent. Meanwhile, the Americans were busy constructing a more or less complete suburb, derived from their own environmental context. The suburb had power, paved streets, recreation areas, American-style houses, schools, etc.[25]

This diverse, multinational group of Arab, East African, South Asian, and Italian workers, who, by failing to possess US citizenship, were not counted as Aramcon, lived in what was originally—and derogatively—called a "Coolie Camp," later referred to as the "Saudi Camp."[26] "Coolie" was the pejorative term for "unskilled laborer," stemming back to the Tamil word *kuli*, which means "wages" or "hire."[27] The term was first used by the Portuguese in India in the latter part of the sixteenth century, only to be inherited by their British colonial-counterpart and subsequently passed on to US companies working in Arabia. The term was used freely until a company-wide public relations campaign

22   Vitalis, *America's Kingdom*, xiii.
23   McMurray, *Energy to the World*, 1:60.
24   Yemen is commonly known as Aden.
25   Jon Parssinen and Kaizir Talib, "A Traditional Community and Modernization: Saudi Camp, Dhahran," *Journal of Architectural Education* 35, no. 3 (Spring 1982): 14.
26   Munira Khayyat, Yasmine Khayyat, and Rola Khayyat, "Pieces of Us: The Intimate as Imperial Archive," *Journal of Middle East Women's Studies* 14, no. 3 (November 2018): 278.
27   See Gaiutra Bahadur, *Coolie Woman: The Odyssey of Indenture* (Chicago: University of Chicago Press, 2014).

"Arab Camp" comprising of makeshift homes and *barastis* (woven palm frond huts) in the foreground and "Senior Staff Camp" in the background, c. 1949. Photograph by Fahmi Basrawi. Munira Khayyat, Yasmine Khayyat, and Rola Khayyat, "Pieces of Us: The Intimate as Imperial Archive," *Journal of Middle East Women's Studies* 14, no. 3 (November 2018): 278.

The Mosque of the Adenese, a gift from King 'Abd al-'Aziz, in the background among the Arab Quarters which were made of *barastis*, c. 1940s. Photograph by Fahmi Basrawi/Saudi Aramco. Scott McMurray, *Energy to the World: The Story of Aramco*, vol. 1 (Houston, TX: Aramco Services Company, 2011), 78. Courtesy of Aramco.

in the 1950s actively erased and omitted the term "Coolie" from all documents and replaced it with the word "Saudi." This move to "sanitize" CASOC/Aramco's rhetoric supposedly came when company executives "recognized that [the] effendi, coolie, raghead situation was wrong and started to do something about it."[28] In line with the renaming of CASOC to Aramco to recast the US company as ally instead of imperial master, this sanitizing move aimed to conceal the harsh realities of how the Saudi hosts were seen and treated. The adoption of "Saudi" further obscures the multinational composition of the "Saudi Camp." Erasing the use of "Coolie," however, did not erase how the US company saw their non-Aramcon hosts and workers; rather, pejorative terms and descriptions are found in abundance in published literature and the camp's own newspaper, *Sun and Flare*, even after the 1950s campaign.[29]

178   December 22, 1934   Jubail C56

Coolie from Bahrain wearing U S A blouse

Photograph and caption of "Coolie" Arab, 1934. Photograph by Joseph D. Mountain. Courtesy of Smithsonian National Air and Space Museum (NASM 92-15945).

Dharhan's spatial segregation took a more radical turn at the end of World War II when not only did more US families arrive but there was also a move to further divide Aramco labor. The postwar years saw a new classification of the camps, which was (supposedly) not based on race but rather on skill. There were now three distinct, fully separate camps: the US Camp would be renamed "Senior Staff Camp" and house the US employees

28   Note by William E. Mulligan to Thomas C. Barger, Folder 2, "History Project," Box 8, William E. Mulligan Papers, Archives and Special Collections, Georgetown University, quoted in Vitalis, *America's Kingdom*, 59.
29   See Loring M. Danforth, "Can Oil Bring Happiness? Alternate Visions of Saudia Aramco," chap. 1 in *Crossing the Kingdom: Portraits of Saudi Arabia* (Oakland: University of California Press, 2016); and Vitalis, *America's Kingdom*, 57–59.

and their families (2,593 people); the Saudi/"Coolie" Camp would become the "General Camp" and would only house male Saudi workers (12,062 people); and lastly, a new camp, the "Intermediate Camp," was established to house those who were more skilled and neither Saudi nor Aramcons (2,516 people).[30]

With the defeat of Mussolini, 1,700 Italians who were left stranded in Eritrea were hired to alleviate a skilled and semi-skilled labor shortage at Dhahran and were housed under bachelor status, alone without their families, in the Intermediate Camp.[31] Aramco designed and operated this new housing scheme on a very strict hierarchal system, in which greater skill (and thus a higher job designation) would correlate with so-called better benefits—although many of the "benefits" acted to exclude specific workers. For instance, Intermediate Camp had its own residential buildings and recreation facilities, including a dining hall, tennis courts, swimming pool, canteens, and a movie theater.[32] With theater forbidden in the Saudi Kingdom, Aramco was effectively prohibiting Saudis from living there, thus defining the Intermediate Camp as inherently non-Saudi.[33] Like many aspects of life in Dhahran, where one could live and thus what one could access was dictated by job level, with level D-1 being the lowest. The higher the number, the higher the job level. This hierarchical system would govern not only accomodations but also salaries, allowances, privileges, exclusions, and exceptions. Thus, Italians who were considered skilled workers by Aramco were designated the job level D-6, but the usual rule that level D-6 workers housed in Intermediate Camp must speak English was waived.[34] This waiver effectively segregated Italians from other nationalities; it was done to reinforce the notion that the established hierarchy was based on skill rather than nationality.[35]

30   Data from Aramco, *1958 Report of Operations to the Saudi Arab Government by the Arabian American Oil Company* (Dhahran, Saudi Arabia: Aramco, 1958), 23.

31   On the hiring of Italian workers and the multinational workforce hired to work in the oil industry, see I. J. Seccombe and R. I. Lawless, "Foreign Worker Dependence in the Gulf, and the International Oil Companies: 1910–1950," *The International Migration Review* 20, no. 3 (Autumn 1986): 548–574; I. J. Seccombe and R. I. Lawless, "Work Camps and Company Towns: Settlement Patterns and the Gulf Oil Industry," working paper (Durham, UK: University of Durham, Centre for Middle Eastern and Islamic Studies, 1987); Gennaro Errichiello, "Foreign Workforce in the Arab Gulf States (1930–1950): Migration Patterns and Nationality Clause," *The International Migration Review* 46, no. 2 (Summer 2012): 389–413.

32   "Intermediate Camps to Open in Dhahran and Ras Tanura: Saudi Intermediates First to Occupy New Quarters," *Arabian Sun and Flare*, September 17, 1952, 1.

33   On the "Housing Priority List," see "And Where Are You on the Housing Priority List?," *Arabian Sun and Flare*, October 27, 1946.

34   Khayyat, Khayyat, and Khayyat, "Pieces of Us," 279; Michael Edward Dobe, "A Long Slow Tutelage in Western Ways of Work: Industrial Education and the Containment of Nationalism in Anglo-Iranian and Aramco, 1923–1963" (PhD diss., Rutgers, The State University of New Jersey, 2008), 138.

However, the reality was that these designations were intentional and racially driven.

U-shaped buildings comprised the residential quarters of the Intermediate Camp, encircling a central grass court with a drinking water fountain; each was to house twenty-four men, twelve on each side, with communal facilities such as a kitchen, storage room, laundry room, and bathrooms with shower facilities in between them. The landscape was planted with grass and screened with a low wall, and air-conditioning was available to rent (but only enough to fulfill 20 percent of demand). Even with its landscapes and architecture, the Intermediate Camp, like the General Camp, only extended to male workers and never their families. Italians, along with Sudanese, Iraqis, Indians, Pakistanis, and Palestinians, were hired under "Bachelor status" and would thus not be included in the Aramco housing schemes for families.[36] For while the nuclear, white US family had to remain intact, especially during the years after World War II, non-Aramcons—i.e., non-US employees—were seen as laborers, and their assigned status meant that their families were not included under Aramco's benefits scheme.[37] The family was crucial for the highly valued US workers, but not other nationalities. The non-English-speaking, non-white, and non-Christian workers were not seen as requiring a family in the same way. Thus, the classification of these workers as "bachelors"—men without families—functioned to dehumanize them and to protect the superior position of the US workers in the hierarchy.

To further bolster these newly established hierarchies of race, religion, nationality, language, and family, Aramco argued that, because it had "grown to be such a large Company, it is necessary to limit the use of facilities [in the Intermediate Camp] to those who, by having earned a certain position level, are entitled to the privileges which go with that position."[38] This statement clearly indicates who belongs where. Aramco was firm on this. When the more skilled Palestinians, Yemenis, and Sudanese sought to move up the ranks, and to the Senior Staff Camp, Aramco responded by hiring intermediate-skilled, single, white,

35   This also placed Italians as inferior to Aramcons.
36   Frank Jungers, *The Caravan Goes On: How Aramco and Saudi Arabia Grew Up Together* (Cowes: Medina, 2013), 47–49; see also Vitalis, *America's Kingdom*, 91–93.
37   On the idea of the nuclear family during the years after World War II, see Elaine Tyler May, *Homeward Bound: American Families in the Cold War Era*, 20th anniversary edition (New York: Basic Books, 2008); and Beatriz Colomina, *Domesticity at War* (Cambridge, MA: MIT Press, 2007). On race and domesticity during the years after World War II, see Dianne Suzette Harris, *Little White Houses: How the Postwar Home Constructed Race in America*, Architecture, Landscape, and American Culture Series (Minneapolis: University of Minnesota Press, 2013).
38   "Intermediate Camps to Open in Dhahran and Ras Tanura," 2.

Newly constructed "Intermediate Camp," Ras Tanura, Saudi Arabia, 1952. Unknown author, Intermediate Camps, Ras Tanura, Saudi Arabia, 1952. "Intermediate Camps to Open in Dhahran and Ras Tanura: Saudi Intermediates First to Occupy New Quarters," *Arabian Sun and Flare*, September 17, 1952, 2. Courtesy of Aramco.

American women to fill the jobs in lieu of promoting capable Palestinians, Yemenis, and Sudanese workers. These women lived in the Senior Staff Camp in a specially built dormitory in an area known as "Hallowed Square."[39] Again, Aramco claimed this was not based on race but on skill: the Palestinians, Yemenis, and Sudanese were not as qualified as these women, and because Intermediate and General Camps were still male-only, these female workers had to live in Senior Staff Camp.

Social Rules and Decorum

In establishing the company town of Dhahran, CASOC, and in turn Aramco, conceived a plan in which the "paternal care" exercised by the company extended beyond the bare-bones architectural requirements of factories. Historians of company towns call this social engineering scheme "paternalism."[40] Due to Dhahran's remote location and the desire to keep the town as an insular entity to house the US employees of CASOC, the

39   Vitalis, *America's Kingdom*, 90.
40   On industrial paternalism, see Andrea Tone, *The Business of Benevolence: Industrial Paternalism in Progressive America* (Ithaca, NY: Cornell University Press, 1997); and Neil White, "Creating Community: Industrial Paternalism and Town Planning in Corner Brook, Newfoundland, 1923–1955," *Urban History Review / Revue d'histoire Urbaine* 32, no. 2 (Spring 2004): 45–58. On the architecture of paternal company towns, see Margaret Crawford, *Building the Workman's Paradise: The Design of American Company Towns*, Haymarket Series (London: Verso, 1995); John S. Garner, *The Model Company Town: Urban Design Through Private Enterprise in Nineteenth-Century New England* (Amherst: University of Massachusetts Press, 1984); and John S. Garner, *The Company Town: Architecture and Society in the Early Industrial Age* (New York: Oxford University Press, 1992).

company made the decision to extend the notion of "paternal care" to its employees. Houses, parks, schools, libraries, and meeting halls were all set within an attractive "green" landscape—all of them evidence of the company's vision of what was required for a "good life."[41] This kind of corporate paternalism also allowed CASOC to exercise exclusionary practices and design the town as it saw fit, without any reprimand. The paternal notion of a company imposing forms of "care" onto its employees extended the legacy of early US mining and British oil company towns in the region, which centered family in their schemes. These company towns drew on an even longer tradition of the "caring employer" dating back to the model villages of industrializing England, where wealthy factory owners provided facilities to improve the lives of their workers and keep them happy enough to continue in their designated roles.

The company town of Abadan in Iran, established in 1912, four years after the signing of the D'Arcy Concession, is considered to be the first oil company town in the region, ultimately serving as the example par excellence of how foreign oil companies should function.[42] Operated by the Anglo-Persian Oil Company (APOC), Abadan's history mirrors that of Dhahran, from the first bungalow and imported materials to the planned suburban expansion based on social and racial segregation.[43] In order to incentivize British personnel to live in Abadan, APOC provided British workers with housing, schools, recreational facilities, and green landscapes—governed by social and racial rules and regulations.[44] Much like Dhahran, Abadan was divided into three distinct housing categories based on race: "fully-furnished housing for British staff and the few senior Iranians; partly-furnished accommodation for non-European junior staff; and unfurnished facilities for wage-earning [Iranian] labour."[45]

41   Garner, The Company Town; Garner, The Model Company Town; and Crawford, Building the Workman's Paradise.

42   The D'Arcy Concession served as a precedent for foreign-operated oil companies in terms of its business model and eventual architectural development. For more on the D'Arcy Concession, see Daniel Yergin, The Prize: The Epic Quest for Oil, Money and Power, (New York: Simon & Schuster, 1991; New York: Free Press, 2008), 116.

43   The Anglo-Persian Oil Company (APOC) was established in 1908 by Burmah Oil, presently British Petroleum (BP), and was renamed as the Anglo-Iranian Oil Company (AIOC) in 1935.

44   Mark Crinson, "Abadan: Planning and Architecture under the Anglo-Iranian Oil Company," Planning Perspectives 12, no. 3 (1997): 341–359; Kaveh Ehsani, "Social Engineering and the Contradictions of Modernization in Khuzestan's Company Towns: A Look at Abadan and Masjed-Soleyman," International Review of Social History 48, no. 3 (December 2003): 361–399.

45   Crinson, "Abadan," 347. This tripartite system was evident in all oil company towns in the region; on this, see Seccombe and Lawless, "Foreign Worker Dependence in the Gulf"; and Errichiello, "Foreign Workforce in the Arab Gulf States."

While Aramco intially only included its Aramcons in those entitled to the benefits of its paternalistic scheme, such as suburban houses, schools, parades, and community spaces, and despite its commitment to the racial, religious, and national hierarchy it imposed, the company was eventually forced to extend these benefits to its Saudi employees in order to placate the Saudi state's growing power. This was achieved by expanding Aramco's medical and education programs.[46] Aramco built three hospitals, one for each camp: Senior Staff, Intermediate, and General; unsurprisingly, the quality of care—and of doctors, equipment, and facilities—at each hospital reflected this hierarchy.[47]

In May 1940, CASOC set up its first "experiment" into education by offering classes to boys in the nearby town of al-Khobar. This was the first instance in which Aramco took an active role in educating its Saudi hosts and employees. This school, followed by a second a month later in the Saudi Camp, was set up as an experiment in teaching Saudi employees the skills required to become effective employees of the company, by offering classes in English, arithmetic, and citizenship, schooling these young Saudi boys into ideal candidates for the Aramco fleet of employees: compliant and orderly. A third school, "Jebel School," was opened inside "Senior Staff Camp," which catered to "houseboys, waiters, and telephone operators with evening hours," so they could combine their education with continuing to work in the mornings.[48]

While these schools gave the impression that Aramco was benevolently offering Saudi employees education and opportunities, the reality was that these schools were re-educating and teaching "new recruits rudimentary language skills in English before they entered the subaltern workforce as office boys, waiters, houseboys, and refinery workers."[49] While pushed to the

46   The narrative that Aramco extended its paternalism to its Saudi employees was taken on and reiterated as "fact"; see Sa'd ibn Sa'īd 'Ā'iḍ Qarnī, Al-Mamlakah al-'Arabīyah al-Sa'ūdīyah Wa-Sharikat Arāmkū, 1352–1401 H/1933–1980 M: Dirāsah Tārīkhīyah / دراسة تاريخية : م ١٩٨٠-١٩٣٣/هـ ١٤٠١-١٣٥٢ ,أرامكو وشركة السعودية العربية المملكة (Saudi Arabia and Aramco, 1352–1401 H/1933–1980: A Historical Study), 6th ed. (Riyadh, Saudi Arabia: al-Jam'īyah al-Tārīkhīyah al-Sa'ūdīyah (Saudi Historical Society), 2008), 88–91; 'Abd al-Raḥmān ibn 'Abd Allāh Thāmir Aḥmarī, "Dawr Sharikat Al-Zayt al-'Arabīyah al-Amrīkīyah (Arāmkū) Fī Tanmiyat al-Minṭaqah al-Sharqīyah Min al-Mamlakah al-'Arabīyah al-Sa'ūdīyah, 1363–1384 H/1944–1964 M : Dirāsah Fī Tārīkh al-Tanmiyah / التنمية تاريخ في دراسة :م ١٩٦٤-١٩٤٤ /هـ ١٣٨٤-١٣٦٣ ,السعودية العربية (Aramco's دور الزيت العربية الأمريكية (أرامكو) في تنمية المنطقة الشرقية من المملكة Role in the Development of the Eastern Province (KSA), 1944–1964: A Study in Development History) (PhD diss., King Saud University, 2007), 89–102.
47   Jungers, American Perspectives of Aramco, 418.
48   Dobe, "A Long Slow Tutelage in Western Ways of Work," 76; Vitalis, America's Kingdom, 112.
49   Khayyat, Khayyat, and Khayyat, "Pieces of Us," 279.

Jebel "Opportunity School," Dhahran, Saudi Arabia, 1949. Photograph by Karl S. Twitchell. Courtesy of Karl S. Twitchell Collection, Special Collections, Fine Arts Library, Harvard University.

periphery of camp, unseen and unheard, this workforce kept the Aramcons' lives operating smoothly. Their acceptance of a low position in the hierarchy was therefore essential to the company's vision of orderly, calm operations that allowed maximum oil extraction with minimum fuss. It was through these schools that Aramco went about systematically imprinting onto Saudi employees the notion of Aramco "citizenship" in which the Saudi men's bodies, actions, and mindset were to be shaped into Aramco's notion of the ideal worker.[50] Much like they viewed the Saudi environment, Aramco's US leaders believed that the "emptiness" of the Arabian desert reflected the Arab's un-sophistication and that it was up to the US company and its US employees to teach and transform the Saudi man into the Aramco man. For CASOC/Aramco,

> as a mass, Saudis constitute an untrained labor supply completely lacking in industrial experience and in work habits. Few can read or write. A recent health check showed 2.4 percent as physically fit... A casual observer would call Saudis small and frail. Their language is exceedingly difficult to learn. Their religion is deep and complex and their social ties and customs are strange. Their legal and political structure differs from ours in fundamental ways.[51]

CASOC/Aramco was not keen on hiring Saudi employees beyond manual labor because they often assumed that Saudis possessed neither the skills nor the drive. The Saudis are often described as "unlettered and untrained, poor and poorly clad," their work habits including "habitual tardiness, undue loafing or insubordination," and it was often on the US employees to help "the [Saudi] Arabs along the road towards greater skill, greater productivity and a higher standard of living."[52] If it were up to CASOC/Aramco, it would not have engaged with teaching their Saudi employees, but if it wanted to continue to operate in the Kingdom, it had to relent, as the 1933 Concession that granted the US company of SoCal exclusive exploratory rights also included what was known as a "nationality clause."[53] This clause, stipulated in article 23 of the 1933 Concession Agreement, effectively gave preferential employment to Saudis, stating that, "as far as practicable, and in so far as the company can find suitable Saudi employees it will not employ other nationals."[54] Even still, CASOC/Aramco's employment system ensured that US employees would stay at the top of the hierarchy. By establishing these schools, Aramco was able to direct what was being taught and how the employees would be allocated based on suitability, and to find employees that it considered more malleable than others. Using "skills" as a measure, Aramco was able to claim that Saudis simply did not possess the skills required for higher employment designation (D-Level) and were thus destined to remain in the Saudi/General Camp.

Moreover, US housewives were encouraged to hire domestic helpers to maintain the landscaping and do the heavy lifting. Domestic work, too, was governed by racial hierarchy and difference. Yemeni, Sudanese, and Saudi men were typically hired to do lawn work and were seldom allowed into the private domain of the Aramcon house. Indian, Goan, and Pakistani men, on the other hand, were hired to work inside the home and were known around camp as "domestics."[55] This reflects the reluctance

50   Originally Aramco only hired Saudi men and all of its training and education
      programs were geared towards Saudi men.
51   "Character of Saudi Employees," Appendix IV in *Aramco's Field Force: A Report
      by the Personnel Planning Committee*, 1950, Box 1, George Rentz Papers, Special
      Collections and University Archives, Stanford University.
52   Roy Lebkicher, *The Work and Life of Aramco Employees*, American Employees
      Handbook Series 2 (New York: Russell F. Moore Company, Inc, 1950), 43.
53   On the "nationality clause," see Errichiello, "Foreign Workforce in the Arab
      Gulf States."
54   *Multinational Corporations and United States Foreign Policy: Hearings before the
      Subcomm. on Multinational Corporations of the Sen. Comm. on Foreign Relations*,
      94th Cong., 2nd sess. (1973), 364.
55   This phenomenon of hiring non-natives was also evident in other oil company towns

of both US and British companies to allow locals into their employee's private sphere and demonstrates who was allowed in and privy to that intimate space. Adding to the complex spatial expression of the racial hierarchy, "houseboys" lived in their own camp on a hill called "Domestic Camp," located outside both Saudi Camp and Senior Staff Camp.[56] In the CASOC/Aramco imaginary, an inheritance from years of British colonial rule, South Asians were assumed by US employees to be "subservient," "docile," and "teachable."[57] Thus, they were deemed predictable and safe to bring into the domestic sphere. These assumptions in regard to Arabs and South Asians were inherently linked to CASOC's assumptions about the Saudi landscape and its environmental imaginary.

To further emphasize the place of non-US employees in Dhahran, Aramco built separate bathrooms for the domestic workers that were placed around the camp in "strategic sites for Middle Eastern personnel, including most public structures," like administrative buildings, schools, and other facilities around camp, such as the theater.[58] Aramcons called these bathrooms *hammams*, the Arabic word for bathrooms, with some homes equipped with a separate, exterior *hammam* for domestic workers that was allocated the same space as a typical garden hose.[59] To keep the Senior Staff Camp as quintessentially "Anywhere, USA," as possible, everything deemed unsightly was kept outside the fence.[60] The fence was not only a physical divide

in the region, where Indians, Goans, and Pakistanis were hired to work as domestic workers. See Reem Alissa, "Building for Oil: Corporate Colonialism, Nationalism and Urban Modernity in Ahmadi, 1946–1992" (PhD diss., University of California, Berkeley, 2012), 53–55; and Anthony D. King, *Colonial Urban Development: Culture, Social Power and Environment*, Cities in the Developing World (1976, repr., London: Routledge, 2010). As can be seen in descriptions by Aramco and other companies in the region, locals were seen as unruly, "savage," "ragheads," "coolies," "backward," and "primitive," and thus unable to interact with Aramcons in a manner deemed appropriate by them. See examples of descriptions of "locals" in *Sun and Flare/Arabian Sun and Flare*. See also Johnson, *You Can Go Home Again*, 42–43; Wallie Ballor, "My Arabian Adventure – Part 7," *Aramco Expats* (blog), February 27, 2005, https://www.aramcoexpats.com/articles/my-arabian-adventure-part-7. See also unedited original documents in William E. Mulligan papers, Archives and Special Collections, Georgetown University.

56   Unfortunately, I cannot confirm the specifics of the Domestic Camp as it was razed and there is no documentation. I learned about the Domestic Camp from an ex-Aramcon and he did not know either. Interview with previous Aramcon, email, April 1, 2019. Name withheld for privacy at the agreement of both parties.

57   Anthony King calls this phenomenon "the colonial third culture," which is the distinct colonial culture of the colonizer in the colonial lands (i.e. British culture in India) that is neither that of the colonizer nor the colonized, resulting in a distinct "third culture." King, *Colonial Urban Development*, 58–66.

58   Interview with previous Aramcon, email, April 1, 2019. Name withheld for privacy at the agreement of both parties.

59   Daniel W. B. Warner, Revised DH 2, Dhahran, Saudi Arabia, 1952. Private collection, Dalal Musaed Alsayer.

60   See Danforth, *Crossing the Kingdom*; Khayyat, Khayyat, and Khayyat, "Pieces of

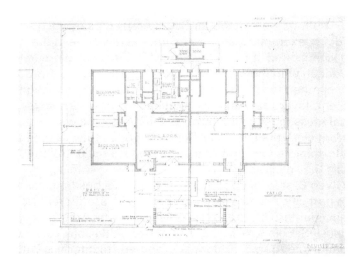

A domestic helper serving dinner in an American home, Dhahran, Saudi Arabia, c. 1952. Roy Lebkicher, *Aramco and World Oil* (New York: Russell F. Moore Company, 1952), 85. Courtesy of Aramco.

Plan of a Duplex house in Dhahran with the *hammam* accessible from the outside. Daniel W. B. Warner, Revised DH 2, Dhahran, Saudi Arabia, 1952. Courtesy of the author.

but also a warning sign for local Saudi employees to stay out of Senior Staff Camp, as it was "adorned" with the dismembered hands and feet of those who stole from Aramco. Through the education programs and other initiatives, Aramco was taking an active role in forging the exemplary Saudi worker. In the same way that the Saudi desert was shaped into a piece of Americana, so would the Saudi employee through training and supervision. The segregation and separateness of the Saudi employees underlined their inferior, racialized position; no matter how "educated" they became, they would never live in the Senior Staff Camp or have access to the salaries, housing, health services, and other services extended to Aramcons.

While it was near impossible for Saudi employees to live in the Senior Staff Camp, external pressure from the king in 1946 ultimately forced Aramco to relent on some of these restrictions. Rare exceptions were made for Saudi Arabs who Aramco saw as model or exemplary, such as Fahmi Basrawi, one of the first teachers hired at the Jebel School.[61] Basrawi, an urbanite from Jeddah who moved to Dhahran to teach at Jebel School, quickly climbed the ranks, and, according to his granddaughters, his US employers saw that his "malleability as an employee, imperial messenger, and interpreter" indicated he was "cut from a different cloth than the local Bedouin worlds they needed to infiltrate, exploit, and control in order to take the petroleum and minerals they desired."[62]

Given Basrawi's upbringing in Jeddah, a bustling, cosmopolitan port city, Aramco executives saw him as different from his Bedouin counterpart. Thus, Basrawi became the Aramco ideal, a model all Saudis working for Aramco should aspire to: he was both Saudi and Aramcon. He was groomed "to interface with the locals to build the human machinery of resource extraction," and, at the same time, he was the poster child for Aramco's success in transforming the Saudi man, in his role "as an elegant and charming translator of the project to local elites and visiting dignitaries. Basrawi became the American's Arabian ambassador, mascot, and medium."[63] But Basrawi was just the exception to

Us," 288; Fadia Basrawi, *Brownies and Kalashnikovs: A Saudi Woman's Memoir of American Arabia and Wartime Beirut* (Reading: South Street Press, 2009), 55–56.

61   According to Danforth, although he does not cite any of his sources, one of the very first young Arab families on the compound was asked to "quietly" leave after "they celebrated the festival of Eid al-Fitra [sic], marking the end of Ramadan, by slaughtering a lamb in their bathtub and roasting it over a fire they built on their living-room floor. When smoke began pouring out of the windows, the Aramco fire department was called." Danforth, *Crossing the Kingdom*, 49.

62   Khayyat, Khayyat, and Khayyat, "Pieces of Us," 279; see also Basrawi, *Brownies and Kalashnikovs*.

63   Khayyat, Khayyat, and Khayyat, "Pieces of Us," 279.

the rule, for Aramco continued to refuse to allow Saudis to live in Senior Staff Camp into the late 1940s and early 1950s. Basrawi and his family were one of the first three Saudi families to move to Senior Staff Camp in 1956, after he completed his studies in Public Relations at the American University of Beirut (AUB) on an Aramco scholarship.[64] Basrawi's ability to negotiate between his "Arabness" and his "Aramconess" was what enabled him to be part of the Aramco orderly, manageable, and malleable fleet. Yet very few people were able to do this. Moreover, Basrawi's inclusion was to some extent only extended to him. Basrawi's wife, who spoke very little English, was often excluded by other Aramcon wives, and their children were often treated differently than their US counterparts.[65] Nonetheless, it was the image of the nuclear family and the ability of the Basrawi family to assimilate, even at the surface level, that maintained hope for other Saudi families to achieve the US dream in the Saudi desert.

Negotiating Aramco Citizenship

While Basrawi's story demonstrates an attempt at inclusion, the reality was that Aramco's racial and exclusionary practices persisted. CASOC/Aramco's extractive practices and adamant desire to create the suburb of "Anywhere, USA," led many Saudis to take matters into their own hands. Not only did they begin settling their families right outside the fence, in small makeshift *barastis* huts, but they also demanded equal rights both from the company and the Kingdom at large. Saudi-led strikes began in 1945, with workers demanding better housing, food, training, pay, and treatment, and continued until 1953.[66] During this period, the company's official newspaper, *Sun and Flare*, failed to report on any of this unrest and instead continued to display triumphant news about Aramcon births, tournaments, and daily happenings in Dhahran and its two other oil company towns in Abqaiq and Ras Tanura. By June 1956, eleven years after

64   Basrawi, *Brownies and Kalashnikovs*, 17.
65   For a first-hand account of growing up in Dhahran, see Basrawi's daughter's auto-biography, Basrawi, *Brownies and Kalashnikovs*.
66   These events in Saudi Arabia were happening concurrently to the US civil rights movement. See Vitalis, *America's Kingdom*, 93, 149–162, 171–175. For a comprehensive account of the demands of the Saudi employees, see Aḥmarī, "Dawr Sharikat Al-Zayt al-'Arabīyah al-Amrīkīyah (Arāmkū) Fī Tanmiyat al-Minṭaqah al-Sharqīyah Min al-Mamlakah al-'Arabīyah al-Sa-'ūdīyah, 1363–1384 H/1944–1964 M: Dirāsah Fī Tārīkh al-Tanmiyah / السعودية,١٣٦٣-١٣٨٤ ه‍/١٩٤٤-١٩٦٤ م: دراسة في تاريخ التنمية دور شركة الزيت العربية الأمريكية (أرامكو) في تنمية المنطقة الشرقية من المملكة العربية (Aramco's Role in the Development of the Eastern Province (KSA), 1944–1964: A Study in Development History), 382–404; For an account of the 1953 strikes, see Jones, *Desert Kingdom*, 147–159.

Dressed in the traditional Arab dress, Fahmi Basrawi (middle) is seen interpreting between the US Aramco official (left) and the Crown Prince Saud (right) during a tour of Aramco's industrial training department and refinery, 1948. Munira Khayyat, Yasmine Khayyat, and Rola Khayyat, "Pieces of Us: The Intimate as Imperial Archive," *Journal of Middle East Women's Studies* 14, no. 3 (November 2018): 280.

Fahmi Basrawi and his family stand in front of their imported US car and the US suburb of Dhahran, c. 1965. Munira Khayyat, Yasmine Khayyat, and Rola Khayyat, "Pieces of Us: The Intimate as Imperial Archive," *Journal of Middle East Women's Studies* 14, no. 3 (November 2018): 286.

the initial strike, another strike occurred in Ras Tanura, where Saudi workers demanded the same benefits extended to those in Intermediate Camp. The king and Saudi Arabian government finally intervened, insisting that Aramco change the status quo and extend better pay and benefits to Saudi employees. Using the threat of nationalization and the barring of US access to oil, the king was able to put pressure on Aramco and gain more profits for the Kingdom and better treatment of Saudi employees.

By 1948, oil royalties had doubled from the previous year and the Saudi government was becoming increasingly dissatisfied with Aramco's unjust practices towards both its Saudi employees and the nation at large. The Saudi government believed that it was its right to reap the benefits of the oil being extracted, and, at the same time, Aramco executives believed that their only responsibilities should be towards their US employees. The hiring of Italians and their resulting accommodations in the Intermediate Camp was a point of great contention for the Saudi government, approved only on the condition that they would not be treated better than Saudi employees; however, as we have seen, this was not the case. With increased pressure from the government and the threat of full nationalization, the strikes and boycotts waned, and Aramco was forced to seriously and ultimately address its shortcomings towards its Saudi Arab employees and share profits with its Saudi hosts.[67]

Aramco attempted to quell unrest by creating the impression that it was giving Saudi employees autonomy and agency over their own lives; yet, this was only a mask for the continuation of racial and ethnic inequity. This about-turn in the Aramco approach represented a huge change in company policy. Since the company's 1944 Planning Committee, Aramco senior officials had argued that they could not finance housing for Saudis as it was far too expensive and, thus, free housing for non-Aramcons was taken off the table. Education followed a similar trajectory; Aramco's instinct was to stop providing this service. This claim was further underlined following a trip to Iraq and Iran in April 1949. Aramco's personnel visited Iraq and Iran to witness first-hand how their British counterparts addressed local workers' strikes so that Aramco could adopt an effective (and cost-efficient) solution to its workers' demands. The Aramco Personnel Planning Committee developed a Force Field Guide that recommended closing all schools for Saudi nationals operating in Dhahran, establishing schools outside of the camp and under Saudi management instead, and developing a system for Saudis to own their houses in order to develop a robust, independent middle class and alleviate some of the political pressure on the company.[68]

The Personnel Planning Committee recommended that, in order to have this strong middle class and avoid the pitfalls of encroaching government-imposed company welfare, as was the case in Iran and Iraq, the company should make homeownership attainable for Saudi nationals. Aramco officials believed that their "paternal" care should only extend to its US employees and that the Saudi government's continued request for Aramco to provide education, housing, and healthcare for its Saudi employees was unfounded. Aramco felt that the burden of educating the younger generation of Saudis should not fall on the company, but rather that the Saudi government should address the nation's educational needs. These beliefs drove Aramco to close its three schools and shift from "an American-type school-oriented education and training policy" for Saudis towards "training by line personnel as an integrated part of the production process."[69] According to Aramco, "If we want to have an independent, secure middle class instead of a group grown dependent on a corporation for the conduct of their personal lives, if we want free men to build a future for themselves and their families, we feel that we must not cut this wish under by company housing."[70]

It should be noted that Aramco continued to maintain schools for Aramcon dependents in Senior Staff Camp and offered co-ed classes, meeting the US standard of education from kindergarten to eighth grade. Obviously, it was assumed that those white US employees in Senior Camp were already robust and middle class enough to survive the pitfalls of free company housing with their work ethic intact. Moreover, Aramco helped fund the extension of the American Community School (ACS) in Beirut to absorb the growing number of ninth-graders who could not be accommodated in Dhahran.[71] Saudis continued to be left out of these "paternalistic" benefits, save for a few "lucky" Saudis who happened to fit into Aramco's scheme of the "civilized Arab," such as Basrawi.

68   For a detailed account of the Personnel Planning Committee's trip to Iraq and Iran, see Dobe, "A Long Slow Tutelage in Western Ways of Work," 104–121.
69   Vitalis, America's Kingdom, 115.
70   Quoted in Dobe, "A Long Slow Tutelage in Western Ways of Work," 108.
71   ACS Alumni, "A History of the American Community School at Beirut," Almashriq, September 1998, archived April 23, 2020, https://lib-webarchive.aub.edu.lb/Borre Ludvigsen/http://almashriq.hiof.no/lebanon/300/370/371/acs/history.

Implementing the Personnel Planning Committee's recommendations, Aramco decided to provide for its Saudi employees far away from Dhahran in the existing Saudi communities of Dammam (approximately 21 kilometers/13 miles northeast of Dhahran) and al-Khobar (approximately 16 kilometers/10 miles east of Dhahran) (also known by the general term "Eastern Provinces"). By providing for its Saudi employees far from the US epicenter, Aramco was able to, first, appease the Saudi Government, and, second, by increasing the distance between the Saudi employee and the US employee, make the differences in their living standards were far less jarring. In order to minimize its financial burden, Aramco devised a plan in which it would build facilities, help establish their operations, and then transfer their management to the Kingdom in somewhat of a Build-Operate-Transfer (BOT) scheme.

In 1953, Saud bin Abdulaziz Al Saud, son of Ibn Saud, became king upon his father's death, and Aramco announced an agreement it had made with the Saudi government "that obliged the firm to build and pay for the operating costs of elementary schools for sons of [Saudi] Arab and Muslim employees."[72] The company acquiesced to these demands so that it would not commit itself to developing a technical institution and so that it would not be forced to re-hire fired employees at the request of King Saud. Aramco officials argued that it was too costly to build a technical institute and that, learning from APOC, now the Anglo-Iranian Oil Company (AIOC), in Abadan, building a technical institute would mean that the management, education, and maintenance would fall on Aramco. This was something Aramco executives wanted to avoid at all costs. In their minds, "dealing with weak, uneducated, disorganized, and irresponsible [Saudi] Arab Muslims" was not a top priority for the company, and the company "need[ed] to win over the employees without falling into paternalism."[73] Ultimately, Aramco executives decided to only extend its "paternal" care to those who were English speaking, white, and Christian.

The first two schools that Aramco built opened in December 1954 in Dammam and al-Khobar.[74] In 1960, Aramco built the first intermediate school in Dammam for grades seven, eight, and

72   Dobe, "A Long Slow Tutelage in Western Ways of Work," 168.
73   Dobe, "A Long Slow Tutelage in Western Ways of Work," 109 and 110.
74   "King Sa'ud Opens Dammam School, First of 10 Scheduled by Aramco," *Arabian Sun and Flare*, December 8, 1954; "King Opens Al-Khobar School, 2nd of 10 in Company Program," *Arabian Sun and Flare*, December 15, 1954; Ahmarī, "Dawr Sharikat Al-Zayt al-'Arabīyah al-Amrīkīyah (Arāmkū) FīTanmiyat al-Mintaqah al-Sharqīyah Min al-Mamlakah al-'Arabīyah al-Sa'ūdīyah," 307–312.

nine—first only to educate the male children of Saudi employees and later to educate all male children living in the area. In the same issue of the company newspaper, it was reported that the Aramcon ninth-grade class consisting of US children "governed" the Dhahran District for a day, during which students "were assigned to the district offices which most nearly duplicate[d] the city positions of an average American community."[76]

Herein lay the realities of Aramco: Aramcons were to rule, govern, and run a community, whereas Saudis were given the bare minimum. Aramco's company-funded care extended only insofar as the recipient was Aramcon, something that Aramco's upper management was clear about.[77] Senior Staff Camp was Aramco's US domain, and extending its services to its Saudi employees was not negotiable; however, with the close proximity of Aramcon and Saudi workers, tensions stemming from Aramco's unjust, racist treatments towards its Saudi employees were inevitable. Saudi employees wanted their families to live with them like their US counterparts instead of commuting to see them on the weekends. The permanent ten-apartment masonry barracks that were built to house Saudi employees instead of the *barastis* huts were simply not enough. Rather than allow Saudis and their families to live in Dhahran, Aramco developed a strategy to establish full-fledged townships for Saudi employees that were in close proximity to Dhahran but still their own separate entities, physically distinct from Aramco. Other non-Saudi, non-US employees would continue to live near Dhahran and would still be without their families. This strategy allowed Saudis to be separated physically and allowed Aramco to distance itself from taking responsibility for the township. The same strategy that Aramco had adopted for schools, building them and then turning them over to the government, was extended to housing and neighborhoods.[78]

Even though these houses were outside of Aramco's physical territory, the company still maintained its control over its Saudi employees. Aramco executives believed that, in the same manner that Saudi employees can be molded through training, their domestic environments could also shape the Saudi employee. Here the company would continue imposing a

75   "Aramco-Built Intermediate School Started in Dammam," *Sun and Flare*, June 22, 1960, 1; Aḥmarī, "Dawr Sharikat Al-Zayt al-'Arabīyah al-Amrīkīyah (Arāmkū) Fī Tanmiyat al-Minṭaqah al-Sharqīyah Min al-Mamlakah al-'Arabīyah al-Sa'ūdīyah," 314.
76   "Ninth-Grade Students 'Govern' Dhahran District for One Day," *Sun and Flare*, June 22, 1960, 3.
77   See for example Dobe, "A Long Slow Tutelage in Western Ways of Work," 205.
78   McMurray, *Energy to the World*, 1:168.

hierarchal structure onto housing loan eligibility: higher grade
would mean higher pay, a bigger mortgage, and thus a better
house. Essentially, in the same manner that Basrawi was molded
into an Aramco man who could fit into Dhahran, the house would
also encourage Saudi employees to better themselves into
exemplary Aramco employees. The company formed a consensus
that "by denying quality housing to the mass of Saudi workers in
lower pay grades, the company would motivate them to improve
their lot by upgrading their skills."[79]

Another factor motivating the company was a growing US
concern of the mid-twentieth century: communism. In typical
US fashion, the single-family home was imagined as the best
defense against the growing threat of nationalist and communist
movements in the post-colonial Arab world. Not only were
Egyptian leader Gamal Abdel Nasser's pro-Arab sentiments finding an audience in Saudi Arabia, potentially threatening US
operations, but the US had also already found a willing consumer
for the "American Dream" of suburban living in South America
and Asia through President Truman's Point Four Program and
the Rockefeller Foundation's International Basic Economic
Corporation (IBEC).[80] By adopting these postwar strategies and
introducing homeownership, Aramco had a two-fold anti-
communist strategy: on the one hand, this tactic of capitalist
homeownership was a way to quell popular uprising by selling
the "American Dream," and on the other hand, it would offer the
Saudi government an alternative to the socialism Nasser was
introducing in Egypt by building a robust middle class.

Aramco wanted middle-class Saudis, but it wanted them
separate from the middle-class US employees living in its
US-style oil town. The strategy for this emerging Saudi middle-
class was to push them further away, into the neighboring cities
of Dammam and al-Khobar by developing an urban housing grid
that was financially more affordable for Aramco, and duplicating
this strategy in other Aramco satellites.[81] The Personnel Planning

79   Dobe, "A Long Slow Tutelage in Western Ways of Work," 108.
80   On the use of the single-family home as a "weapon" against communism, see Dalal
      Musaed Alsayer, "Architecture, Environment, Development: The United States and
      the Making of Modern Arabia, 1949–1961" (PhD diss., University of Pennsylvania,
      2019); Greg Castillo, Cold War on the Home Front: The Soft Power of Midcentury
      Design (Minneapolis: University of Minnesota Press, 2010); Nancy Kwak, A World of
      Homeowners: American Power and the Politics of Housing Aid (Chicago: University
      of Chicago Press, 2015); G. McDonald, "The Modern American Home as Soft Power:
      Finland, MoMA and the 'American Home 1953' Exhibition," Journal of Design History
      23, no. 4 (December 2010): 387–408; Colomina, Domesticity at War; Nathan J Citino,
      "Suburbia and Modernization: Community Building and America's Post–World War II
      Encounter with the Arab Middle East," Arab Studies Journal 13/14, no. 2/1 (Fall 2005/
      Spring 2006): 39–64.

Sun and Flare   - 4 -

Students 'Govern' Dhahran for a Day

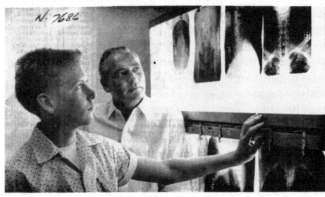

Jeff Nelson explores the problems of Public Health with W.K. Lanuis, Medical department.

"Mayor
Dhahra

Third grader Norman Reed maneuvers his bicycle through a handling test devised by the Safety department for one-day "Principal" Susan Swindig and Principal of the Dhahran Senior Staff School, William Riley.

Photograp

Acting Assistant District Manager Jack Reed and "Assistant Mayor" Tom Handzus observe installation of a soda fountain at the new Youth Center,

Diana Sherman takes
Transportation under th

- 5 -   June 22, 1960

N-7692

"City Engineer" Cory Milam in conference with H.N. Lane, Engineering.

N-7693

"Fire Chief" Mary Teel discusses fire hazards with Dhahran's Fire Chief G. H. Totten.

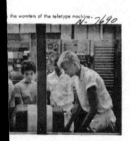

the wonders of the teletype machine.

N-7690

N-7694

Jane Tomaselli (left) and Danee Sullivan (right) check the Recreation and Community Services duties of Carl Jackson, (left) U.V. Stewart (right).

The student city government meets in a round-table session with the "Mayor."

N-7695

Aramcon ninth grade students undertaking various jobs as they "govern" Dhahran for a day. In the same issue, the front cover shows the beginning of the intermediate school program. "Students 'Govern' Dhahran for One Day," *Sun and Flare*, June 22, 1960, 4–5. Courtesy of Aramco.

Committee argued that the costs for housing in the Saudi Camp were far too great and that Saudi Camp itself was simply inadequate to meet the housing shortages. It envisioned a home ownership plan that would allow eligible Saudi employees to apply for a home loan through Aramco. The committee further stated that it was "quite clear that such home ownership must be a real incentive to the individual worker and not simply a matter of casual choice."[82] So while Aramcons were still given homes in Senior Staff Camp, Saudi Arab employees who had worked hard enough could now earn the privilege of housing. The Personnel Planning Committee developed the Home Ownership Program (HOP) in 1951 for Saudi employees only by offering "free-interest loans to build on government land."[83]

Architects, engineers, and planners for the towns of the Eastern Provinces were all provided by Aramco using the same technical expertise that the company had developed in Dhahran.[84] Aramco agreed to build 10,000 houses (6,000 for Saudi families and 4,000 bachelor quarters for Saudi men) from 1951 to 1959. The 4,000 bachelor quarters expanded on the existing 3,536 permanent bachelor rooms made available after the 1947 riots; family housing, on the other hand, had to be in what Aramco called "natural communities," a problematic term that Aramco used to describe existing Saudi communities near the oil towns.[85] The fenced-in suburban town of Dharhan was seen as the opposite of the "natural" environment of Saudi living, but of course it was considered "natural" for US employees to live in this

81   Vitalis, *America's Kingdom*, 109; Al-Mubarak, "Oil, Urban Development and Planning in the Eastern Province of Saudi Arabia," 41–44; Mashary Al-Naim, "Identity in Transitional Context: Open-Ended Local Architecture in Saudi Arabia," *Archnet-IJAR, International Journal of Architectural Research* 2, no. 2 (July 2008): 129; Aḥmarī, "Dawr Sharikat Al-Zayt al-'Arabīyah al-Amrīkiyah (Arāmkū) Fī Tanmiyat al-Minṭaqah al-Sharqīyah Min al-Mamlakah al-'Arabīyah al-Sa'ūdīyah" 161–197; Saleh A. Al-Hathloul, "Tradition, Continuity and Change in the Physical Environment: The Arab-Muslim City" (PhD diss., Massachusetts Institute of Technology, 1981).
82   Aramco, "Housing Facilities," sec. 5 in *Aramco's Field Force: A Report by the Personnel Planning Committee* (Dhahran, 1950), 2, Reel R-84, Aramco Folder, IBEC Housing Corporation (IHC): Middle East: Saudi Arabia, Series R: IBEC Microfilm, International Basic Economy Corporation (IBEC) records, RAC; on the Home Ownership Program (HOP) as a money-saving strategy for Aramco, see Vitalis, *America's Kingdom: Mythmaking on the Saudi Oil Frontier*, 23.
83   Al-Mubarak, "Oil, Urban Development and Planning in the Eastern Province of Saudi Arabia," 45; see also Al-Hathloul, "Tradition, Continuity and Change in the Physical Environment," 160. For the details of the 1938 government scheme requirements, which include building in concrete and stone, see Al-Mubarak, "Oil, Urban Development and Planning in the Eastern Province of Saudi Arabia," 41.
84   Al-Mubarak, "Oil, Urban Development and Planning in the Eastern Province of Saudi Arabia"; Abdul Aziz Abdullah Alkhedheiri, "Urban Infil: A Rational Policy for Land Use in the Kingdom of Saudi Arabia" (master's thesis, Massachusetts Institute of Technology, 1991); Aḥmarī, "Dawr Sharikat Al-Zayt al-'Arabīyah al-Amrīkiyah (Arāmkū) Fī Tanmiyat al-Minṭaqah al-Sharqīyah Min al-Mamlakah al-'Arabīyah al-Sa'ūdīyah," chap. 2.
85   Aramco, "Housing Facilities," 7.

privileged environment. This notion of "natural" was essential for Aramco to racialize and spatially other its Saudi employees. In the same manner that certain behaviors described earlier, such as "habitual tardiness, undue loafing or insubordination," were seen as "natural," so was the environment in which Saudis lived, and in the same manner that education was to transfer habits, so was housing.[86] Priority for Saudi family housing was to be extended to those of higher rank until 1954, when loans from HOP would be offered to Saudi bachelors. To offset costs and to ensure that these communities were indeed what Aramco deemed to be "natural," Aramco decided to include non-employees in their housing schemes, but they would not be responsible for any of their associated costs. In the same manner that US towns were drawn up with racial exclusions, Aramco planned these communities as a place that would define a segregated Saudi township. Plots were to be occupied by a specific ethnic and religious mixture, with some areas housing more Bedouins than others. Aramco would provide the infrastructure, and for its employees, it would also provide a housing loan.[87] It was decided that 12,000 plots would be made available in each of the three neighboring Saudi communities—Rahaima (447 acres), Dammam (670 acres), and Hofuf (225 acres)—with half of those plots for Aramco employees and the other half for non-employees.[88] Moreover, under this program, Aramco would establish its own development company that would be responsible for site selection, site acquirement, finances, and the construction of infrastructure, while paying no more than 50 percent of the loan.[89]

In true Aramco fashion, the Personnel Planning Committee established a classification for what constituted a house that it would fund: "The lot should contain at least 2,000 square feet and be enclosed within a compound wall no less than seven feet high. Provision should be made for mejlis [equivalent to formal living room and was male-only], an additional room for sleeping, kitchen, storeroom and washroom containing toilet and separate shower."[90] Similar to the training programs in General Camp that governed the ways in which Saudi employees would act, the house became another place in which Aramco would seek to govern and regiment proper citizenship and decorum. Drawings

86   Lebkicher, The Work and Life of Aramco Employees, 43.
87   Aramco would use water supply as strategy for urban development by supplying
      water to places it wanted to develop in the future and denying water access to places
      it deemed "undesirable." See Aramco, "Housing Facilities," 20.
88   Aramco, "Housing Facilities."
89   Aramco, "Housing Facilities," 24.
90   Aramco, "Housing Facilities," 31.

were prepared without consulting the future occupants, and a bid extended to Saudi contractors for a "house and compound wall [that] would be built of native masonry like the houses Saudis build for themselves."[91]

In addition to the basic houses, higher grades (and thus more elaborate houses) were also submitted for bidding, and a scheme was devised that assigned four different house types to four grades, with D-2 being the lowest and D-5 the highest.[92] These four "Saudi" prototypes were to be "native" and "natural" in the design, construction, and occupancy, in comparison to the prototype Aramco called "Arab-American" (AA), which was designed to be a hybrid between Arab and US houses. The AA house combined the Saudi compound wall, courtyards, and useable flat roof with the "convenience in layout, greater storage space, and adequate plumbing installations" of the suburban US house.[93] Beyond the flat roof and the spatial divisions of the house, the Saudi desert climate and social structures (of extended families) were not taken into consideration. It appeared that the company felt that the suburban US home would overcome everything, no matter where it was built or what environmental and cultural conditions it encountered.

For Aramco, the suburban US home was more than just a structure—it was an architecture that could change behavior and introduce new social and spatial norms. This idea that the suburban house could modify and mold bodies and practices stems from both the US's New Deal and Point Four's use of suburban housing to aid in rapid development and modernization. The US house, and the "American Dream" that accompanied it, was the key weapon in the US's march against communism and in effectively dealing with a place that was environmentally different from the US. The committee's report states that the AA house would appeal to Saudis and Aramcons alike. Anyone reading this document without an understanding of Aramco's racialized and discriminatory history would assume that these houses are for Arabs and US employees equally, but that is a far cry from the truth. Although Aramco's AA House was to cater to the needs of both Saudis and US employees, finances hindered its application. AA houses were never built in these communities but instead were only memorialized in company documents. Herein lies the realities of Aramco's intentionally racial practices: it was always concerned with the appearance of care. Just as the

91   Aramco, "Housing Facilities," 31.
92   Note that D-6 is the required grade for occupancy in the Intermediate Camp.
93   Aramco, "Housing Facilities," 38.

divisions of the camps "appeared" to address Aramco's racial practices by using skills as a gauge, so did these houses through their superficial attempt at developing a Saudi-US prototype.

In July 1955, construction began on thirty-five concrete two- and three-bedroom homes for Saudis in the Dammam townsite.[94] This first batch of homes was intended for higher-grade employees and were designed as flat-roofed single-family detached houses set back from the perimeter of the plot. Here Aramco was setting the example for lower-grade employees that the "Aramcon dream" of the single-family home was achievable; all one had to do was emulate the higher-grade Saudi employees. While the original plan was to construct "native" homes using "native" materials, it seems that Aramco shied away from this strategy, deciding instead to construct all houses under the HOP in concrete since it was faster, more reliable, and more "modern." Aramco saw concrete as a tangible representation of how it was transforming the desert and bestowing modernization onto the Kingdom. On the occasion of the completion of the 5,500th house in March 1965, the company's weekly newspaper, Sun and Flare, splashed the news on the first page, complete with an image showing the proud home owner, Abdullah ibn Hameed al-Abdul'al, with W.L. Crampton, Assistant Dhahran District Manager, and Shaykh Hassan al-Jishi, Director of the Qatif Municipality.[95] These houses were propaganda strategies aimed at settling ongoing labor unrest and demonstrating to the Saudi government that Aramco was keeping up its end of the bargain of offering equitable housing. These HOP homes introduced the single-family, detached house to the Kingdom. For many in the Eastern Provinces, this was the first time that concrete, electricity, running water, and a (Western) bathroom were available to a Saudi family.[96] Aramco touted these homes as beacons of the success of HOP and as an attainable dream for Saudis, as long as they were prepared to strive hard enough for it.[97]

---

94   "Housing Under Construction At New Dammam Townsite," Sun and Flare, September 21, 1955, 1.
95   See "Ceremony Marks 5,500th Home," Sun and Flare, March 31, 1965, 1.
96   See Al-Hathloul, "Tradition, Continuity and Change in the Physical Environment"; Alkhedheiri, "Urban Infil"; Al-Naim, "Identity in Transitional Context"; and Mashary Al-Naim, "Dammam Saudi Arabia," in Architecture and Globalisation in the Persian Gulf Region, ed. Murray Fraser and Nasser Golzari (London: Routledge, 2016), 57–76. These three Saudi scholars also criticize the HOP's lack of sensitivity to Islamic and traditional architectural elements. See also Aḥmarī, "Dawr Sharikat Al-Zayt al-'Arabīyah al-Amrīkiyah (Arāmkū) Fī Tanmiyat al-Minṭaqah al-Sharqīyah Min al-Mamlakah al-'Arabīyah al-Sa'ūdīyah," chap. 2; and "367 Homes Built or Brought Under Loan Plan," Sun and Flare, January 15, 1958.

Concrete house constructed through the Home Ownership Program (HOP) with the new homeowner, Abdulla al-Quereshi standing in the door, talking to the builders Isaac N. Richa and Frank Lincoln of the Home Ownership division, Arab Development department, Thugba, Saudi Arabia, 1957. "Employee Uses Home Loan Plan," *Sun and Flare*, November 13, 1957, 2. Courtesy of Aramco.

HOME OWNERSHIP MILESTONE

Ceremony Marks 5,500th Home

Ceremonies on March 23 marked the completion of the 5,500th home constructed with a loan made available under Aramco's Home Ownership Program.

OWNER OF THE new home is Abdullah ibn Hameed al-Abdul'al, a baker in the Dhahran Bakery. He has been an Aramco employee since May, 1950. Al-Abdul'al and his wife have two sons and two daughters.

The home, where the ceremonies were held, is located in the Qatif oasis in the village of Umm al-Khamam, northwest of Saihat. The two-bedroom home has a mejlis, kitchen, family

room, and car port with overhead veranda.

SPEECHES marking the occasion were delivered by W.R. Crampton, assistant Dhahran district manager, who briefly explained the intent of the Home Ownership Program, and Shaykh Hassan al-Jishi, Director of the Municipality of Qatif.

In his address, Shaykh al-Jishi complimented the Home Ownership Program, then discussed several projects which will affect Umm al-Khamam. He mentioned paving of the road to Umm al-Khamam and construction of a meat and vegetable market.

The 5,500th home was designed

by 'Umar Bushnaq, architect, and constructed by Hassan al-Bashrawi, contractor. Al-Bashrawi was present for the final inspection and ceremony.

AMONG THE Aramco officials present were L.T. Weathers, manager, Arab Industrial Development Department, and Frank E. Patterson, coordinator, Home Ownership Division. Also attending were representatives from Home Ownership in all three districts.

The loan program to build homes for eligible Saudi Arab employees began in 1951. The 1,000th home was finished in

(Continued on Page 8)

Municipality Director Speaks

PARTICIPANTS in the ceremony marking the 5,500th home completed under Aramco's Home Ownership Program were (from left) Abdullah ibn Hameed al-Abdul'al, owner of the home in the village of Umm al-Khamam, Assistant Dhahran District Manager W.L. Crampton, and Shaykh Hassan al-Jishi, Director of the Municipality of Qatif. (Ghamidi)

MISS ALDERS

Districts Plan Holiday Dances

The Henry May Orchestra with vocalist Nancy Alders, brought from Rotterdam by the AEA for 'Id al-Adha festivities, will open their local appearances at a dance at the Dhahran Industrial Cafeteria Friday, April 9. Starting time will be 9 p.m. Admission will be by ticket and control card.

Tickets, SR 10 each, will be on sale from 5 to 6 p.m. in the booth outside the Family Issue Store each working day starting Saturday.

In Dhahran, those wishing to make table reservations should contact Aline Boudreaux at 4120.

The Abqaiq dance will be held April 10 at 9 p.m. on the Clubhouse Patio. Tickets, priced at SR 10, may be obtained at the Recreation Library or from AEA representatives.

Ras Tanura's spring dance will begin at 9 p.m. April 11 on the Surf House Patio — co-sponsored by the Ras Tanura Women's Group and the AEA. Tickets, at SR 10, are available from Women's Group officers or AEA representatives.

Sun and Flare

Vol. XXI, No. 13

Published by Aramco — Phone 3129
Printed by Al-Mutawa Press — Dammam

March 31, 1965

ENTRANTS, VIEWERS INVITED

Garden Show on Thursday

The Dhahran Garden Group is inviting everyone in the community to participate in the 1965 Spring Garden Show this Thursday, April 1, in the Industrial Cafeteria.

Entries will be received between 10 a.m. and noon. Featured will be arrangements for all types of parties, from baby showers to farewell banquets.

Home-grown or purchased materials may be used for arrangements employing fresh, dried, or artificial flowers, foliage, fruits, and vegetables.

The Garden Group is hoping that green-thumbers will turn out in force to enter the categories for all types of indoor and outdoor plants, flowers, vegetables, and herbs.

The show will be open from

3 to 5:30 p.m. In addition to the main attraction, there will be music and refreshments, courtesy of the Dhahran Women's Group, and door prizes.

The Dhahran Art Group will display some ceramic pieces made by members and the Ras Tanura Garden Group will have a special display of orchid plants and corsages.

Dietitian's Talk To Be Saturday

Hospital Dietitian Betty Whitney will discuss nutrition this Saturday in the last class of the Dhahran Women's Group health and charm course. Dr. Mary Barretto will speak on "Functions of Vitamins and Minerals in the Body." The class will begin at 7:30 p.m. in the Recreation Portable.

There have been three classes since the course began March 13.

Movies

Vacation-month movie programs for children will be presented in Aramco theaters according to the following schedule:

Abqaiq — 2 p.m. on April 3, 10, 17, and 24.

Dhahran — 2 p.m. on April 2, 9, 16, and 23.

Ras Tanura — 4 p.m. on April 4, 11, 18, and 25.

FESTIVAL TONIGHT
Doors open tonight at 7:30 for the Tri-District Music Festival in the Dhahran School Gymnasium.

Dr. Taher Addresses AIME

DR. ABDULHADY TAHER, Governor of the General Petroleum and Mineral Organization, spoke to a gathering of AIME members last Saturday in Dhahran, discussing "Industrial Development and Planning in Saudi Arabia." Taher, who earned his doctorate at the University of California, is an honorary member of the Saudi Arabia Section of the Society of Petroleum Engineers of AIME.

Don't Forget To Set Clocks

Dark and early Friday morning — at 12:01 a.m. — company clocks will be advanced one hour, putting company operations on daylight saving time until Friday, Sept. 3.

Artists' Works To Be Displayed

The works of several local artists will be on display in company facilities during the next three months, a project sponsored by the Dhahran Art Group.

A "one man show" will feature paintings in various media by Jane Taylor. These will be exhibited in the theater lobby.

A collection of collages will be on display in the Snack Bar — works of Gloria Titcomb, Dorothy Kellenberg, Kiko Johnson, Norma Hoke, and Virginia Swann.

The Recreation Library will have paintings by Nancy Weeks, Shirlee Blank, and Eunice Banks. For further information, call Beverly Swartz, 5889, or Eunice Banks, 4682.

ARABIC CLASSES

Arabic language classes in Dhahran will resume Saturday for those registered to attend on either an assigned or voluntary basis.

The Weather

March 22-29

		Temp.	Hum.
Abqaiq	Max.	93	99
	Min.	61	15
Dhahran	Max.	92	89
	Min.	62	14
Ras Tanura	Max.	89	96
	Min.	59	23

Ceremony marking the 5,500th home completed in Umm al-Khamam, under the Home Ownership Program (HOP) showing home owner Abdullah ibn Hameed al-Abdul'al (left), with Assistant Dhahran District Manager W.L. Crampton (middle), and Qatif Municipality Director, Shaykh Hassan al-Jishi (right). "Employee Uses Home Loan Plan," *Sun and Flare*, November 13, 1957, 1. Courtesy of Aramco.

Everywhere and Nowhere

Dhahran was the site of many firsts in the Eastern Province, a region that was mainly home to nomadic Bedouin tribes who had a deep and intricate relationship to their desert landscapes. The first US airplane in the region arrived in 1934, piped water and prefabricated homes in June 1936, Western wives in the spring of 1937, the first airport in 1945, the first brick school in 1946, the first green lawn in 1947, and the first film was shot in 1948.[98] The settlement also brought the first paved road, the first electric generator, the first hospital, and the first signs of industrialization: the refineries in Dhahran and Ras Tanura. Coupled with Aramco's full-fledged propagandist public relations department, the company came to symbolize development, modernization, and triumph of technology. But Aramco was fueled by US exceptionalism and "paternal" care, and these so-called "firsts" were made available only to Aramcons. Upon setting up camp, everyone who was not Aramcon was kept outside of their fenced-in camp, establishing a hierarchy along racial and class lines. Dhahran as a sort of US "suburb" became emblematic of technological prowess, development, and modernization. This story of the transplantation of the US suburb to the Saudi Arabian desert sheds light on the ways in which US oil companies sought to define a specific model of urbanization exported from the US that centered around the single-family home, a model that was then duplicated by budding nation-states as an ideal way to become "modern."

The airplane, the pipeline, and the car traversed deserts, overcoming them, taming them, and ordering them into a little piece of US suburbia outside the US. There, Aramcon families lived in suburban homes with their green lawns along the quaint streets of Dhahran, in a place akin to *The Truman Show* (1998).[99] Dhahran was in reality Anywhere, USA. The desert was a mere background, rendered flat, replaceable, changeable. For Anywhere, USA, was indeed anywhere, somewhere, and nowhere at the same time.

97   See "The House That Ibrahim Built," *Aramco World*, March 1953.
98   Richard Lyford, *Miyah, a Story of Water*, video (United States: Arabian American Oil Company, 1950).
99   Peter Weir, *The Truman Show* (Hollywood, CA: Paramount Pictures, 1998).

Emblems of Modernization: Tapline, Saudi, and Airplane. Saudi Aramco, the Trans-Arabian Pipeline, Saudi Arabia, 1951. Scott McMurray, *Energy to the World: The Story of Aramco*, vol. 1 (Houston, TX: Aramco Services Company, 2011), 122–123. Courtesy of Aramco.

Alla Vronskaya is professor of History and Theory of Architecture at Kassel University. Her book *Architecture of Life: Soviet Modernism and the Human Sciences*, which explores the intersections between architecture, labor management, and human sciences in modern Russia, is forthcoming from University of Minnesota Press. Vronskaya received her PhD in the History, Theory, and Criticism of Architecture and Art from Massachusetts Institute of Technology in 2014, and has since taught at ETH Zurich, Illinois Institute of Technology, and Kassel University. She was a member in residence at the Institute for Advanced Study in Princeton, and received residential fellowships from the Getty Research Institute and the Dumbarton Oaks Research Library. She has published and presented widely, and is a coeditor of the former Soviet Union section in the *Bloomsbury Global Encyclopedia of Women in Architecture* (forthcoming).

ALLA VRONSKAYA

THE WHITE SEA CANAL AND THE RHETORICAL DESERTIFICATION OF KARELIA

№ 76

Kor'ašša kuluu iltakoite,
vieronašša vierȫy iltaviečora,
laitošša lankieu päivänlašku.
Eikä viečora viihyttäis,
kun en voi laitto laulua,
kun on lanken laulusika,
jo on vierryn viekaš aika.
Laulan iänellä lankennuolla,
šoitan iänellä šortunuolla.
Lakki on šortan laulun aijan,
sorokka on šortan šoitto aijan.
Laulu on kuin lauvan vešto,
goolossu on kuin koiran haukku.
Kun olis laatnoi laulukieli,
ta olis šomana šoittoaika,
luatisin laulut laihinoista,
vetäsin virtyöt veloista.
Aijä kun šyytta šyrvätäh,
Šijä tauvitta tallatah.

В горе проходит закат,
в печалях протекает вечер-вечерок,
в тоске исходит заход солнца.
И вечер не веселит,
и не могу печальная петь,
ведь отошло время песен,
и укатилась пора игровая.
Пою голосом упавшим,
напеваю голосом сорвавшимся.
Чепец покончил с порой песенной,
сорока завершила время игр.
Песня, что тесание досок,
голос подобен лаю собаки.
Был бы ладным голос певчий,
да красивым время игр (музыки),
создала бы песни из долгов,
затянула бы вирши из недоимок.

The sunset is spent in sorrow,
The evening passes in grief,
The sun declines in anguish.
The evening does not bring joy,
And I, full of sorrow, cannot sing,
Because the time of songs is over,
And the age of games is gone.
I sing with a faltering voice,
Hum with a strained voice.[1]

1   Karelian *joiku* (folk song) from Kaleval'sky district, Karelia, Russia. Shown here in both Karelian (top) and Russian (bottom). N. A. Lavonen, A. S. Stepanova, and K. Kh. Rautio, *Karel'skie yegi* (Petrozavodsk: Karel'skii nauchnyi tsentr RAN, 1993), 156. Translated from Russian by the author.

Тяжело сдавили своды,
Тяжело гнетёт тюрьма.
Мутным призраком свободы
За решёткой дразнит тьма.

Спит тюрьма и трудно дышит,
Каждый вздох — тоска и стон,
Только мёртвый камень слышит,
Ничего не скажет он.

Но когда последней дрожью
Содрогнётся шар земной,
Вопль камней к престолу Божью
Пронесётся в тьме ночной.

И когда, трубе послушный,
Мир стряхнёт последний сон,
Вспомнит камень равнодушный
Каждый вздох и каждый стон.

Михаил Фроловский
1925

The vaults press hard,
The prison oppresses heavily.
As an opaque mirage of freedom,
Darkness teases from behind the bars.

The prison sleeps and breathes with trouble.
Each breath is [full of] sorrow and moan.
Only the dead stone can hear it,
But it will keep silent.

But when the earth will shake
In its last shiver,
The scream of stones to the throne of God
Will rush through the night's darkness.

And when, obedient to the horn,
The world will shake off the last slumber,
The indifferent stone will recall
Every sigh and every moan.[2]

2   Russian engineer Mikhail Florovsky (1895–1943) had served in the Red Army before
     his first arrest in 1925, when this poem was written. After spending three years in the
     notorious Solovetsky prison camp (formerly a revered monastery on the islands in
     the White Sea, not far from where the White Sea–Baltic Canal would soon be built),
     he was exiled, before being arrested again in 1941. He died in Karaganda labor camp
     in Kazakhstan. See Elena Volkova, "Poetry Lesson: Stone and Cross of the GULAG,"
     History Lessons, December 19, 2011, https://urokiistorii.ru/article/2746. Handwritten
     and translated by the author.

Socialist colonialism remains an elusive figure. Postcolonial theory, developed for the analysis of such colonial empires as the French and the British, has yet to fully account for the logic and mechanics of extraction, control, and exploitation within state-socialist countries such as the Soviet Union. Despite positioning itself as an alternative to colonial empires, the Soviet Union, which was formed in 1922 on the territories of the former Russian Empire under communist governments' control, often maintained similar practices of domination. If during the first postrevolutionary years the term "colonization" (*kolonizatsiia*) was often used in Russia in the positive sense to refer to the economic development of a region, by the late 1920s it was replaced by "the conquest of nature," an expression that betrayed the militaristic, aggressive character of this development.[3]

3   Andy Bruno, *The Nature of Soviet Power: An Arctic Environmental History* (Cambridge: Cambridge University Press, 2016), 32–33, 68. Introduced in the Soviet Union during the interwar period, the term "conquest of nature" was used across the Socialist Bloc during the Cold War, becoming a part of its rhetoric and ideology. See, for instance, Sergio Diaz-Briquets and Jorge F. Pérez-López, *Conquering Nature: The Environmental Legacy of Socialism in Cuba* (Pittsburgh: University of Pittsburgh Press, 2000). On this notion in the Soviet context, see Bruno, *The Nature of Soviet Power*, 29–72; Paul R. Josephson, *The Conquest of the Russian Arctic* (Cambridge, MA: Harvard University Press, 2014); and Alla Bolotova, "Colonization of Nature in the Soviet Union: State Ideology, Public Discourse, and the Experience of Geologists," *Historical Social Research* 29, no. 3 (2004): 104–123.

"The conquest of nature," which was understood as the heroic subordination of a resistant nature to man, was, indeed, justified not only by the economic needs of the industrializing country but often also by military considerations.[4] This essay will trace the historic roots of this "conquest of nature" in both Russian social democratic culture and Western imagination in the early twentieth century to show how such constructs as "civilization," "the desert," "savage," and "development" were mobilized for the Soviet colonial project.

Seen as an obstacle to modernization and economic prosperity, the desert was the first among many landscapes to be conquered in the name of development—an attitude that was by no means unique to the Soviet Union. For instance, in North Africa, pastoral nomadic populations were blamed for "desertification" (a now-contested theory that stipulated that the desert zone was rapidly expanding) and deforestation (which, colonial scientists falsely claimed, was triggered by their cattle).[5] The Russian Empire began its assault on the desert in Central Asia shortly after colonizing the region; this assault was amplified in the late 1920s and early 1930s, when American experts helped devise irrigation systems, transforming the region's economy from one of diverse agriculture for local consumption to a cotton-based monoculture.[6] In other words, the designation of a region as a "desert" implied that it required a "conquest"; it was thus a rhetorical instrument that sustained colonization politics. Such designation often included portraying entire populations, based on their presumed relationship to the desert, in binary terms, as either those who preferred to adapt to it and remain "savages" or those who chose the "dignified" fight against it and thus "civilization."

This essay focuses on a historic attempt to dialectically sublate this binary opposition within the notion of "socialist

4   The city of Murmansk on the Kola Peninsula has been an important naval base since the nineteenth century and was all but destroyed during World War II. Severodvinsk on the White Sea is the main base of the Russian nuclear submarine fleet.

5   David S. G. Thomas and Nicholas J. Middleton, *Desertification: Exploding the Myth* (Chichester: John Wiley & Sons, 1994); Diana K. Davis, *Resurrecting the Granary of Rome: Environmental History and French Colonial Expansion in North Africa* (Athens: Ohio University Press, 2007), 5. The North American Dust Bowl crisis of the 1930s further augmented these fears, and during the Cold War period, the counter-desertification measures within the framework of the UNESCO Arid Zone Program would become one of the few spheres of smooth international collaboration. On this program, see Perrin Selcer, *The Postwar Origins of the Global Environment: How the United Nations Built Spaceship Earth* (New York: Columbia University Press, 2018), 97–132.

6   Imperial irrigation projects were centered in Mirzacho'l Steppe on the left bank of the Syr Darya River in contemporary Uzbekistan. On early Soviet irrigation projects, see Maya Peterson, "US to USSR: American Experts, Irrigation, and Cotton in Soviet Central Asia, 1929–1932," *Environmental History* 21 (2016): 442–466.

development." Examining the rhetorical making of the desert in Russia, it moves between ideology and the material infrastructure that supported it, between fiction and reality—and between planets. It traces how the image of the desert impacted the reality of the Soviet Union's colonization of its north while reading philosopher and revolutionary Alexander Bogdanov's early twentieth-century novel *Engineer Menni* alongside one of the darkest and most gruesome episodes of Soviet history, the construction of the White Sea–Baltic Canal (often known as simply the White Sea Canal) in a marshy and wooded Northern-European region that was climatically anything but a desert.

Fiction can help elucidate the real built environment as a symbolic form. "All the deserts of the world have a future," concluded Bogdanov's protagonist Menni, announcing a demiurgical ambiton of transforming them into productive oases.[7] As this essay will argue, this productivity was identified with civilization: in Russian social-democratic and early Soviet thought, the desert was seen as the necessary cradle of civilization, which stimulated the development of human ingenuity and collaboration, but only inasmuch as it was the challenge that had to be overcome. A key part of colonial discourse and practice, which employed *mission civilisatrice* as both a rationale for colonial domination and a program of colonial development, the rhetoric of civilization betrays the colonial ambitions of symbolic desertification in the Soviet Union.

The Great Project

Established in 1894, the Lowell Observatory in Arizona was named one of "The World's 100 Most Important Places" by *Time* magazine.[8] It was here that Pluto was discovered in 1930. The observatory was named after its founder, the US scientist and spiritualist Percival Lowell, whose three major publications, *Mars* (1895), *Mars and Its Canals* (1906), and *Mars as the Abode of Life* (1908), popularized the belief that markings on the surface of the planet were evidence of intelligent life forms. This belief persisted among scientists until the post–World War II period, when technological advances revealed that the markings were an optical illusion resulting from the inadequacies of early telescopes. First recorded by the Italian astronomer Giovanni

7   Alexandr Bogdanov, *Engineer Menni*, in *Red Star: The First Bolshevik Utopia*, ed. Loren Graham and Richard Stites, trans. Charles Rougle (Bloomington: Indiana University Press, 1984), 158.
8   The designation was made in 2011. See "About Lowell Observatory," Lowell Observatory, https://lowell.edu/discover/about-us.

Schiaparelli in 1877, the markings were described as *canali*, which can be translated as "canals," "channels," or "gullies."[9] Choosing the word "canals," Schiaparelli's English translators interpreted the original term as a constructed irrigational infrastructure, encouraging speculations about an intelligent civilization that created it. In believing that they had discovered a civilization on Mars, scientists both provided the planet with a historicity and asserted its colonial dimension, based on a presumed difference between the "civilized" and the "non-civilized."

Created in Denmark, this Mars globe reflects the popularity of Lowell's vision. Emmy Ingeborg Brun, *Mars efter Lowell's Glober*, 1909. Courtesy of the Royal Museums Greenwich.

According to Lowell, the arid, dying landscape of Mars reflected the decline of an old civilization, which was forced to build giant canals to bring water from the polar caps. A similar

9   Giovanni Virginio Schiaparelli, "Osservazioni astronomiche e fisiche sull'asse di rotazione e sulla topografia del pianeta Marte fatte nella reale specola di Brera in Milano coll'equatoreale di Merz durante l'opposizione del 1877: memoria del socio G. V. Schiaparelli," *Atti della Reale Accademia dei Lincei: Memorie della Classe di scienzefisiche, matematiche e naturali* 3, no. 2 (1877–1878): 3–136. See K. Maria D. Lane, "Mapping the Mars Canal Mania: Cartographic Projection and the Creation of a Popular Icon," *Imago Mundi* 58, no. 2 (2006): 198–211.

pessimistic view of "civilization" as associated with old age was shortly after employed by German historian Oswald Spengler in his influential *Der Untergang des Abendlandes (The Decline of the West)*, whose first volume appeared in 1918. A milestone of German romantic conservative thought, *Der Untergang des Abendlandes* distinguished between *Kultur*, rooted in blood, vital force, and tradition, and *Zivilisation*, which was cosmopolitan, materialist, lifeless, rationalist, and capitalist.[10] In the same manner, the binary oppositions of the old and the young, the modern man and the savage, reason and vital force were mobilized by the colonial project in Soviet Russia (just as they were elsewhere), translating into the dialectical opposition of civilization and the desert.

Inspired by Schiaparelli's discovery and other astronomical observations of the planet, science fiction writers around the world began to speculate about life on Mars, projecting earthly concerns onto literary descriptions of Martian civilization. Among the most influential novels were *Uranie* (1889) by French writer and astronomer Camille Flammarion; *Auf zwei Planeten (Two Planets*, 1897) by German author Kurd Lasswitz; *The War of the Worlds* (1898) by English author H. G. Wells; and *A Princess of Mars* (1912) by US writer Edgar Rice Burroughs. In Soviet Russia, Mars emerged as a stage-set for discussing contemporary politics. Alexei Tolstoy's 1923 novel with a Spenglerian title *Aelita, or the Decline of Mars* described two systems of Martian canals: the first, hardly detectable, was an old, dried-out, abandoned network, overgrown with cacti; the second was a newer, functional, and clearly visible system.[11] The Martian imaginary had already been incorporated into the Russian political imaginary before the 1917 revolution, as the observed red color of the planet was linked to the political symbolism of the revolutionized society. Influenced by Lasswitz's book, Bogdanov published the novel *The Red Star* in 1908 (the same year he publicly debated the principles of communism with Lenin, challenging his principles from the left), in which he depicted a communist society thriving on Mars.[12] Its sequel *Engineer Menni* (1913) described

10   For a critical analysis of the notion of civilization in German conservative thought, see Jeffrey Herf, *Reactionary Modernism: Technology, Culture, and Politics in Weimar the Third Reich* (Cambridge: Cambridge University Press, 1984).
11   The novel was turned into a popular silent film, directed by Yakov Protazanov, the following year.
12   The novel, set in 1905, described the journey of a Russian revolutionary to Mars, where he encountered a technologically advanced communist civilization. For more on this and other Russian science fiction novels see Asif Siddiqi, *The Red Rockets' Glare: Spaceflight and the Russian Imagination, 1857–1957* (Cambridge: Cambridge University Press, 2014).

the construction of canals as the context of the political struggle during the period of the transition of Mars to communism.

Engineer Menni focuses on the life and work of Martian engineer Menni Aldo, who possesses an ambitious vision for the transformation of nature on a planetary scale. The book follows Menni's work on the development of Libya—a region distinguished by early astronomers and still recognized today as Libya Montes, a highland terrain on Mars. In his fictional book The Future of Libyan Desert, Menni outlined "The Great Project"—a system of canals that would channel water to an artificial sea, turning the uninhabitable desert into fertile agricultural land:

> At present this is nothing but an arid desert whose surface stratum of sand has been ground into a fine dust that is injurious to the lungs and eyes... All this will change if we succeed in creating an inland sea in Libya. The moisture evaporating from the surface of the water under the tropical sun will be retained by the mountains surrounding the depression and will return down their slopes as streams and rivers that will provide sufficient if not abundant irrigation. According to our analyses, the soil of the desert is rich in the salts necessary to vegetation, and the water will immediately render it fertile. If agriculture is organized on a scientifically correct basis, the country will be able to feed 20 million persons of our entire present population of 300 million.[13]

The canal promised an answer to the impending crises of overproduction. "You are aware that at regular intervals during the past 150 years we have been beset by serious financial and industrial crises," Menni testifies. "At such times credit falls, the market shrinks, thousands of enterprises are ruined, and millions become unemployed."[14] Breaking this cycle, his proto-Keynesian construction program aimed to trigger economic growth, to give people work, to stimulate consumption and production, and to eventually incorporate a whole new territory into the economic sphere.

This program came at a heavy human price. The site of the tragedy, which eventually cost Menni his position and freedom, was the work on a 200-kilometer-long section of the canal known

13   Bogdanov, Engineer Menni, 154.
14   Bogdanov, Engineer Menni, 155.

The cover of Bogdanov's *Engineer Menni* depicts the protagonist holding a Lowell's globe of Mars as he conceives the transformation of Martian geography. A. Bogdanov, *Inzhener Menni* (Petrograd: Sovet rabochikh i krest'ianskikh deputatov, 1919).

as the Rotten Bogs. This was an uninhabitable territory, where deadly fevers abounded. 300,000 workers worked up to the waist in water. Diseases proliferated, thousands died each month, and the workers' unrest intensified.[15] Menni had foreseen the difficulties and explained his decision: although the canal could have been moved east, bypassing the Rotten Bogs, this would have meant passing through a zone of high Mars-quake risk. Although there had been no quakes for a long time, such risk was inadmissible because it would have destroyed the cities built around the canal, causing hundreds of thousands of deaths. Thousands of lives had to be sacrificed to the interests of future civilization—in Bogdanov's words, "It was not Menni who did that, but necessity."[16]

15   Menni was imprisoned for killing an engineer who tried to reroute the canal in order to pacify striking workers. However, the workers later realized that the conditions of their labor were worse under the new management and demanded Menni be reinstated as the head of construction.

16   Bogdanov, *Engineer Menni*, 168–177, 183.

The White Sea–Baltic Canal

Not coincidentally, canals were noticed on Mars when earthly canal construction was booming. Reports from canal construction sites dominated both newspaper headlines and the public imagination across the globe: the Suez Canal was completed in 1869 (predating Schiaparelli's discovery by eight years); it was followed by France's unsuccessful attempt to build the Panama Canal in 1880. The builders—Egyptian peasants in one case and Black Antillean Islanders in the other—endured dismal living and working conditions, which were widely known and criticized.[17] The French Panama Canal project was abandoned in 1881 due to engineering problems and a high worker mortality rate, caused by mosquito-spread diseases and insufficient food and housing. The project, taken over by the United States in 1904, finally opened in 1914.

As a reflection on the tragedies that plagued the construction of the Panama Canal, Bogdanov's *Engineer Menni* would itself contribute to normalizing the atrocities that were to follow in the Soviet Union. Like the great irrigation projects of ancient Mesopotamia and modern transportation canals, Menni's Great Project challenged the technological, social, and even moral standards of the time. In the Soviet Union, these standards were soon radically and proudly subverted during the years of industrialization, as new industrial sites were constructed en masse, with the builders' living and working conditions no better (and often worse) than those in Panama and Suez, and as the network of the GULAG (the Main Directorate of Camps) spread throughout the country, fed by Stalinist mass repressions.[18] The construction of the White Sea Canal in the north of Russia became the site where terror and modernization came to be most poignantly intertwined. The canal's economic purpose—or rather, the oft-noted lack thereof since it ended up being too shallow to be passable for most ships—has puzzled historians. It was, as

17   See Gustave Anguizola, "Negroes in the Building of the Panama Canal," *Phylon* 29, no. 4 (1968): 351–359; and May Farouk, "Forced Labor during the Excavation of the Isthmus: A War of Words and Novelistic Representation," *Sociétés & Représentations* 48, no. 2 (2019): 143–155.

18   Numerous historians have explored this subject. On the building of new industrial cities, see, for instance, Mark Meerovich, Evgeniia Konysheva, and Dmitrij Chmelnizki, *Kladbishche sotsgorodov: gradostroitel'naia politika v SSSR 1928–1932 gg.* (Moscow: Rosspen, 2011). For more focused studies in English, see Stephen Kotkin, *Magnetic Mountain: Stalinism as a Civilization* (Berkeley: University of California Press, 1995); and Heather D. DeHaan, *Stalinist City Planning: Professionals, Performance, and Power* (Toronto: University of Toronto Press, 2013). On the history of the GULAG, see Oleg Chlevnjuk, *History of the Gulag: From Collectivization to the Great Terror* (New Haven: Yale University Press, 2004), among many other academic and popular publications.

this essay suggests, not transportation but development itself, broadly understood as a project of "civilization," that was the canal's primary mission.

Stretching between the Arctic Ocean's White Sea in the north and the Gulf of Finland in the west, the White Sea–Baltic Canal passed through Karelia, a sparsely populated region that since the fourteenth century has been divided between Sweden (subsequently Finland) and Russia. Like Bogdanov's Martian Rotten Bogs, Karelia is marshy, although cold and covered with the subarctic wooded forest, *taiga*. Karelians, who settled in the region at the end of the first millennium, pursued a traditional economy of hunting and fishing. Karelia remained a double periphery—of Russia and of Finland—and the two powers repeatedly clashed over their influence.[19] Following the revolution of 1917, the region was recognized as the Karelian Autonomous Republic, led by the government of "the Red Finns"—Finnish communist émigrés under Edvard Gylling.[20] Driven by a vision of "Greater Red Finland," Gylling strove, in the words of historian Nick Baron, "to accelerate the evolution of Karelians into Finns."[21] Following his government's dismissal in 1935, the Soviet Union began an aggressive politics of assimilation, integrating Karelians into Russian culture: whereas 37.42 percent of Karelia's population (100,781 people) identified as Karelian in 1926, only 7.08 percent (45,570 people) did so in 2010.[22]

Both Finnish and Soviet propaganda touted the alleged "primitiveness" of the Karelians to support the claims of political and cultural hegemony over the region they promised to modernize.[23] Constructed seven years before the Soviet Union attacked Finland in what would be known as the Winter War (1939–1940), the White Sea Canal became one of the physical and symbolic tools of this modernization, and, most crucially, the spine of future territorial development. As former

19   Karelian language is closely related to Finnish, but over time Karelians converted to Orthodox Christianity and developed their own dialects, while the Finns converted to Lutheranism; the relationship between the two nations was not always peaceful. See Nick Baron, *Soviet Karelia: Politics, Planning, and Terror in Stalin's Russia, 1920–1939* (London: Routledge, 2007), 9–19. See also Bruno, *The Nature of Soviet Power*.
20   Karelian Autonomous Soviet Socialist Republic was founded in 1923 within the Russian Soviet Federative Socialist Republic. Gylling and his team remained in power until 1935; in 1937, he was arrested and later executed.
21   Baron, *Soviet Karelia*, 36.
22   Central Statistical Office of the USSR, "Vsesoyuznaia perepis' naseleniia 1926 goda. Natsionalnyi sostav naseleniia po regionam SSSR," 1928–1929, Demoscope Weekly, http://www.demoscope.ru/weekly/ssp/rus_nac_26.php?reg=53; and "Informatsionnye materialy ob okonchatel'nykh itogakh Vserossiiskoi perepisi naseleniia 2010 goda," Federal State Statistics Service, December 14, 2011, http://www.gks.ru/free_doc/new_site/perepis2010/perepis_itogi1612.htm.
23   Baron, *Soviet Karelia*, 18.

Tsarist economist Gennady Chirkin, who became the head of the Colonization Department of the Murmansk Railway—which had been constructed in close proximity to the future White Sea Canal during the 1920s, prefiguring its colonizing ambitions—had put it, "In the Old World, nations built their railways; in the New World, the railways created the nation."[24] Chirkin, who would soon find himself working on the economic program of the White Sea Canal, could have included canals in the same category of modern nation-building colonization projects.

Although the strategic necessity of a canal that would connect the White and the Baltic Seas had been discussed in the Russian Empire since the early eighteenth century, it was rejected because of its high cost. The costs did not impede the Soviet regime. In the 1930s, Vyacheslav Molotov, the head of the government, pronounced that "a giant construction of artificial waterways"—the unification and expansion of water transportation systems within the European part of the USSR, including the White Sea–Baltic canal—was a key goal of the Second Five-Year Plan of Economic Development (1933–1937).[25] The construction was predominantly conducted by forced GULAG labor at the White Sea–Baltic Prison Camp, managed by the political police, OGPU (Ob'edinennoe gosudarstvennoe politicheskoe upravlenie, or Joint State Political Directorate), which placed it outside of the control of the Karelian government.[26] According to the OGPU chief Genrikh Iagoda, the project aimed to "colonize these areas and exploit their natural resources by means of the use of prisoner labor."[27] Not only did the canal rely on

24   G. F. Chirkin, Sovetskaia Kanada (Karelo-Murmanskii krai) (Leningrad, 1929), 1, quoted in Baron, Soviet Karelia, 76. Chirkin cited an unnamed American professor.
25   Vyacheslav Molotov's report on the XVI Congress of the Communist Party of the Soviet Union in 1934, quoted in M. Gorky, L. L. Averbakh, S. G. Firin, eds., Belomoro-Baltiiskii kanal imeni Stalina: Istoriia stroitel'stva, 1931–1934 (Moscow: OGIZ, 1934; reprint by unknown publisher, 1998), 67. Translated to English by Amabel Williams-Ellis as The White Sea Canal, Being an Account of the Construction of the New Canal between the White Sea and the Baltic Sea (London: John Lane, 1935).
26   Both those who broke the law and those who did not found themselves in the GULAG. The educated were frequently falsely accused of espionage and industrial sabotage, peasants of being "kulaks" (prosperous farmers who hired paid labor), and women of prostitution.
27   Politburo, June 27, 1929, RGASPI 17/3/746/2, 11, quoted in Baron, Soviet Karelia, 119–120. As Baron concluded, the more pragmatic rationale behind the canal construction was provided by "the OGPU's need to create demand to meet an explosion in the supply of forced labour resulting from collectivisation, and Iagoda's desire to carry out a prestigious project to prove the economic efficiency and propaganda value of using convicts and exiles to conquer, colonize and assimilate peripheral regions." Baron, Soviet Karelia, 129. Iagoda himself would be arrested in 1937 and shortly after executed. On the use of forced labor in the Soviet Union, see Paul R. Gregory and V. V. Lazarev, eds., The Economics of Forced Labor: The Soviet Gulag (Stanford, CA: Hoover Institution Press, 2003). On the use of forced labor in infrastructure projects in other colonial contexts, see Kwabena Opare Akurang-Parry, "Colonial Forced Labor Policies for Road-Building in Southern Ghana and

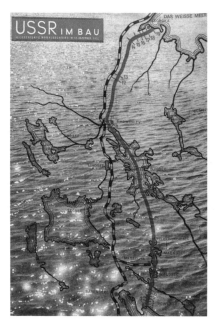

This map shows the northern section of the White Sea Canal between Povenets on Lake Onega and Soroka on the White Sea (in red), as well as the Murmansk railroad. Map by artist Alexander Rodchenko. From the magazine *USSR im Bau* (*USSR in Construction*), no. 12 (December 1933). Courtesy of Artists Rights Society.

incarcerated labor from all over the country, but also, just as fictional engineer Menni, its experts and planners, including the economist Chirkin and chief engineer Sergey Zhuk, were imprisoned.[28]

    The construction of the 227-kilometer-long canal in the midst of the "northern desert" began at the end of 1931 and took only twenty-one months to complete: in the course of this time, more than 100 hydro-technical structures and nineteen canal locks were erected; more than 2,500 kilometers of railroads were laid to support the construction.[29] The speed of construction

International Anti-Forced Labor Pressures, 1900–1940," African Economic History, no. 28 (2000): 1–25. See also Frederick Cooper, *Decolonization and African Society: The Labor Question in French and British Africa* (Cambridge: Cambridge University Press, 1996); Alice L. Conklin, *A Mission to Civilize: The Republican Idea of Empire in France and West Africa, 1895–1930* (Stanford: Stanford University Press, 1997); and Opolot Okia, *Communal Labor in Colonial Kenya: The Legitimization of Coercion, 1912–1930* (New York: Palgrave-Macmillan, 2012).

28   Chirkin was arrested in 1930 and then again in 1938 declared a participant of the never-existing counter-revolutionary sabotage organization Labor Peasant Party, while Zhuk was falsely accused of participating in a counter-revolutionary officer organization. Other specialist labor was provided by the so-called Industrial Party trial in 1930, which led to the charging of over 2,000 Soviet specialists—including the entire Central Asian Hydrology Department—as saboteurs. Baron, *Soviet Karelia*, 135.

One of the canal locks today. Photograph by Alexxx1979, 2018, via Creative Commons.

came at an enormous human cost. Causalities were amplified by the use of self-made equipment, often resembling that of the ancient world. Of the 250,000 imprisoned workers, 12,800 (roughly 5 percent) died according to the official statistics—contemporary historians estimate the total was likely double this figure, and possibly as high as 50,000 people.[30]

Despite its gruesome history, and even though its technical details were guarded as a state secret, the White Sea Canal was widely celebrated at the time in books, journals, newspapers, and films. Yet, unlike the Moscow River–Volga Canal—which was constructed immediately after, passing through Russia's core territory and adorned with sculpture and Neoclassical structures by celebrated architects—the White Sea Canal was described as engineering rather than as architecture.[31] Moreover, it was commonly presented not as a finished project but as a process of heroic construction that civilized both the unproductive environment and the "savage" imprisoned workers. For one, Alexander Lemberg's propaganda film *White Sea–Baltic Waterway* (1932) portrayed the construction as an act of heroism, which both transformed the criminals and "dekulakized" nature (stripped it of wealth) by making it work.[32]

29   *USSR im Bau*, no. 12 (December 1933), inside rear cover.
30   The violent history of the canal and its propaganda became the subject of multiple publications. See, for instance, Joachim Klein, "Belomorkanal: Literatur Und Propaganda in Der Stalinzeit," *Zeitschrift Für Slavische Philologie* 55, no. 1 (1995): 53–98; Cynthia Ann Ruder, *Making History for Stalin: The Story of the Belomor Canal* (Gainesville: University Press of Florida, 1998); A. N. Iakovlev, ed., *Stalinskie stroiki GULAGa, 1930–1953* (Moscow: MFD, Materik, 2005); and Anne Brunswic, *Les eaux glacées du Belomorkanal* (Arles: Actes Sud, 2009).
31   The construction of the Moscow River–Volga Canal began in 1932.

Alexander Rodchenko's photocollages juxtapose the stasis of the Karelian landscape and the militant dynamism of the people transforming it. *USSR im Bau* (*USSR in Construction*), no. 12 (December 1933). Courtesy of Artists Rights Society.

Propaganda publications celebrated the use of forced female labor as an instrument of emancipation and moral re-education. Alexander Rodchenko, *USSR im Bau* (*USSR in Construction*), no. 12 (December 1933). Courtesy of Artists Rights Society.

Former Constructivist artist Alexander Rodchenko paid three long visits to the construction site between 1931 and 1933, documenting it for the official propaganda journal *USSR in Construction*.[33] His photographs and photocollages juxtapose a calm, desolate Karelian landscape with the vibrant energy of the humans transforming it. One spread shows the site, a hill covered with snow and trees, before construction; the project's masterminds, depicted as giants towering above trees that barely reach their knees, point the way, supported by a rally of workers who march under the banner "Give Water" and a surveyor who has already commenced the work. "To the attack on earth!" declares another page, depicting war-like explosions, "With spade, ammonal, fire, iron!"[34] Moreover, as the resistant northern nature was taught to work, the incarcerated "social parasites," who had alledgedly been made such by the old society, were re-educated as good and industrious citizens. Far from hiding the use of forced labor, including that of women, Soviet propaganda promoted it as a tool of re-education.[35] Rodchenko's spread

32   The campaign of "dekulakization," or the struggle against prosperous peasants, the so-called *kulaks*, was a major source of captive labor for the canal construction.
33   Alexander Rodchenko, "Belomoro-Baltiiskii kanal im. Stalina," *USSR im Bau*, no. 12 (December 1933). See also Aglaya Glebova, "Elements of Photography: Avant-garde Aesthetics and the Reforging of Nature," *Representations* 142 (Spring 2018): 56–90.
34   *USSR im Bau*, no. 12 (December 1933): n.p.
35   One example is former prostitute Zinaida Yurtseva, once allegedly prone to

depicts women toiling with spades next to an image of the banner "[Give] way to the woman"; nearby is a group of socially transformed women celebrating Woman's Day. "I learned a lot at the canal construction... I know that now I am a totally different person," admits a former correction house inmate. Importantly, not only did the former idlers need the desert for their personal transformation, but their abundant "savage" energy was indispensable for this desert's civilization: an understanding of their important role, as it were, empowered the workers, contributing to their development.

In August 1933, together with construction managers, Rodchenko greeted the streamliner *Karl Marx*—and the group of 120 writers and artists on board led by the revolutionary romantic writer Maxim Gorky, Bogdanov's long-time friend and collaborator—as it arrived to celebrate the completion of the White Sea Canal. Back in 1895, Gorky had made his name as the author of "Old Izergil," a story that recounts the legend of Danko, a brave young leader who sacrificed his life to guide his people out of a dark forest by pulling out his flaming heart to light their way. In the group was the author of *Aelita*, Aleksei Tolstoy, and the former formalist Viktor Shklovsky, whose brother was in the "Canal Army," as the prisoner-workers were officially named.[36] After the visit, the writers published a collective volume, edited by Gorky, which acknowledged the risk and hardship endured by laborers as the inevitable price of the conquest of the North.

The book celebrated the canal as an instrument of a double transformation: the transformation of the hostile northern desert into productive land and the transformation of corrupt criminal personalities into enthusiastic builders of socialism.

> Deserted shores. Silent villages. Virgin lands covered with boulders. Untouched forests. Perhaps too many forests, they have invaded the best soils. And the swamps? The marshes creep in, bordering on man's very dwelling, devouring the roads, making life unkempt and dull. [Stalin says:] The Karelian Republic is right, it is tired of being called "harsh and swampy," it wants to be called "cheerful and bountiful."[37]

fighting and breaking windows. Channeled into the constructive course, Yurtseva's overabundant energy made her the leader of a women's brigade. Gorky, Averbakh, and Firin, *Belomoro-Baltiiskii kanal imeni Stalina*, 227–228.

36   Vladimir Shklovsky would be released in 1933, but again arrested and executed in 1937.

37   Gorky, Averbakh, and Firin, *Belomoro-Baltiiskii kanal imeni Stalina*, 552.

In the future, the book announced, "Arctic regions — half-savage and backward — will revive."[38] Barley, oats, wheat, forage grasses, and potatoes (a cross-breed of early-ripening varieties with cold-resistant ones from the Andes) would be harvested there.[39] Civilization, in the form of industry, culture, and urbanization, was juxtaposed with the backward lifestyle of the Indigenous Karelian hunter:

> Cities, factories, settlements, highways will emerge, they will cut forests, while cereals and forage grasses will rustle on dried swamps, and brown-icy waters of rivers will rush into the snails of turbines, lightening stern nights of the polar circle. Houses of culture, theaters, clubs will occupy the sites of winter camps, where just yesterday the man slept on fir-tree branches next to a dying camp fire, and the Master (or He, as he is known here — the bear) cautiously approached to smell the smoky human odor.[40]

Turning a remote northern region into a vital transportation hub, the White Sea Canal was intended to mark "the beginning of a harmonious system of socialist development (*osvoenie*) of the region," one in which logging would stimulate industrialization and urbanization.[41]

As soon as the canal was completed in 1933, the White Sea–Baltic Prison Camp was re-organized into the White Sea–Baltic Combine (*kombinat*), which, although centered on wood-processing and cellulose industry, included all forms of production, from mining rare metals to agriculture. Directed by OGPU, it was among the early examples of a typology that would define the Soviet development-focused approach to urban planning during the Cold War era — the territorial-production complex, an economic region defined by several production sites that share infrastructure and workforce.[42] Universalizing colonial logic, the territorial-production complex postulated economic development as the end goal of modern urbanism.[43]

38   Gorky, Averbakh, and Firin, *Belomoro-Baltiiskii kanal imeni Stalina*, 69.
39   Gorky, Averbakh, and Firin, *Belomoro-Baltiiskii kanal imeni Stalina*, 558.
40   Gorky, Averbakh, and Firin, *Belomoro-Baltiiskii kanal imeni Stalina*, 555.
41   The term *osvoenie*, used by the authors, had the connotation of making use of a resource.
42   The first, largest, and most widely publicized territorial-production complex, the Ural-Kuznetsk Combine, was founded in 1929.
43   See Kenny Cupers and Igor Demchenko, "Projective Geographies between East and West," in *East, West, Central*, ed. Ákos Moravánszky, vol. 2, *Re-Scaling the Environment: New Landscapes of Design, 1960–1980*, eds. Ákos Moravánszky and Karl R. Kegler (Basel: Birkhäuser, 2016), 135–151.

The peaceful, submerged landscapes of the White Sea—Baltic Canal hide the violent history of their creation. Photograph by Alexxx1979, 2018, via Creative Commons.

Although the notion of development is often dated to Harry Truman's inauguration speech in 1949, which made it the beacon of global Cold War economic programs, its roots go back to the colonial period, when the development of human and natural resources was used not merely as an economic imperative but as a moral one—the defining quality of civilization.[44] Later, colonial development programs transitioned to postcolonial ones, which aimed not to abandon development but to reroute its benefits towards newly independent nations. Seen in this light, the Soviet project of "hijacking" colonial development for the benefit of the people rhetorically pioneered the programs that would appear in "developing countries" in the aftermath of decolonization.

As a rhetorical construct that could be used, as the case of Karelia demonstrates, to justify dictatorship, forced labor, and imperial domination, in the course of the twentieth century, "the desert" appeared in colonial thought as a territory in need of moral and economic development, while an artificial waterway emerged as a material, architectural sign that defined a land-scape as a desert. Moreover, rooted in the neo-romantic myth of heroic self-sacrifice (to which both Gorky and Bogdanov contributed in their literary work), the rhetoric of empowerment allowed the Soviet colonial project to cynically claim that it treated land and people not as disposable objects but as an active life force

44   Wolfgang Sachs, introduction to *The Development Dictionary: A Guide to Knowledge as Power*, ed. Wolfgang Sachs (London: Zed Books, 1992), xvi; and Arturo Escobar, *Encountering Development: The Making and Unmaking of the Third World* (Princeton: Princeton University Press, 1995), 3.

that stayed dormant and idle until endowed with the mission of building civilization.

The Great Man-Made River: A Postscript

The story of the canal as an instrument in the development of the desert continued into the twentieth century. In 1984, Colonel Muammar Gaddafi, the ruler of earthly Libya, laid the foundation stone of The Great Man-Made River, an extensive network of wells, pipes, and reservoirs, which brought water from underground natural repositories to cities.[45] In Western liberal societies, however, enthusiasm about the civilizing potential of the fight with the desert had waned by then, as civilizations were imagined to be of two kinds: liberal and despotic, the difference often explained by the environmental conditions under which they had formed. In the 1950s, historian Karl Wittfogel, a disillusioned communist, argued (relying on Marx's early and subsequently abandoned theory of the Asiatic mode of production) that the challenge of conducting large-scale irrigation projects in hostile natural environments led to the emergence of not simply civilizations but "Oriental despotisms," among which he included Russia.[46] In 2011, the Great Man-Made River was bombed by NATO forces in the course of military intervention, depriving the civilian population of access to fresh water. In contrast to its modernist precedents, this twenty-first-century story has been written along the lines of re-desertification: the destruction of the water system was to support the destruction of Gaddafi's "Oriental despotism." The solution to the ethical dilemma that had been formulated by Bogdanov—the death and suffering of thousands versus the destruction of "civilization" associated with many more deaths—which had been resolved by Menni in favor of the former as the least of the two evils, has been reversed. Yet, the opposition of the desert and civilization, rooted in conservative and colonialist discourse, is still waiting to be rejected.

45   Ali M. El-Gheriani, "The Great Man-Made River Project," *La Houille Blanche* 89, no. 1 (2003): 99–101.
46   Karl Wittfogel, *Oriental Despotism: A Comparative Study of Total Power* (New Haven: Yale University Press, 1957). Marx espoused this theory, which associated early civilizations with the absence of private property on land and with the despotic power of the state, in the 1850s. In Russia, it was supported by the intellectual leader of early Marxism, Georgy Plekhanov, who linked the mode of production with the natural environment, but was officially rejected in the Soviet Union in the 1930s.

I am deeply indebted to Samia Henni, Isabelle Kirkham-Lewitt, Joanna Joseph, Adam Jasper, Amjad Alkoud, Hannah Chazin, Regine Pruzsinszky, Igor Demchenko, and the participants of the "Designing the Deserts" session at SAH 2020, chaired by Samia Henni, for their suggestions. Work on this essay was enabled by a membership at the Institute for Advanced Study, Princeton, New Jersey, during the 2019/2020 academic year.

Timothy Hyde is a historian of architecture at the Massachusetts Institute of Technology whose research focuses on the political dimensions of architecture from the eighteenth century to the present, with a particular attention to relationships of architecture and law. His most recent book is *Ugliness and Judgment: On Architecture in the Public Eye* (Princeton University Press, 2019), and he is also the author of *Constitutional Modernism: Architecture and Civil Society in Cuba, 1933–1959* (University of Minnesota Press, 2013).

TIMOTHY HYDE

ARCHITECTURE ADRIFT IN THE ANTARCTIC DESERT

The particulate matter of the Antarctic Desert is not grains of sand but microscopic crystals of ice. Formed from the limited moisture of Antarctica, these crystals have accumulated in countless numbers over millennia to become the continental ice sheets that give Antarctica its endlessness, its scalelessness, its hazard, and its lure.

These crystals of ice are also a map of time, recording in their assembled layers the passage of climatic events in a temporality incommensurable to human experience. Continuous ice cores from Antarctica can span the extent of 800,000 years, a vastness of time made material by the accumulation of small, individual crystals of ice. The temporality of Antarctica seems to reflect its appearance; it is both so expansive, so remote that it flattens to perception. Its specificities and contingencies are only brought into view by a concerted attention that conjures perspective, allowing the expanse to recede into background.

This concerted attention might be scientific, the kind required by a laboratory analysis of an Antarctic ice core. It might be experiential, as a human being tries to orient themself to small landmarks in the seemingly undifferentiated Antarctic landscape. Or it might be historical, aiming to draw an interpretive significance from the events and artifacts of the Antarctic Desert. But is there a place for history in this Antarctic Desert, distant from and hostile to human settlement and technics? There is history in deserts, of course, and the elision of history from deserts conceals and protects acts of appropriation, violence, and neglect. But historical attention too has its own limits, its own latent tendencies, which appear all the more sharply in the Antarctic Desert, a desert without Indigenous habitation, without permanent settlement, without shared experience. How does history grasp this desert, beyond offering only renditions of arrivals (and retreats) and elaborate descriptions of the expectations that precede visits to the continent? Historical attention brings to the desert techniques of explication, narrative, and interpretation that arrive already half-formed, and architectural historical attention brings to the desert methods of seeing and manners of thought that position the buildings and structures of Antarctica as architecture.

History risks a different kind of elision of the desert. To encounter Antarctica as a space beyond, as the end of the earth, is to encounter it through a temporality and appearance at a historical and conceptual distance. When buildings arrive in the Antarctic they may possess the attributes of architecture, such as the act of structuring shelter or the reenactment of human techniques of making, but by being in this ungraspable context, their purposive dimensions are transformed. They become objects indifferent to the social or ecological concerns from which they sprang; they become material participants in the accumulations and variations and extremities of their environment. In the Antarctic Desert, these objects escape history and become time. In the inevitable cessation of their usefulness, in the attenuation of their origins, in the estrangement of their cultural significance, they escape history; measured in the contractions induced by temperature or by the erasures carried out by wind and snow, they become time. Thus, in order to encounter them without restoring them or confining them to a purely historical presence, they might perhaps be glimpsed by historical attention only in refracted views, like in the passages that follow, neither regarded nor explained in full.

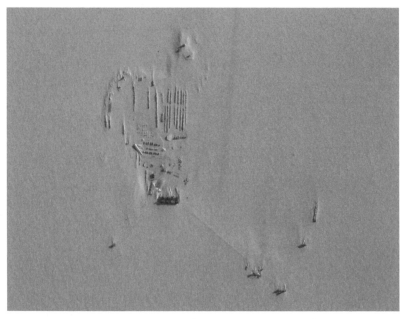

Aerial View of Scott-Amundsen South Pole Station, 2010. Courtesy of NASA, Digital Mapping System group.

Footprints

Human footprints in Antarctica do not endure for long, abraded by wind or filled by snowfall. Architectural footprints are another matter; architectural footprints may survive for years in Antarctica.

A footprint should be evidence, direct and irrefutable, but this famously indexical sign unfolds into calculated interpretation. For the colonizing perspective of Crusoe, it was the unmistakable and unexpected evidence of presence and occupation, and therefore evidence of encounter, an unwelcome threat or needed solace. For the more recent solutionist perspective facing climate crisis, the footprint has become evidence of consequence, a denotation of harm or recovery.

The footprint of architecture is dimensional, width times length, the occupation of an area of ground that could be, before the architecture arrived, more aptly measured in some other way. In Antarctica, that measurement could be the seasonal accumulation of layers of snow forming into ice, the deep time of geology, or the constant shower of massless neutrinos travelling at the speed of light. Compute the dimensional footprint of architecture here and it seems that it is an insignificant presence in Antarctica, almost invisible—and even when visible, it takes on the appearance of natural forms or *fata morgana*.

Seen from the air, the collected buildings of the Amundsen-Scott South Pole Station are granular marks upon an otherwise unbroken surface of snow. Architectural qualities are reduced to one defining binary: a footprint and its ground. But look closely: the footprints of these buildings extend past their walls as striations of snow—piles on the windward side and troughs on the leeward. Here is the reminder that the footprint of architecture is not only dimensional, but also systemic, a calculus of the interaction between architecture and environment.

"Footprint of architecture" often now, in the moment of climate crisis, refers to this interaction as a larger measurement of extraction, movement, and consumption. What was required to manifest this architecture in this place—at the South Pole or elsewhere—and what will be the residual consequences of that placement? In Antarctica, where the physical presence of any architectural object is minute in relation to the continent, it is precisely the distance that that object must travel to arrive there that expands its effect. The footprint of an architectural object is much greater than it appears.

Why, though, call this a footprint? The directness of the footprint, its irrefutability—are either of these evident in the broader equation? But this is precisely why the footprint *is* invoked, to propose exactly the indexical relationship as the culmination of a chain of contingencies. The footprint is a category of moral or ethical judgment precisely because it is a measurement of excess, a measurement of what is no longer there.

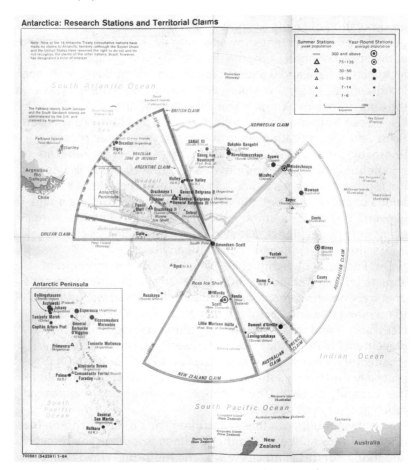

"Antarctica: Research Stations and Territorial Claims," 1984. Courtesy of United States Central Intelligence Agency.

Nobody's Place

Is there a place for architecture in Antarctica?

Architecture has been built in Antarctica, despite the climatic extremity of the continent, many times over the past 120 years. Early voyages, from those likely undertaken by Māori sailors centuries ago to those of European sailors early in the nineteenth century, concluded with brief sightings of the frozen coast. But subsequent expeditions, motivated by geographic exploration, by the possibility of unknown resources, and by nationalist adventure, built shelters, research stations, and supply depots; footings were set, walls raised, roofs laid and tied down. But the building of architecture is not exactly the same thing as the placing of architecture.

Antarctica itself is a particular kind of place. The legal designation *terra nullius*, "nobody's land," emerged in the late nineteenth century, in part out of the desire of expansionist nations to resolve territorial claims in the exploration of the polar regions, areas where permanent settlement was deemed impossible and where geographic contiguities did not exist. *Terra nullius* asserted the principle of a territory occupied by no one— and therefore possessed by no nation—that might be claimed through use of the territory instead of by symbolic gesture. Used in some parts of the world by colonizing nations to retroactively claim lands already occupied by Indigenous peoples, *terra nullius* in Antarctica prompted simultaneous overlapping claims, peculiarly accentuated by the convergence of longitude at the South Pole. In 1959, twelve nations signed the Antarctic Treaty to establish Antarctica as a territory outside the structure of nations, an ungoverned legal entity constituted by the terms of the treaty, which exists today in the fragile coexistence of competing but unrecognized national claims.

Is there a place for architecture in the nobody's place of Antarctica?

The place of architecture requires more than a physical site, and more than the privileging of that site. The place of architecture also consists of its location within an apparatus of property and legal regulation (in some settings) or within a framework of rules of customary practice and traditional entitlements (in others). These intangible surroundings, as much as footings or cable ties, hold architecture in place. They frame architecture with an orientation, a permission, a past, and a future. Antarctica has been given such an apparatus, fashioned in treaty and custom, but, like the weakened light of the sun always hanging low on the horizon, it lacks definition, precision, contrast. There is a place for architecture in Antarctica, yes, but uncertain, transient, unmoored from the stronger nets of placement in architecture's settled environs.

Ernest Shackleton expedition hut, 1908. Courtesy of Joseph Kinsey Collection, Alexander Turnbull Library.

Smallness

Perhaps some architecture is too small to judge—small enough that it appears to be something else entirely, small enough that its presence withdraws from attention rather than capturing it. Such a withdrawal might be received as humble, a respect for context through a determined utility or a deliberate abnegation. Architectural humility, though, is a deceptive category, depending as it does upon motive—a willing desire to withdraw from attention. Could a withdrawal from attention—specifically aesthetic attention—be prompted otherwise?

An architecture too small to judge suggests a different category altogether: an architecture with terms of construction and placement oriented toward a larger, much larger, context, such that the correspondence of one to the other appears vanishingly slight. From this slightness arises a kind of inattention and disregard, and from this inattention and disregard an aesthetic indifference, an indifference that is not the intention of the small architecture but its actuality.

The first architecture of the Antarctic mainland was a pair of huts constructed in 1899 by the British Antarctic Expedition. Timber-framed, sheathed in planking, and insulated with papier-mâché, these two huts were positioned side by side, separated by a small access space and forming an open working area covered with canvas and sealskin. The huts were simple forms, anchored to the ground with wooden foundations and roofs tied down to withstand the winds.

These huts were followed by other structures that varied slightly in size and in construction details, as each new expedition staked its success upon a carefully thought-out shelter: wooden structures, attached by various means to the frozen ground, clad and insulated with tarred paper, cork, felt, or seaweed. Spaces to augment these huts were carved out of the ice, like rooms to provide storage or for instrumentation or workshops. Dug by hand with pickaxes and shovels, these Antarctic rooms resemble diminutive mineshafts. Above the ice, stacks of crates of provisions created insulating walls or stood separately in piles. Small compounds were fashioned out of these huts, caves, and piles.

Over the decades, more compounds were placed across the continent, by the agencies of nations from all of the other six continents. At the coastline, at interior sites, at the South Pole, though larger than the original huts, all of this Antarctic architecture is small—too small to judge. For what, in the scope of the surrounding landscape, could be the compass to orient, compare, and assess? Set in relation to the vastness of the continent—a vastness made infinite by its shapeless, monochromatic surfaces—these architectural objects are vanishingly small, more building blocks than buildings. The smallness of this architecture resonates in several forms: the weight and volume calculus of logistics, the frailty of the human body, the contingency of technological change.

But with all these resonances it is also, profoundly, the actuality of an architecture's relationship to a context that is overwhelmingly difficult to grasp. The context of these buildings is not a context of structures, it is a context of weather; it is not a context that the buildings—and thus their inhabitants—defy, it is one that they endure. In this endurance is a kind of deference, a deference that is not at all an indifference to the continent but that is therefore an acceptance of indifference to anything not of the continent.

Frank Debenham, "Priestley stands on a snow-covered beach holding up a piece of seaweed," c. 1910. Courtesy of Scott Polar Research Institute.

Insulation

The Antarctic Desert contains architectural resources, though, like many deserts, its appearance of bounty is discernable only by an eye accustomed through cultural knowledge. Materials that would have seemed to announce their architectural purpose to the first European expeditions—forests of trees, for example, or expanses of clay—are not to be found in this arid environment. Encircling the South Pole, a barren surface of snow and ice offers only a ground to be dug into, and with time and with human effort or mechanical resources, expedition and research teams have carved tunnels and rooms into the ice. These architectures of ice have provided sufficient and effective insulation to be used for storage, for kennels or stables, for laboratories or even sleeping quarters.

Near the Antarctic coastline, in areas where the ice gives way to the ocean, expeditions have found and occupied patches of exposed ground, permafrost just below the surface of pebbles or rocks or beds of stone. These patches do not yield building materials sufficient to compose and assemble structural elements. It has always been necessary for expeditions to bring their architecture to this desert, rather than find it there. But this coastline does offer—sparingly—architectural resources. The rocks have been piled as weights to hold down ties securing roofs against wind, or stacked to create half-walls that give an additional layer of protection to the vulnerable fabric of tents.

The Antarctic coast offers another, less apparent architectural resource in the bands of seaweed that collect on the shore. In 1910, the British Antarctic Expedition led by Robert Scott brought their prefabricated hut to Cape Evans, and, as they assembled their shelter, they used seaweed, sewn together into quilts and pressed between the planks that made up the walls and roof, as a layer of insulation, answering a vital architectural need.

While other expeditions in the early years of Antarctic exploration brought with them cardboard or newly invented building felts, the resourcefulness of Scott's 1910 expedition created one of the very few transformations of the materials of the Antarctic Desert in architecture. More than a century later, that seaweed insulation, still pressed between the wooden plank walls of the hut on Cape Evans, remains both architecture and nature.

Grommet detail from South Pole geodesic dome, c. 1970. Courtesy of United States Antarctic Program Photo Library.

Cold

All of the fasteners used by the US Navy Seebees in the assembly of the South Pole geodesic dome were required to be at least 3/8″ in diameter. This kind of specification would normally be based only on structural considerations. In this case, however, the requirement resulted from the climate—3/8″ was the smallest dimension that could reliably be held while wearing the heavy insulated gloves needed during construction. A number of similar material decisions arose from this environmentally determined site. Engineers designed the dome as an aluminum, not steel, structure, aluminum having more suitable cryogenic properties, remaining ductile and strong at subzero temperatures instead of becoming brittle. It is also lightweight, crucial for an assembly that had to be shipped to Antarctica from North America and that would need to be quickly raised with a minimum of applied mechanical power. The design was calculated so that no single part of the assembly—struts or panels—weighed more than 50 pounds.

But those 3/8" diameter lock bolts are a telling detail—a minute particular—in revealing how body, building, and environment are bound: the act of building, increasingly so effortless in the tale of modernity, poised on the struggle to grasp a fastener securely in gloved hands—temperature as a commandment.

From the first huts, the difficulty of assembling the architecture of Antarctica in wind and cold resonated through human bodies, through hands most of all. Carrying, lifting, holding: gestures of effort in any circumstance took on an extremity, with foundations most of all, as holes for pilings were drilled with a hammer and chisel. These foundations and fastenings were the interface between imagining and reality, architecture and weather. They carry a meaning for the historical imagination—in the commensuration of the precision of machined fasteners and the clumsiness of cold, gloved hands.

Robert Scott expedition discovery hut. Courtesy of United States Antarctic Program Photo Library.

On the Veranda

When a British expedition overwintered on the coast of Antarctica in 1902, they brought with them a hut acquired in Australia. It was, according to the memoir of expedition leader Robert Scott, "a fairly spacious bungalow of a design used by the outlying settlers of that country." He was referring to the colonial settlers then carving out an existence in the desert climate of the Australian outback, who employed architectural techniques (themselves inherited from other places) to mitigate the (to them) unfamiliar harshness of the surrounding environment. The pyramidal roof of the wood-framed hut, which drew air inward and upward for ventilation, and the encircling veranda, which shaded the interior, were characteristic architectural accommodations against sun and heat.

Despite its starkly different climate—with winds to be blocked out rather than invited in, and with direct sun desirable but scarce in summer and absent entirely in winter—the Antarctic Desert was an environment of extremity, like the outback, and thus it was thought a building type for the one could provide shelter in the unknown conditions of the other. With its perimeter eventually filled with packing crates, the veranda did provide an insulating airspace of sorts, but the foundation system of posts intended to be dug several feet into the ground, as they would be in the original type, presented a challenge in a site where permafrost lay only inches below the surface.

As a response to the problem of designing architecture for an unknown location with no local building resources or pre-cedents, the use of an existing building type had a certain logic. And yet that logic rendered not the proximity of these two deserts but their distance. Where the technological accommo-dation of one environment might give rise to social habits and behaviors, shaping sleeping patterns or encouraging a thoughtful repose on the veranda, the accommodation of the other super-seded entirely any social dimension of architecture, leaving in its place a curious architecture, migrated from one desert to another, to become less a human invention than a non-human participant in the sweep of wind, snow, and cold.

Anders Beer Wilse, Amundsen's hut under construction in his garden at Svartskog, Norway, 1910. Courtesy of National Library of Norway.

Amundsen's Deception

In the first decades of Antarctic exploration, beginning from 1898, the utter lack of anticipatory knowledge exacerbated the difficulty of planning architectural shelters to endure Antarctica's extreme climate. With so few prior reports to learn from—and those in any case limited to minute areas of a vast continent—each expedition arrived with almost no foreknowledge of actual conditions or topography. Many expeditions ended up building at alternate sites after the intended site proved unfeasible. The architectural imaginings necessitated for the Antarctic were thus undertaken by way of prefabrication, with each expedition making, cutting, and fitting materials into a built form before embarking.

Ernest Shackleton, an Anglo-Irish merchant-mariner-turned-explorer, commissioned the hut for his 1907 expedition from Humphrey's Limited, of Knightsbridge, London, a leading manufacturer of iron-framed prefabricated buildings that could answer to all the endeavors of British imperialism. The geodesic dome erected by the United States government at the South Pole in 1975 was equally a global traveler, as these domes were constructed in almost every region of the world during the twentieth century. But in this universality, in this architecture of everywhere, is another architecture—not of nowhere but of another place.

In 1910, the Norwegian explorer Roald Amundsen had a shelter for his expedition team built by two carpenters, who first assembled it in the garden of Amundsen's house in Norway. Wanting to keep his intention to be the first explorer to the South Pole secret, Amundsen encouraged the assumption that the hut would be an observation station for a planned Arctic exploration; not a shelter, and not intended for Antarctica. Once completed and tested in his garden, Amundsen had the hut dismantled and packed for its voyage south, where, in 1911, it would be reassembled on the barrier ice.

Amundsen's deception was unintentionally part of a larger pattern of misdirection, and architecture's involvement in that pattern was no small matter. His prefabricated hut was the making of something that was not—the making of a negation rather than an affirmation. The other prefabricated structures were similarly acts of architectural imagining, all of them thus architecture for another place, a place other than Antarctica.

That other place may be one of manufacture, where hands forge, plane, cut, mold, or weld; that other place may be social, like a domestic garden in Norway. But that other place holds and determines the architecture, even as it travels, so that in its final setting it is still an architecture that deceives, claiming to be placed somewhere else.

Herbert George Ponting, "Sledging ration for one man for one day," c. 1911. Courtesy of Scott Polar Research Institute.

Inventory

The material presence of Antarctic architecture possesses a defining, inescapable importance. After all, the physical properties of wood, canvas, aluminum, and all of the other materials imported to the continent are decisive in their capacity to slow the transmission of temperature differentials or the pace of their decay through the abrasions of countless minute particles of ice. At a visible or microscopic scale, in conditions experienced by a human nervous system or conditions that unfold over decades, these materials, their physical reality, are decisive.

And yet much of Antarctic architecture is captured in lists; much of Antarctic experience as a whole is captured in lists. The geographic and climatic extremity of Antarctica renders all encounters with the continent a matter of logistics. Planning and preparation must account for every needed resource, and each resource must be enumerated as a quantity, a volume, a weight, so that each can be transported; once arrived, each resource remains a number, further divisible and inserted into new chains of calculation. Everything in Antarctica is an inventory, including architecture.

Before the Shackleton Hut could house the fourteen members of the 1907 British Antarctic Expedition who would spend a full year on the raw coast of Antarctica, it had to be described on four typewritten pages. A few hundred words describe the details of a small timber-framed "Portable House," 33 feet long, 19 feet wide, 8 feet from floor to eave. For portability, the wood frame of "strong yellow deal" was to be mortised and tenoned, so that it could be easily erected, dismantled, and re-erected. Tongue and groove boarding was to clad the exterior and interior walls; windows and doors were to be of good quality. Two details within these minimal specifications stand out. First, the framing members for this small structure were "to be so constructed and attached as to give great strength at each joint. Principals to be secured to Main Posts by wrot [sic] Iron Straps and belts, and provided with Iron Tie Rods." And second, the structure was to be well-insulated, with all its surfaces lined with the new Stoniflex patent felt roofing material, and the air space between interior and exterior boards to be packed with Slag Wool.

These, of course, are requirements specific to the demands the environment will impose upon the hut, demands whose exact nature is unknown but whose extremity is inevitable. Before the iron can resist the tensile pull of a katabatic wind, and before the sub-zero air across the ice and the air heated by a coal stove can overlap within the weave of patent felt, each element must find its place on a list.

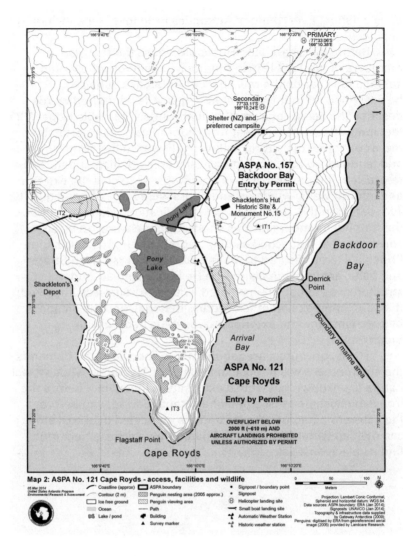

Map 2: ASPA No. 121 Cape Royds - access, facilities and wildlife

Site topographic map of Antarctic Specially Protected Area No. 157. Courtesy of Secretariat of the Antarctic Treaty.

Two Utopias

Antarctica now has dozens of areas that are administered by government agencies and NGOs either to conserve the historic presence of sites such as the expedition huts or to conserve the existing environment against human presence. The contradiction—between history and environment—is a contradiction of rivaling utopias.

The regulatory apparatus designed to preserve a single hut of almost unfathomable geographic remoteness is also to maintain the ideal of that remoteness. The expedition huts themselves are understood to embody a motive that is utopian in its instinct—the intention to enter into the unknown seeking the possibility of a different knowledge, a utopianism of imagined surcease from the inevitabilities of known "civilization." But when, in 1959, the signatories of the Antarctic Treaty agreed to place Antarctica outside of geopolitical calculus, Antarctica became another utopia, in the sense of a no-place set legally outside the structure of nations as nobody's place; another utopia in that the treaty promulgated an aspiration of peaceful existence with the promise that Antarctica would never become an object of discord between nations. Thus far, the several dozen research stations operated year-round by several different nations have fulfilled this aspiration.

The utopia of Antarctica could only be written in these terms once its shores had been mapped, its interior explored, its environment understood. Therefore, the paradoxical presence of two differentiated utopias must be confronted: one historical and the other still a future, and yet *both* require preservation. The paradox is manifest in the protected areas, which designate the preservation of the human history of Antarctica *and* the preservation of an Antarctica that has never been touched or seen. Two utopias are to be preserved, one historical and the other environmental, sharing a single continent that is the common heritage of humankind. Antarctica and its legal mechanisms suggest a curious process of interference and non-interference, in which the presence of architecture at the end of the world becomes a measure for the persistence of an imagining of world yet to come.

Wreckage of Little America III, seen from *USS Edisto*, 1963. Courtesy of United States Navy.

Drift

The cleaving of a tabular iceberg opens a building to a lateral view, with an archeology not of sifted vertical strata but of a sudden cut that exposes its interior. This is the wreckage of Little America III, the third in a sequence of US research stations on the Ross Ice Shelf initiated in 1929. Layers of accumulating snowfall buried all but the tops of a few high telephone poles bearing antenna wires. But all the while the snowpack accumulated on its rooftops, America III was moving, drifting. Built atop a massive shelf of ice, the position of its prefabricated architecture was never still. The ice shelf moves, fed at one side by glaciers and eroded at the other by ocean. The architecture drifts on currents of ice.

Two decades after it was built, America III left the Antarctic continent as part of an ice shelf calved off and set to sea as an iceberg. In February 1963, a US Navy icebreaker spotted the base at S 77°32'30', E 174°22'30'. An exploration of the surface of the iceberg revealed no way to enter the rooms of the base from above, so photographs of its open side captured a moment of this architectural journey. Sometime after, perhaps later in the warming waters of that Antarctic summer, the drifting architecture would have settled into the sea as flotsam, to float, sink, dissipate.

All of the architecture constructed upon the Antarctic ice is adrift, adrift on a ground that is constantly moving, sliding sideways across the earth's surface. There are buildings along the edge of the continent whose foundations are set into *terra firma*, and these are securely moored, but others are not. At the South Pole, even the column that marks the pole itself has to be reset periodically, to correct for the movement of the ice into which it is planted.

This constancy of architectural movement, its drift, binds these buildings to environmental contingency: to the weight of snow, to thermal differential, to glacial flows, to ocean currents. In the use of these buildings—as writing cases for the precisions of scientific work—compensations must be made *against* drift. This drifting architecture is coordinated not to human endeavor but to environmental pressure.

All of the architecture constructed upon the Antarctic ice is adrift, loosened from its attachments to cultural custom or social apparatus, loosened from the frameworks of economic value or political purpose. This drifting architecture reveals the gaps and cracks in the conventions of an architectural history that attempts to fix in place this architecture's usefulness, origins, or significations. The translation—from position in space to position in time—embodied in the architecture that drifts across the Antarctic Desert loosens the grip of history.

Notes

A survey of the cultural and historical resonances that Antarctica has precipitated can be found in Elizabeth Leane's *South Pole: Nature and Culture* (London: Reaktion Books, 2016).

Footprints

The Amundsen-Scott South Pole Station was established by the United States in 1956 and has been continuously in use since, supporting research under the auspices of the National Science Foundation and hosting international research. Scientific research undertaken at the South Pole and elsewhere across the continent is described by G. E. Fogg in *A History of Antarctic Science* (Cambridge: Cambridge University Press, 2005).

Nobody's Place

The most recent research into the likelihood of Māori voyages to the edges of Antarctica is presented in Priscilla M. Wehi et al., "A Short Scan of Māori Journeys to Antarctica," *Journal of the Royal Society of New Zealand* (June 2021), https://doi.org/10.1080/03036758.2021.1917633.

The most useful accounting of the concept of *terra nullius* and its colonizing application can be found in Michael Connor, *The Invention of Terra Nullius: Historical and Legal Fictions on the Foundation of Australia* (Sydney: Macleay Press, 2005); and Andrew Fitzmaurice, "The Genealogy of Terra Nullius," *Australian Historical Studies* 38, no. 129 (2008): 1–15.

For the complex legal constitution of Antarctica, see Ben Saul and Tim Stephens, eds., *Antarctica in International Law* (London: Bloomsbury, 2015).

Smallness

At present, thirty or more nations, at least one from each of the six other continents, maintain research programs in Antarctica, many in permanent research stations; for a compilation of Antarctic information, consult Beau Riffenburgh, ed., *Encyclopedia of the Antarctic* (London: Routledge, 2007). For a narrative account of early exploration of the continent, the most visceral is Apsley Cherry-Garrard's memoir of the 1910 expedition, *The Worst Journey in the World* (London: Constable & Co., 1922).

On the Veranda

Robert Falcon Scott, *Voyage of the Discovery*, vol. 1 (NewYork: Charles Scribner's Sons; London: Smith Elder & Co., 1907), 160.

Amundsen's Deception

Roald Amundsen, "Plan and Preparations," chap. 2 in *The South Pole: An Account of the Norwegian Antarctic Expedition in the "Fram," 1910–1912*, vol. 1, trans. A. G. Chater (London: John Murray, 1912).

Inventory

Chris Cochran et al., "Conservation Report: Shackleton's Hut, British Arctic Exploration 1907–09, Cape Royds, Ross Island, Antarctica," unpublished report for the Antarctic Heritage Trust, 2003, 118–121.

Two Utopias

The twelve signatories of the Antarctic Treaty in 1959 were the governments of Argentina, Australia, Belgium, Chile, France, Japan, New Zealand, Norway, South Africa, the USSR, the United Kingdom, and the United States. An additional thirty-eight nations have subsequently acceded to the Treaty, the text of which can be found at: https://www.nsf.gov/geo/opp/antarct/anttrty.jsp. Although there is no government or executive that enforces the treaty, a number of committees operate under its auspices to coordinate and facilitate scientific research on the continent. In addition, dozens of NGOs, many based in the original signatory nations, direct efforts in environmental protection. Other NGOs with an interest in historic preservation represent the national perspectives of the early expeditions, whose huts are the objects of their conservation efforts.

Photographs by Bruno Barrillot, the co-founder of the Observatoire des armements in Lyon, France. The images were taken during a visit to France's nuclear sites in Reggane and Ecker in the Algerian Sahara, with the filmmaker Larbi Benchiha and his team in November 2007. Courtesy Observatoire des armements (www.obsarm.org). On the context of these nuclear wastes and radioactive landscapes, see the introduction to this book.

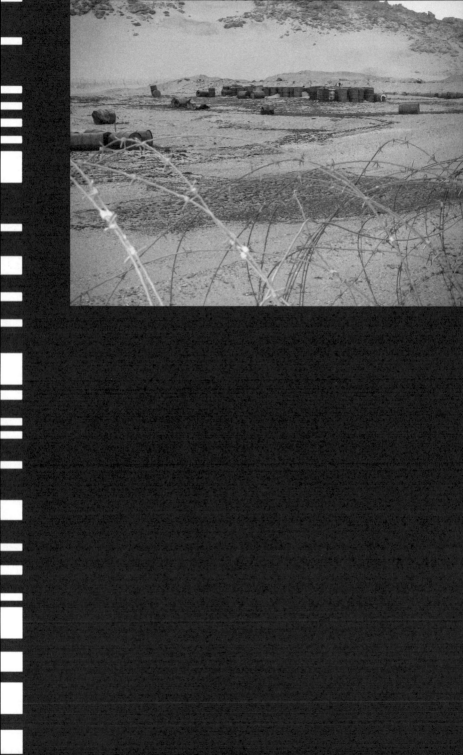

This book has been produced through the Office of the Dean, Amale Andraos, and
the Office of Publications at Columbia University GSAPP.

This project was supported in part by the Preston Thomas Memorial Lecture Series
Fund at the Department of Architecture, Cornell University.